The Process of Drama

The Process of Drama demonstrates how dramatic meaning emerges, shaped by its multiple contexts, and illuminates the importance of all participants to the dramatic process.

Starting with the notion that the over-used word 'process' may be defined in terms of negotiating form, the book provides a unique model of the elements of drama in context and explains how these are negotiated to produce dramatic art. Unlike most texts in the field, *The Process of Drama* does not start and finish with the audience, nor with the playwright, director and actors. Instead it views the dramatic event as a whole, and investigates the experiences of all the participants, and their roles in the creation of the work.

Illustrated with scores of examples from both improvised and scripted forms, and looking at drama created in the classroom as well as the theatre, *The Process of Drama* is the most comprehensive and rigorous analysis available of the dramatic process. Essential reading for students and teachers of drama.

John O'Toole is Senior Lecturer in Drama at Griffith University, Australia. His previous books include the highly-acclaimed *Theatre in Education*, as well as *Dramawise*, written with Brad Haseman.

"The Process of Drama"

Negotiating Art and Meaning

John "O'Toole"

ROUTLEDGE

London and New York

First published 1992
by Routledge
11 New Fetter Lane, London EC4P 4EE

Simultaneously published in the USA and Canada
by Routledge
a division of Routledge, Chapman and Hall, Inc.
29 West 35th Street, New York, NY 10001

© 1992 John O'Toole

Typeset in 10 on 12 point Baskerville
by Witwell Limited, Southport
Printed in Great Britain by
Clays Ltd, St Ives plc

British Library Cataloguing in Publication Data
   O'Toole, John
      Process of Drama: Negotiating Art and Meaning
      I. Title
      792

Library of Congress Cataloging in Publication Data
   O'Toole, John.
      The process of drama: negotiating art and meaning/
         John O'Toole. p.   cm.
      Includes bibliographical references and index.
      1. Theater. 2. Drama. I. Title.
   PN1655.087   1992
   801'.952—dc20   92-7785

ISBN 0-415-08243-9   ISBN 0-415-08244-7 (pbk)

Contents

Introduction

1 PRELIMINARY DEFINITIONS

Defining process

This book sets out to investigate the notion of *process* in drama, with particular reference to the genre which is known by its practitioners, mainly in Europe, the UK, Canada and Australia, as 'drama in education'. However, this is a book about the art form of drama, rather than education. One of the main ideas in the book is that drama is not literature, words on a page. That is just a playscript, and has the same relationship to drama as a score has to music. Drama itself *happens*, and never accidentally;[1] it is a dynamic event which is always part of its context. Since schools form an important part of the context in which this genre usually happens, schooling practices and educational ideas and structures do feature prominently, as a background to the aesthetic.

The word 'process' is rarely, if ever, defined. It is a word often used in drama these days, as it is ubiquitously in education, and seems to denote anything that keeps on going on, and hasn't come to something called a 'product', which has somehow stopped. To look at the grammar of these words may be revealing, because it shows how we deal with reality, and reconstruct knowledge and ideas in our society. You may notice that 'process' is a noun, a thing, that has become quite detached from its base verb 'to proceed', though what process denotes is actually verbal, doing. Our thinking in formal contexts of knowledge like education, history and science is dominated by the *objective* – making reality into discrete objects, that is nouns. This tendency to reify knowledge goes back at least to Newton and Descartes, who showed us the promise of the 'objectivity' of scientific discourse. We in the knowledge business joyfully learned to devalue subjectivity, kinships and verbs, thereby creating any number of misleading dualisms and giving a false status of 'truth' to nominal constructs. Our thinking is enslaved by nouns. This is not true of all epistemologies: while post-European culture has 'history', 'religion' and 'myth' – three blockbusting and compartmentalising nouns – Australian Aborigines have 'dreaming' – very much a verb, which may be one of the reasons why we have difficulty in valuing or comprehending their culture.[2] Similarly, the Balinese – that most artistic of races – have no traditional noun for art; they just do it.[3] Even in western scientific thought, it is nearly a century since Einstein showed that the substance of the physical universe is relationships, not things. Yet in much of our thinking we remain enslaved to his predecessors. There is much more to this argument, and it will be taken up later in this book, as we struggle to comprehend drama (noun), which is really a verbal event that can only be truly apprehended as it happens.

This is why it is necessary to define 'process', which carries embedded assumptions. Take for instance the phrase 'the rehearsal process' – doesn't it sound more imposing than simply 'rehearsing'? Is there a difference between 'the drama process' and 'process drama' – imposing phrases, both? Verbalising the nouns, we know what is meant by producing drama, but does proceeding in drama mean anything? If not, why is the word 'process' so popular? Is dramatic product the same as a dramatic production? And do they embody process, or are they the opposite? These questions are not rhetorical but depend for answer on a clear definition of this elusive pimpernel of a word. Process in drama may be defined as:

> negotiating and renegotiating the elements of dramatic form, in terms of the context and purposes of the participants.

Defining the territory

Some genres of drama entail more negotiation, more 'process', than others. This book looks at a number of genres, mostly modern, which do involve negotiating the art form. The genre of drama in education has been chosen as the main focus for scrutiny because it is extremely processual (unfortunately the noun does not come with a ready-made adjective, so please learn to put up with this rather ugly derivative).

And while we're on the subject of vexatious words, already some readers familiar with linguistic and literary theory, and particularly the work of sociolinguists like Halliday,[4] will be irritated by my use of the word 'genre' to describe drama in education and similar forms. I am using the term as formerly it was popularly used (as it translates from its French roots) to describe generic forms of drama – and I understand it is still used so in dance, where 'ballroom', 'contemporary', 'jazz ballet' are termed genres. However, linguists have appropriated it to describe very specific and small-scale language transactions defined by their purpose and context, and 'genre theory' has become one of the hot areas of controversy.[5] One colleague reading a draft of this book rightly, if tetchily, dismissed my usage as 'loose and outdated'. His razor-sharp and much more modern description of drama in education is as follows:

> not a single genre but a complex area of related activities composed of a multiplicity of genres which exist as the specific structural elements and together with the specific contexts determine the text of the drama.[6]

So, wherever you stand on linguistic theory, you are justified in throwing tomatoes. The trouble is, I can't find a better word – or at least one short enough to be readable as often as I shall use it in this book. There are too many categories of dramatic activity for the words available. The word 'form' already refers here to drama as distinct from other art forms, and the activity of forming that art. 'Style', 'Mode', 'Convention' are all used, interchangeably, to describe categories like comic/tragic, mystery plays/Restoration drama/Victorian melodrama, realism/absurdism, soliloquy/tableau/alienation device . . . and so confusion multiplies. So please, as you have with 'processual', please put up with 'genre' to describe a category of (quite big) lumps of drama of approximately the same order, including drama in education, theatre in education – mercifully shortened in common use to TIE – street theatre and community theatre.

Drama in education is here defined not as the whole corpus of work in drama which takes place in schools, but specifically as the form of dramatic activity centred on *fictional role-taking* and improvisation which has become known by this title. If you are not sure what that entails, there are numerous descriptions throughout the book of role-taking and the various other activities which together comprise the genre to give you a more than generalised picture. It normally takes place among a class of schoolchildren and their teacher, not in a theatre but in a classroom or studio within a school. The genre had its formal beginnings in the mid-1950s in Britain, passed through a number of formative stages, and was consolidated by the late 1970s into what is recognisably a stable genre with a shared terminology, explicit claims to the status of 'art form' and a body of shared practice which is current in a number of countries, including Australia, Britain, Canada, some countries of Northern Europe and a little in the USA, as well as a developing body of scholarship.

Drama in education is very dependent both on the specific group of people taking part, and on external conditions over which they have little control, and so they must continually renegotiate the way in which they can manage and manifest the basic elements of dramatic form. It is therefore always very processual, and has the potential to operate at quite extreme forms of processuality. The purposes of the participants and their **real context*** impose constraints upon some or all of the elements of dramatic form which demand their renegotiation.

The functions of participants in most genres of western drama – that is, *playwright, performer, audience, director* – are performed by separate people with discrete tasks and responsibilities. This is not so in drama in education, where those functions are subsumed in other functions and roles and another network of relationships – the real roles and purposes of people in school. This actually allows for greater flexibility through less primacy. This analysis of drama in education may prove helpful in revealing that in many other, more conventional genres of drama the separateness of these functions and roles is more apparent than real.

Some attention is also given in the book to the closely related genre of participational theatre in education. This too is a specialised title, denoting teams of performers, or 'actor/teachers' as they are sometimes called, working in 'programmes' which incorporate both performance and active audience participation,

* Words in bold type are defined in chapter 1.

with groups of school students. The actor/teachers sometimes present these programmes in a theatre, sometimes travel from school to school. This genre may usefully be regarded as midway in processuality between drama for performance and drama in education.[7]

Any dramatic event may have significant processual elements, so examples of playwriting for performance have been included, mostly taken from fields whose workers perceive themselves to be processual – such as community theatre and youth theatre. Each of these examples demonstrates a significant and different processual emphasis.

Defining dramatic form

The first recorded book on drama, Aristotle's *Poetics*,[8] attempted to define what drama is. Since then, the shelves of libraries have become crammed with books about drama, but very few indeed explain what the elements of the art form actually are – perhaps because they seem obvious. Perhaps, too, most people still more or less implicitly use Aristotle. Perhaps it is time for a new definition. The basic tenet of the following model is that there are identifiable elements which are present in all drama, and which all have to be present for an event to be called a drama.[9]

There are many quasi-dramatic performance events which have the semblance of drama but not all the elements, such as 'war games' and other forms of simulation training, 'performance art' and 'happenings', and some public sporting activities. In addition, there are a number of 'real-life' human activities which embody certain dramatic elements, particularly activities connected with dramatic play, such as children living through operative fantasy, adults consciously adopting role-model behaviour, and certain forms of publicly performed ritual and ceremony.[10] These proto-dramatic activities are examined where they are relevant to this enquiry; study of children's fantasy/dramatic play and of role theory are both important in the development of drama in education.

However, the key elements of a properly dramatic activity are interrelated and interdependent but distinct and distinguishable, as indicated in Figure 1.

But beware: this model is not objective truth, no universally valid definition of the elements of dramatic form, though it does

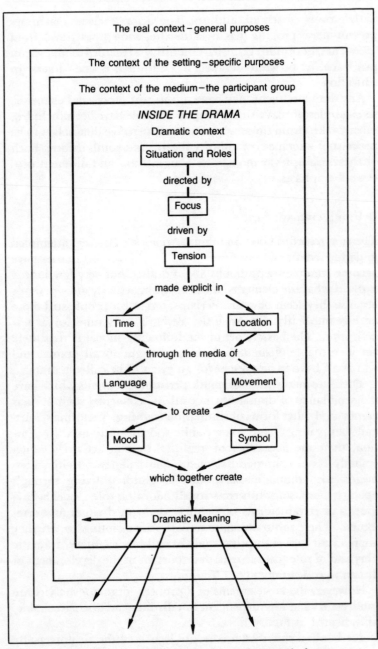

The real context – general purposes

The context of the setting – specific purposes

The context of the medium – the participant group

INSIDE THE DRAMA
Dramatic context

Situation and Roles

directed by

Focus

driven by

Tension

made explicit in

Time   Location

through the media of

Language   Movement

to create

Mood   Symbol

which together create

Dramatic Meaning

Figure 1 Dramawise + model: the elements of dramatic form

sit still conveniently and authoritatively upon a page, a thing to be received or analysed. It is certainly not processual. To try and *com*prehend cognitively, as a series of statements embodied in a book and diagrammatic models, a dynamic form which its participants *ap*prehend both cognitively and affectively, subjectively and objectively, implies a major structural and epistemological transformation of that form where the processual is removed from the process. Both diagram and book are nothing more than a temporary and potentially misleading holding form, through which, however, we may perceive dramatic process sufficiently for some of its operation, its underlying structures and its social and ideological functions to become evident.

Education, like art, is a dynamic process which people apprehend subjectively, though even more industry and energy are spent on the objectivisation and nominalisation of education and learning[11] than of art. Since this study primarily concerns the genre of drama *in* education, we shall be investigating the nexus between these two subjective, dynamic processes.

I have already asserted several times that drama is dynamic. Let us investigate what this means on a number of levels.

1 It normally exists in physical action, in three dimensions, and in time – both in the moment, and in the passage of time.

2 Drama is a group art, involving a number of people directly and indirectly in the action, with a number of different functions, taking part simultaneously as individuals, as sub-groups clearly identified by function, and as a whole group within the dramatic event.

3 Modern literary theory shows that in any literature the relationship between artist and audience is almost infinitely negotiable, and the meanings emergent between them are inevitably dynamic and shifting.[12] In drama, where there is a degree of direct communication with the audience, this negotiability becomes palpable, and sometimes conscious. In the genre of drama in education, the audience become to a degree artists, and the notion of audience ceases to have independent identity as a definable function distinct from playwright and actor.

4 Drama is 'multi-medial'.[13] The contexts in which drama presents itself are invariably complex and never exactly reproducible. By its nature it operates in at least two and up to four contextual frames simultaneously, each of which has its own sign systems and its own cultural and ideological referents (this is

explained and explored in chapter 1). Attempting to codify the signifiers in such 'multi-medial texts' is a task akin to counting sand. The drama practitioner *and* scholar Martin Esslin, actually proposing a practical semiotic approach to the study of drama, ironically notes that at a conference on the semiotics of drama, 'the assembled scholars . . . were deeply disappointed when one of the most distinguished directors of one of the world's leading theatres told them that he had found it all useless and impenetrable'.[14] This multi-contextual dynamic peculiarity of drama is explored in detail throughout this study.

Drama and literature

The place of drama in literature has perplexed scholars and taxonomists through the ages. Yet drama has, uneasily, been perceived to be part of literature within the Western European tradition. For both Aristotle and Horace, the essence of drama lay within the verse. Both discussed drama under the heading of poetry. Aristotle classified as the essential elements of drama *plot, character, diction, thought* – all shared with other literature – along with two others which were not, *melody* and *spectacle*, which he then demoted into 'accessories'. From then on, the pattern was set.[15] Noted poets Philip Sidney and John Dryden both published analyses of drama entitled defences of poetry.[16] Ben Jonson, accomplished as both poet and playwright, in fact, praises Aristotle as 'the first accurate critic'. In the same work he compares the 'verses' of Euripides with those of Virgil, making no distinction whatever that might place the two writers as operators in a different art form.[17]

However, the classification of drama *as* literature does raise more problems than it solves, and always has done. This is partly because drama does not stand still like a book to be reified. The notion of literature as dynamic and negotiable is very recent in western thinking, a startling proposition by the Russian Formalists in the 1920s, reasserted systematically only since the 1970s by literary deconstructionists and post-structuralists in the wake of modern linguistics.[18] We should, however, remember that it would perhaps be not at all strange to those cultures which partake of a shared oral and performative tradition of literature, such as the Australian Aborigines, where the audience is part of a simultaneously poetic, narrative, dance and dramatic event, and the event is seen as part of a continuous remaking of culture and history.[19]

I have already suggested that within the western dramatic tradition the various participants in a dramatic event may have significantly different perceptions about that event from those of an audience alone, and that to see drama only from the point of view of the audience, or the critic, is to miss much of its structure and significance. This is particularly so in the genre of drama in education, where there is usually no audience as such, and some of the other conventional functions of theatre are combined and subsumed in each other. Accordingly, the word 'participants' will be used for those who are actively engaged in making the drama – in conventional terms the playwright, director, production team and actors – while the word 'percipients' will be used throughout to denote *all* those who take part in a drama, including the audience if it is separable, who all have their proper *perceptions*.

The two most influential dramatic theorists of the twentieth century, Stanislavski and Brecht, were both practical men of the theatre, whose theory was more *a posteriori* than *a priori*. Brecht for instance may have been initially influenced by the Russian Formalists in developing his theory of alienation effect, but it was for a similar pragmatic purpose of explicitly remaking culture and history that he developed it, and it underwent considerable modification in the light of his practical experience as a dramatist and director.[20] Much influential modern writing about drama is by those involved in *practice* like Peter Brook and Augusto Boal,[21] whose contribution is recognised later. The word 'text' now is taken almost universally to denote the dramatic event, not just the playscript. The social context is no longer to be outlawed as corrupting of the author's intention.[22]

The last twenty years have seen a well-documented change towards 'director's theatre' led by directors such as Brook, where audiences now welcome the right of the director and performers to modify *explicitly* the conventions and the written text even of classics like Shakespeare. In recent years I have sat in audiences quite unfazed by a *Henry V* with direct visual references to the Falklands War (English Shakespeare Company, 1988); *King Lear* in a circus tent (Footsbarn Players, 1984); and even a *Hamlet* reduced to fifteen minutes in length (*The Marowitz Hamlet*[23]).

This kind of process is not entirely contemporary. It would be unrealistic to suggest that directors and actors have not *always* been (a) reinterpreting the plays of Shakespeare in terms of the ideology and cultural mores of their time (Davenant's *King Lear* with its happy ending is a case in point); (b) adapting the plays to the audience expectations and the theatres of their time (it is revealing to contrast Restoration productions of *The Merchant of Venice* starring a red-wigged Shylock strutting a Palladian stage with Charles Kean's nineteenth-century version of the same play in Drury Lane with a flooded stage complete with gondolas and a 300ft × 20ft high moving diorama of Venice specially painted by Stansfield, and the actors hardly evident); (c) cutting and rearranging Shakespeare's text (Charles Marowitz may hold the record for brevity, but *Hamlet* is rarely if ever produced in full, and one-hour versions by touring theatre groups for country stages or for schools have been common since Shakespeare's time). However, all these modifications have often been covert and unacknowledged, with the assumption postulated by the providers and accepted by the audience that the production is attempting to reach the essence of Shakespeare's meaning, and certainly not trying to corrupt it.

Static, product-centred, traditionally literary models of drama are better replaced by a dynamic, processual model. This has always been true of most practice, and is now affirmed by the critical literature. However, it is important to see *process* and *product* not as dichotomous but as points on a continuum. This processual model may be characterised by:

- redefinition of the givens
- to start with much more specific givens
- which act as constraints within which the author's control over content, context, style and convention have to be renegotiated
- which in turn entails renegotiation of some of the elements of the drama itself.

To put it in terms of conventional forms of theatre and drama, many playwrights write with and for specific groups of performers and audiences, sometimes with other writers (especially for film and television). Directors and dramaturges renegotiate the playtext itself, sometimes with the writers (at least living ones – the dead ones they seek to recreate, effectively to transform, in terms of contemporary relevance), and then with the actors, almost invariably using forms of improvisation. The whole development of Fringe theatre in the UK, Europe and Australia – which includes the genre of theatre in education (TIE) – is very much a part of this change of thought, with its emphasis on ensemble performance, on the writer as part of a team, on writing with particular, often polemical purposes, and on catering for specific audiences. The practice of a director taking a script, blocking it to the writer's instructions, real or assumed, and demanding obedience to these constraints from the actors (described tongue in cheek by the French critic Derrida as 'interpretive slaves who faithfully execute the providential designs of "the master" . . . the Author-creator who, armed with a text, lets representation represent him through representatives'[24]) is now thoroughly discredited.

Or mostly, at least at the top of the trade. Old perspectives die hard, however, among the practitioners as among the critics. At an International Conference of Young Playwrights, the delegates from round the world nearly all seemed to share a number of assumptions about the nature of a playwright.[25] Together, the assumptions may be expressed as a proposition, based on the primary premise that *a play is the sole creation of a playwright.*

This may be further expanded thus:

1 A (single) playwright finds his or her (but usually his) way through the elements of drama to create, alone, a finished play upon the playwright's own terms ('the writer in the garret contemplating the empty page') with his own choice of subject matter and style, and an audience conceptualised (if at all) merely as 'the public'. This is as nearly realised as possible in the text: including detailed design, all possible stage directions for director and actors, and descriptions of appropriate characterisations, expressions and moods – sometimes including lighting.

2 Director, designer and actors (the 'interpretive slaves') reproduce this as faithfully as possible, and their job includes trying to find its essence. They perform it to 'the public'.

3 That audience, undifferentiated, perceives it, while having effectively no say upon it – they receive the experience, and they all receive the same experience.

(margin note, handwritten: have discussion or change in script)

4 It is put in a book, called a playscript, and may be revived, with due attention to its essence.
5 Critics of the performance next day, or students of the script in future generations, may try to pin down that essence.

These assumptions were not always borne out in the different ways the young playwrights created their own plays – some at school for assignments, some at home with friends, some as members of local youth theatres. However, instead of questioning the assumptions, most of the writers had further assumed that their own practice was just a deviant from the norm. In subsequently teaching Playwriting to successive groups of undergraduate drama students, I have found the same assumptions underlying many of the students' perceptions. We may suppose, since all the students were interested people just starting out on the practice of drama, that these assumptions are ones carried with them from public lore. The assumptions may be mythical; but they seem to be the generally assumed method of writing plays. Further evidence of this is provided in the way many adults set out to write plays. One of the most frequent shortcomings of scripts sent for assessment to the Australian National Playwrights' Centre each year is that the authors have not conceptualised their audiences sufficiently nor taken them into account as part of the event. Another major criticism is that the authors, most of whom are relatively inexperienced in theatre practice, are not sufficiently aware of the creative contribution to be made to the script by the director, the design and production team, and the actors.[26] In other words, like the youngsters, these budding professionals are unconsciously articulating and to a greater or lesser degree following a set of assumptions and ideologies which are no longer current.

Some playwrights, of course, are not in the position to write for a given audience, actors, or commission – the circumstances of the context are negotiable, because they do not yet exist.

For other playwrights, and certainly for teachers who are effectively being playwrights in drama in education, these givens are specific, and entirely non-negotiable because they belong to a very real external context. The elements of the drama have to be negotiated around them. And that brings us to the two really big words of Figure 1 and the book, both extensively used already: *context* and *elements*.

Defining dramatic context

As percipients of any dramatic event, whether as active participants or audience, we are engaged in two different contexts simultaneously – the art form of drama depends on that for its existence. In simple terms, when we go to a play or act in one we are metaphorically transported into a fictional world, inhabited by fictional characters, a pretend world in which we are made to believe, as, in Coleridge's term, we willingly suspend our disbelief.[27] Our real selves may be forgotten, but they do not disappear – we are still here, and unless we have a schizoid disorder we can reassert our consciousness of what is real at any time we like. Throughout this book, the percipients' reality – what we know to be real, and what we bring to the drama in terms of our cultural background, experience, and attitudes – is termed the **real context**, while the make-believe world of the drama which we have agreed to believe in together is termed the **fictional context**. While the drama is happening, we are operating in both of these contexts, and it will be shown that they are operating on each other. That is part of what is romantically called the 'magic' of theatre; however, I shall unromantically term it 'metaxis',[28] because it is a very substantial and definable component of the experience itself, which needs to be understood if we are to comprehend the dramatic aesthetic and the dramatic meaning.

However, there is even more to any dramatic event than that. As I have indicated in Figure 1, the percipients' **real context** embodies at least one specific internal context very crucial to the operation of the drama, the **context of the medium**, and sometimes a second, the **context of the setting**. These are explored and further defined in chapter 1.

2 THE ELEMENTS OF DRAMATIC FORM

To establish and define the elements of dramatic form as they are used in this book, and their relationships to each other, you may find it useful to refer again to Figure 1, for this is the terminology which is used throughout.

At times it will be necessary to distinguish between those *elements* such as role, tension and time which can be seen to be properly within the **fictional context** as it has been defined here, and those that are more strictly *conditions* which mediate that context (such as purpose and participant group – both of which feature in the diagram as part of the **real context**). However, all these elements have particular manifestations of their existence both within and beyond the **fictional context** itself: for instance, the playwright's *real purposes* dictate the selection of a particular situation and characters; those characters' *fictional purposes* dictate the cause and effect of the narrative. Since charting the close and interdependent relationship between the **real** and the **fictional contexts** is a central theme, in this book they are all considered elements in functional terms.

This is how the book is organised. Each chapter explores an element, in approximately the order reading down Figure 1. There are exceptions to this, where grouping elements together helps to illuminate their function: purpose dictates focus, inside and outside the drama; similarly dramatic tension is a product of the management of time; mood, symbol and meaning are effectively outcomes of the other elements.

1 The fictional context

The **fictional context** may be defined as comprising *situations* embodying *characters* who interact with each other, and their physical, social and cultural environment as presented in the fiction. These characters are representations of human subjects (or beings with recognisably human qualities) in dealings with each other in a more or less recognisable human situation. Tom and Jerry, though not human, are anthropomorphic, and even Samuel Beckett, who tested the furthest boundaries of situation, cannot stray far from *la condition humaine*.

The contextual situation

One major aspect of the fictionality is that the **fictional context** is finite and selective – in other words it is a selection, with established parameters, of the human subjects, their relation-ships and the environment which would exist if the **context** were in fact real. It is a *model*. The word is used here as it frequently is in fields connected with education, like biology and geography:

Models can be viewed as selective approximations which by

the elimination of incidental detail allow some fundamental relevant or interesting aspects of the real world to appear in some generalised form.[29]

This definition by educationalists, true of the plastic skeleton and the polystyrene contour map in their classroom, is equally true for the playwright. The **fictional context** may be seen to be a model in both the theoretical and everyday use of the term.

As such, the contextual situation is the first element of the drama to be *negotiable*. Another educationalist describes the more sophisticated use of models at work in proto-dramatic exercises and simulations in geography:

> In practice, models are chains of ideas linked together and observed at work; skeletons which can be made to dance at the command of the observer.[30]

In traditional genres of western adult drama, it is the makers, the playwright and actors, who make the skeleton dance. In some participant processual genres like drama in education, or Boal's 'theatre of liberation', the observer, or audience, may be invited to assist in choreographing the dance, and even building the skeleton. In the classroom most of the dancing is at the command of the teacher, rather than the 'observers', though as participants they inevitably get to build and choreograph a little, sometimes a lot.

The situation being fictional, the people inhabiting it are fictional – in other words they do not have an existence beyond and independent of the drama. There is often confusion and controversy among practitioners and audiences particularly in the more extremely processual forms of drama as to the truth of this assertion. Whether there is a twilight area between drama and reality has been a matter of interest for dramatic experimenters particularly since the 1960s, though of questionable residual effect. In one famous dramatic event – a dramatic performance or a proto-dramatic experiment, depending on your definition of drama – Ed Berman and his troupe of actors laid a (really) dead dog down in the street, and stood round discussing its demise, encouraging a crowd of passers-by to congregate, and they then used that crowd as participants. They knew they were pretending (i.e. engaging in drama by willingly suspending their disbelief), but the audience did not, at least to begin with. In this book, the close metaxis but essential independence between the real and the fictional is examined in detail. I would not assert, for instance, that drama is entirely inconsequential in either the literal or the figurative sense of the term; however, its consequences can and need to be limited as part of the contract which the participants engage in. In other words, for normal people, who are able to dissociate the **fictional context** from the **real context**, the drama will end, and enemies within the drama can still be friends in life. The **fictional context** may, however, have proved sufficient of a refraction of the **real context** to leave residual, even operative, traces. Drama practitioners with different ideological standpoints, such as phenomenological and Marxist, often have differing perceptions of the nature and potency of this effect. This too is examined in detail in chapter 1.

Internal contextual frames

Referring back to the 'Dramawise' model in Figure 1, the **fictional context** appears as the central box framed within a number of other boxes representing aspects of the percipients' **real context**. The relationship between these is dealt with later, throughout this study. The **fictional context** consists of people and events existing within the *frame* of the art work itself. However, within this frame, the **fictional context** may have a number of internal frames. (This concept of framing is defined and investigated later in this chapter and in chapter 3.) Those internal frames may be concentric or concurrent. Explicitly, a play-within-a-play may occur, or, implicitly, other forms of deception which create subtextual frames, concentric with the focus event. Some scholars in the field of drama in education[31] propose that the richness of a drama and the quality of dramatic tension are directly linked to the number of these internal concentric frames in operation. Alternatively, the dramatic situation may be reframed concurrently within a drama, to reveal and explore the focus events from other perspectives, and even in other styles and time-frames. Shakespeare constantly does this, particularly in his later plays, showing for instance the meeting of Antony and Cleopatra in that play through the eyes of the hardened soldier Enobarbus; he even consigns a major part of the denouement of *The Winter's Tale* to the prosaic gossip of minor characters. And, just as Shakespeare often reframed his own sources, reframing *Hamlet* provided Tom Stoppard with a new play, *Rosencrantz and Guildenstern are Dead*. In drama in education, participants frequently move between frames within the overall structural frame of the dramatic context.

2 Roles and relationships

In the **fictional context** the human subjects within the model express their relationships to each other and to the situation through their behaviour, which forms the primary text of dramatic action. As in real life this behaviour is not random, but is a product of the tasks and constraints imposed by the situation mediated by the capabilities, limitations and other personal characteristics of the individuals. This is the *role* of each character, and when participants 'take role', whether as actors upon a stage or as role-players in a drama in education, they are taking on those tasks, constraints and characteristics, as they do in real life.

Role in **real life contexts** has been defined as the 'clusters of rights (socially sanctioned claims) and obligations within a social unit . . . the parts that every member has to play'.[32] Sociologists and social psychologists have noted the similarity between the operation of role in real life and dramatic and theatrical conventions; it has almost become an informal movement in social psychology. Its roots are with earlier social and anthropological writers like Frazer,[33] picking up the Renaissance concept of *teatro mundi* – succinctly but by no means originally expressed as 'all the world's a stage'. By the 1960s the writers were re-evaluating that, abandoning it as a valid explanation of behaviour, but acknowledging their debt to it. Those influenced by it sufficiently to refer to it in their writings literally or metaphorically are from very diverse schools of thought sociologically, including for instance Erving Goffman, R.D. Laing, and Eric Berne,[34] three very popular and very disparate writers of the period. This is mentioned as significant because these writers were themselves all influential upon the teachers and dramatic artists developing drama in education at the same period, and there would appear to be a palpable correspondence of thought where the two disciplines influenced each other.

As in real life, dramatic characters have multiple roles to play. The primary role of being Hamlet, for instance, incorporates the secondary roles of son, stepson, lover, prince-elect, revenger, cynical observer, etc., throughout the whole play, and periodically takes on specialised tertiary roles according to the situation – prisoner, escapee, murderer, madman, etc. For example, the actor plays (1) Hamlet throughout the play; (2) loving son in the scenes with Gertrude; (3) her accuser and conscience in the bedroom scene.

Part of the importance of the fictional model is that the situation can be selected out and focussed to make these roles finite enough to be visible and manageable by percipients, whether as *actors, role-players* or *audience* (titles which are themselves roles within the **context of the medium**). This is particularly important in role-play, where many and varied responses are possible from the other role-players. Moreover, personality, cultural and relationship factors from the **real context** may potentially interfere in the fiction. This genre therefore imposes demands upon the participants for clarity of signalling and a very clear definition of the roles they are playing, for the drama to be sustained at all. For instance, relative *status* is an important situational factor inside and outside drama, and among a class of school students and their teacher there are normally very strongly upheld status positions. These may be partially suspended within the drama, but particularly if the teacher is participating they need to be taken into account and appropriately managed to prevent them from subsuming the status levels of the characters within the **fictional context** and either destroying or corrupting the drama in action.

The following constraints upon role operate significantly in dramatic fiction as in real life:

Social characteristics

Status (as part of the 'rights and obligations') is of course one of the major social and cultural characteristics of the dramatic role, part of the social *field* in which it is set. Other important characteristics of the field are: the cultural norms, customs and conventions; the moral and ethical limitations; and the ideological setting.

Relationship characteristics

Narrowing the field, the role is further characterised by particular behaviour patterns appropriate to the relationships with the other characters within the situation, such as the degree of kinship or familiarity, and the consequent level of formality, the amount of 'closed' interactions such as ritual and so forth.

Personal characteristics

In addition to these social characteristics delimiting the character's behaviour is a set of personal characteristics, including the basic psychological drives, the degree of motivation to the purpose and task, personal styles of behaviour and social skills, and attitudes – by which are denoted the usually unconscious emotional fixed reactions both culturally and personally derived, which each character holds towards other persons, ideas or environments.

One of the most fruitful fields for the creation of dramatic tension, and arguably the basis for the majority of dramatic subject matter, has always been the dissonance between these sets of characteristics, which impose constraints, often conflicting and contradictory, upon the characters. In the language of the real-life social psychologist, together they interact to create each character's postures towards the situation and the other characters which make up the behaviour of the role. The simultaneous management of status, role and posture within the **real context** and the **fictional context** is a key component of the metaxis between the two, as we shall see.

3 Purpose and task

General purposes beyond the fictional context

The religious origins of drama in the Western European tradition suggest that a function beyond 'art for art's sake' was perceived for drama from its chronologically earliest form. Plato in his *Republic* nervously contemplated its potential for destabilising society.[35] Aristotle, on the other hand, perceived its power for reinforcing socially acceptable behaviour both through the explicit messages it could carry (such as avoiding hubris and placating authority sources like the gods) and through its affective potential, which he codified into his theory of catharsis, purging the excess of dangerous emotions.[36] The validity and modern relevance of this is investigated in detail in chapter 4. For both these writers it is implicit that the experience should by its nature be pleasurable and entertaining.

By Roman times, a rather more dualistic perception seems to have emerged:

> Poets wish either to profit or to delight . . . the seniors rail against everything that is void of edification; the knights disregard poems which are austere . . . he who joins the instructive with the agreeable carries off every vote.[37]

This dualistic view of the edifying and the pleasurable would still have currency today, not only in drama in education, which after all takes its cues from the education system in which it is embedded, but among the public's perceptions of the role of the arts, which are inevitably influenced by that same education system.

The same dualism comes more directly into that system, via the legacy of Puritanism, from the nineteenth century, in the wake of both Romantic thought and commonly held perceptions of social class and work. This gave us a clearly demarcated and still ferociously held distinction between 'high' art and 'low' entertainment. The apologists and protectors of high art during the Victorian age further divided themselves equally ferociously between the notion of 'art for art's sake' (Pater, Wilde *et al.*) and the notion of the usefulness of art (Ruskin, Morris *et al.*). These two movements may both be seen to have derived from the Romantic revolution, where on the one hand art was seen as being a retreat from the base and utilitarian values of the society and a temple to preserve the higher aspirations of mankind, and on the other hand art was espoused as a potential rallying ground and way of subverting the same base and repressive power structures. Both these perspectives appear clearly evident together in works like Wordsworth's Preface to the *Lyrical Ballads* - as they still do in school arts staffrooms. Nowadays, terms like 'heritage art' and 'community arts' have replaced Wordsworth's, though perspectives and terminology still owe a lot to the Romantics: a national policy paper on the arts in Great Britain from the Government's own arts funding body (1984) was

entitled *The Glory of the Garden*, a title that was particularly
provocative to artists working as agents of social change.

The terms 'drama in education', 'theatre in education' and
'community theatre' all implicitly denote purposes beyond the
art form itself. These implications have caused dramatic artists in
response to man barricades in recent years in defence of the purity
of art form. These modern aesthetes do not always question
whether the dichotomous assumptions underlying their response
to these terms are in fact valid. In 1983, a respected theorist and
practitioner of drama in education, Gavin Bolton, was attacked
by two equally noted arts in education philosophers, John Fines
and Malcolm Ross, both of whom have contributed significantly
to the genre. Ross accused Bolton of betraying what he elsewhere
calls the 'holy' art form of drama to the less worthy functional
imperatives of education, while Fines accused him of selling out
education to the pretensions of the high art lobby.[38]

I would maintain that while both ideological and polemical
differences of attitude need to be acknowledged, the question of
purpose in dramatic activity is not a matter of simple polarity,
and that binary notions of art/entertainment and use/ornament
are unhelpful in understanding the complexities of a fusion of
already complex disciplines, such as arts and education, or arts
and community.

In order to clarify the general purposes of the arts, in this book
we take from the field of educational research some definitions of
the functions of *play*, particularly children's play. I believe that
drama, and all the arts, may usefully be viewed as playful
activities. As such they are inherently collective and processual,
and thus both socially and individually developmental.

Play is a word which may be seen naturally to fit into both the
world of education and the world of drama. Naturally, but
somewhat uneasily, in both worlds. In schools, while it is natural
for children to play, isn't the classroom the place to work, while
play is left outside in the playground? In theatre, too, actors
play in plays, but not for fun, they do not play about. *Play*, with
its rarely acknowledged but strongly implicit assumption:
work = serious / play = trivial, is a word which causes as much
distress, antagonism and oppositional behaviour among the
utilitarians who often and historically control educational systems as it does among the proponents of the high seriousness of
art. We have no axe of social control to grind, and so theories of

play and examples of dramatic play activity are well worth examining for the light they shed both on the natural and formal development of children, and on the nature of drama itself as a human artistic activity. This can then be usefully related to the reconstruction of this playful behaviour into dramatic *process*. The constraints from the educational contexts act upon the artistic purposes, entailing continuous renegotiation, not only of the elements of drama, but of the educational contexts and purposes themselves.

Specific purposes beyond the fictional context

The percipients in any dramatic activity will have different purposes, general and specific, conscious and unconscious, according to their role and function in the **context of the medium** (the whole event that is the drama). A person adopting the function 'playwright' may intend to instruct his/her audiences with a polemic or moral, to explore with an audience a specific context, to enable the audience to forget their everyday concerns and escape into a world of comfortable fantasy, to give the audience an uplifting experience, to make money, to gain fame, to prove that he/she is capable of writing a play, to fulfil a commission, to express a community concern, or in fact usually to fulfil a combination of purposes. Participants holding the roles of actors, directors, role-players, audience, etc., will also have personal purposes which may be identical, complementary or conflicting. Participants may also be carrying out more than one function at a time. It is not uncommon for an actor in theatre in education and community theatre projects also to be joint playwright, director, designer, company administrator as well as actor and role-player. The teacher in a classroom drama is normally simultaneously the primary playwright, primary director and designer and perhaps role-player; the students may be role-players, actors, subsidiary playwrights and directors and, at times, audience.

These participants carry into the activity purposes from those multiple roles. In genres with a highly specific functional component of purpose, such as drama in education, the purposes are explicit to at least some of the participants. In these genres, for the drama to be successful, the participants' sets of purposes must match. This involves an elaborate (though not always explicitly elaborated) set of *contracts* – of obligations and expectations. Much of the disappointment and sense of failure among percipients of any dramatic event, which is often put down vaguely to 'subjective reaction', springs from a mismatch of contractual expectations among participants, whose perceptions may well all be accurate but are inevitably limited to a great degree by the parameters of the contract they negotiated or assumed.

Almost invariably in drama in education, and frequently in theatre in education, general purposes such as the above may underlie the undertaking of the activity, but there are very specific purposes from beyond the drama which dictate its **fictional context**. Drama in education normally has two contextual settings, each of which which indicates a somewhat different approach and degree of specificity of purpose. Where the activity is taking place among a group of students under the name of 'Drama', though the subject matter will be constrained by the limitations of the school ethos and the comfort levels of the participants, it will normally be relatively negotiable, and particularly susceptible to initiatives from the students themselves. Their consciousness of the art form is likely to be relatively high. On the other hand, where the dramatic activity is subsumed under another subject heading, in what is commonly termed 'functional role-play', the subject matter is more severely constrained – in fact the drama is usually being invoked merely in order to explore that subject matter. The **fictional context** is almost invariably chosen by the teacher, and although there may be some negotiation of particular elements among the group, all the processual organisation of the drama is managed by the teacher in pursuit of very specific objectives, normally set in advance. The consciousness of the art form among the group is usually low. However, it is not always so cut and dried; some differences of approach to functional role-play do allow for a degree of flexibility in the learning expectations.

When one group of participants is involved at different processual levels from another, their particular expectations and demands need to be made most explicit. In a piece of theatre in education, the actor/teachers, the student audience/participants and the watching schoolteachers all have their sets of purposes; the educational purpose which is supposed to be the *primary* purpose is frequently confused or subverted quite accidentally, with each set of participants coming away with quite different perceptions of the action and the event. This also applies to other genres, such as youth theatre (i.e. performance work *by* young people). I was aware of an apparently mystifying difference of opinion among the various sets of percipients in a recent group-devised play that I was reviewing. It can in fact largely be explained by the piece's varying success at meeting different expectations:

> Whose truth do we believe? The truth for the performers (who in this case are the most important part of the project) is that it was worthwhile and a success. The truth for this supporter of La Boite Theatre is that it was a worthy venture. The truth for this adult theatregoer is that it was worthy . . . The truth for some of the players' contemporaries was that it was admirable . . . and the truth for one of Brisbane's adult critics was that in the end it was a bunch of kids with pretensions being pretentious.[39]

Purposes within the fictional context

Strictly speaking, it is the purposes within the **fictional context** which comprise that element of the dramatic form. Purpose within that context, as an element of the drama itself, is essentially a function of *role*. In order to examine this element, and the use that will be made in this study of the word 'task', it must be perceived from inside the outer frame of the drama. The dramatic narrative may be perceived as a story from outside that frame (i.e. by an audience). This is not how the characters, were they not fictional, would perceive it. It is only in rare moments in real life that we humans perceive ourselves to be characters enacting a story. For most of the time we live in the present, do what needs to be done in this moment, solve the problems presented by our environment, and plan our next moments according to our perceptions in this present. We move from one activity and *task* to the next, managing our lives according to the roles and attached purposes we perceive for ourselves. The characters of the drama may all be said to have purposes according to their roles and their personal characteristics. For some the purposes will be major goals subsuming many others, such as killing the king, finding the treasure, expiating a guilt or attaining the loved one. Those subsumed may include keeping secrets, dealing with rivals, exercising power, maintaining or changing status. The purposes may even be passive, such as waiting for an undefined goal like Chekhov's three sisters, enduring suffering, or attempting to continue without change. These purposes, like the roles themselves, are limited by the boundaries of the particular internal frame. I propose to use the general term 'task' to define the expression of these purposes in action within the drama. This term may readily be seen to have a particular helpfulness in the organisation of drama in education, especially in the management of dramatic tension, where the characters' tasks generate texts and subtexts of action and dialogue. This may usefully be studied to reveal the internal negotiating and concealing of purposes which form a notable part of the total dramatic action.

4 Focus

Framing reality

Erving Goffman, who developed the theory of *frame analysis* of social reality,[40] was not the first actually to apply the notion of framing either to social reality or to drama. The concealed metaphor of 'framing' dramatic narrative itself is found as far back as Sir Philip Sidney in his celebrated defence of the freedom of dramatists: 'a tragedie . . . is not bound to follow the story but having the liberty either to faine quite a new matter, or to *frame* the history to the most tragicall conveniencie'.[41] Sidney expatiates with many examples that clearly illustrate the flexibility afforded the dramatist by this 'liberty'.

Bateson's notion of the *play-frame* is extremely helpful in defining the basic function of dramatic make-believe as a human activity, and in support of the concept of art as playful activity.[42] Play is seen as essentially metaphorical rather than actual, expressed in a set of signals accompanying behaviour, which *frame* that behaviour as 'not-meant'. For our purposes, the fact that it is 'not-meant' allows extensions of the behaviour unacceptable in real behaviour, and simultaneously provides participants with protection both within the play and from 'real' consequences beyond it.

Bateson's definitions of 'map' and 'territory' also give warning of any too simplistic distinction between fact and fiction:

> in the dim region where art, magic and religion meet and overlap, human beings have evolved the 'metaphor that is meant', the flag that men will die to save . . . [where] we can recognise an attempt to deny the difference between map and territory.

It must be acknowledged in the light of this quotation that the categorical distinction I made earlier, between the **real context** – with its subsidiary **contexts of setting** and **medium** – and the unreality of the **fictional context**, is perhaps something of an over-simplification. However, for the sake of a clearer understanding of conventional practice in drama and drama in education the distinction needs to be maintained, mediated by the metaxis between them. Bateson further goes on to discuss the contextualised 'outer frame' which 'tells the viewer that he is not to use the same sort of thinking in interpreting the picture that he might use in interpreting the wallpaper outside the frame'[43] and which is a constraint both crucial and natural within drama in education.

To sum up, the act of entering a **fictional context** may be said to be entering a play-frame. Inside this frame the perspectives and apparent reality will be different from outside. It is by agreement 'not-real' – the most celebrated exponent of drama in education, Dorothy Heathcote, expressed it in now cant parlance as 'agreement to the big lie'.[44] It provides *some* protection from external consequences for those who step inside it. Its messages have entire currency within the frame only. In Bateson's terms, when Brecht's devices seek to make audiences alienate themselves from the drama to look at it 'from outside', the playwright is merely asking them to step outside the frame, or, later on in more sophisticated constructions of the *Verfremdungseffekt*, to place one foot inside and one out. Much the same is implicit in Brecht's instructions for acting – and the styles of 'Brechtian' acting which have emerged since.

Focussing the moment

Once the overall frame for the drama has been chosen, and the particular selection of picture depth (role-distance) and surface (convention) has been made, consideration must be given to the moment-by-moment operation of the action. There are a number of components used in common by drama participants and by teachers, which provide clarity of focus in the moment, and which are further investigated in chapters 3 and 4, with particular emphasis on the crucial nature which questions play in focussing the moment.

5 Tension

Dramatic tension is one of the most identifiable elements of any drama, yet it is one of the least defined. It is an element of no substance, entirely existent within the action and within *time*. In that sense the word is merely a construct to define a set of emotional reactions which percipients of a drama experience individually and as a group. However, it is one of the driving forces of drama, its presence or absence is immediately recognisable, and the success of any drama owes some measure to the appropriate management of dramatic tension. 'Like the rubber band which drives a model aeroplane, tension is the force which drives our drama.'[45] For the purposes of this study the source of tension may be defined as *the gap between the characters and the fulfilment of their purposes.*

Clearly, tension has to do with the passage of time, real time and narrative time. Neo-classical theories of unity were founded on the notion that dramatic power and tension were most heightened if the narrative time was concentrated – if not into an absolute congruence with real time, then at most into one calendar day.[46] Long after the Romantics like Hugo with plays such as *Hernani* at one end of the nineteenth century, and Realists like Ibsen at the other end, had broken the thrall of dramatic *practice* to these neo-classical notions, the Russian Formalist critics usefully ended this scholastic dispute. They proposed the concept of 'impedances' or 'retardation' as the source of narrative tension, being the devices by which an author prevents the reader reaching the end of the story. Drama in education theorists rarely use either of those words, preferring the term 'constraint'. The dramatic tension lies in the constraints faced by the characters in their pursuit of the resolution of their purposes. 'Drama is the art of constraint.'[47]

The term 'constraint' may be usefully used for processes

relating to the audience as well as to the characters. To some degree, even in a play where alienation is the aim, the audience is asked to identify with a **fictional context** sufficiently to want to know what eventuates in the situation. The more constraints put in their way, the greater will be the dramatic tension, until the audience's frustration level is greater than their desire to know, and the tension snaps. This is normally managed within the situation itself by the constraints upon the characters – particularly those characters with whom the audience is asked to identify. A common but simplistic and largely discredited view of drama places *conflict* as the basis of all dramatic tension. This view flourished during the early days of the development of drama in education, and led to forms of practice full of torrid and stultifying confrontations and slammed classroom doors. Conflict certainly is a significant component of dramatic tension, but by no means the only, nor even the primary source.

There have been a number of recent attempts in the field to define and categorise tension.[48] I propose four main categories, three entirely within the **fictional context**, one a product of the metaxis between **real** and **fictional**.

The tension of the task

In order to achieve their purposes, the characters within the fiction undertake tasks in which they are naturally absorbed, and which take time to complete, even if there are no other constraints to prevent their completion. There is a tension implicit in the very undertaking of these tasks. Realising this has been particularly helpful in refining the practice of drama in education. The earlier convention used by classroom teachers of 'acting out a story', far from being an easy activity, actually put the children into the difficult position of operating inside and outside the frame of the fiction simultaneously, being characters and narrator/actors together. It is now more sophisticated common practice in drama in education and participational theatre in education for teacher/playwrights to define the sections of the drama when empathetic role-play is appropriate, that is, when the children will be *in-role* as characters within the situation, and then to construct the dramatic action as a series of tasks for them to carry out before 'they' can reach their goals. These tasks may consist of physical action, or of verbal negotiation, of decision-making or planning. For instance, before the 'State Emergency Service Workers' can rescue the family trapped in the bushfire, they have to decode the faint Mayday radio message that has been received, and locate the house on a map, two very real and time-consuming tasks, with an urgency provided by the fictional situation.[49]

The tensions of relationships

The most commonly recognised sources of tension in drama are the relationships within the **fictional context** and among the characters. These tensions of relationship may be involuntary or voluntary.

We can distinguish three common involuntary forms. The first, *conflict*, is the constraint provided by the characters' *attitudes* to each other acting on their motivations. In the second, *dilemma*, which is arguably the most significant, the constraint is essentially provided by the *situation* in which the characters find themselves and involves either a choice between two purposes/goals, or between two potentially disadvantageous courses of action in pursuit of the purpose/goal. The harder the dilemma and the more risky the choice, the greater the tension. The third form, *misunderstanding*, may be attitudinal, situational or both.

Voluntary tensions of relationship exist in those interactions which the characters may have sought out for themselves, or willingly find themselves engaged in, but which have the effect of suspending the pursuit of purpose through time, which is why they embody tension. These include, on an individual level, *intimacy*, where characters share the significance of a moment, prolonging the time before reaching their ultimate goals. *Ritual* is the group equivalent, the formalised and ceremonial sharing of a moment perceived to be significant by all those concerned. Rituals may also include tension of the task, where the characters are depending on the operative effectiveness of the ritual to fulfil their purposes.

The tensions of surprise, mystery and secrecy

These tensions include both the shock of the unexpected and the shock of the expected, after that expectation has been withheld or delayed, or where the expectation carried a particularly high charge of significance, or where there is a mismatch between the expectation and the 'reality'. All of these tensions operate for instance in a play such as Synge's *The Playboy of the Western World*. Perhaps surprisingly, they operate even more strongly in a processual genre, through a phenomenon known as the 'dual affect', which forms an important part of percipients' response to drama, and is dealt with in detail in chapter 3.[50]

An important source of dramatic tension is the withholding or retardation of knowledge, either from the audience by the playwright, or from the characters: in other words, suspense. This discrepancy of knowledge is frequently seen as the principal source of dramatic tension by those who believe that the main line of communication in theatre is one-way, from the playwright to the actors, and thence through the characters and plot to the audience.[51] Some key practitioners of drama in education believe that suspense is a vital form of tension, and use it with sophistication in their practice.[52] However, while there is some validity in the notion, the tension produced by withholding information is actually a product of a broader dynamic, embodying a dialectic of power and control.

Metaxis: the tension of the real

There is a fourth tension only partly connected with the drama itself, and this is crucially found within the interaction, or *metaxis*, between the **fictional context** and the **real context**. In drama in education, where the **real context** also incorporates a dominant **context of setting**, and where the whole **fictional context** needs to be negotiated taking that **context of the setting** into account, this metaxis is always present. It is potentially a source of learning and dramatic meaning, as well as tension. If the urge for power and control mentioned above is at the centre of the negotiability of dramatic tension, then this metaxis is even more significant dramatically.

6 Time

Real time and narrative time

Drama shares with some other art forms like the novel the significant passage through time of its action. Barthes, Fish and the reader reception theorists have noted that the construction of meaning in any work of art, even a short lyric poem such as a haiku, has a temporal aspect, through the time taken by the audience to perceive it. A painting may, too, have an *implied* narrative. Narrative as it is normally understood is by definition temporal in the most basic way in that it describes the passage of events and the passage of people through them.

Both literary theorists and psychologists have proposed that narrative is very basic in another sense, that it is a central way by which humans organise experience into reality and identity for themselves: 'the child needs ideas on how to bring his inner house into order, and on that basis be able to create order in his life . . . The child finds this kind of meaning through fairy tales.'[53] The theatre director and theorist Eric Bentley relates it succinctly to drama: 'story is halfway house between Life and Plot'.[54]

Drama departs from other narrative art forms in that part of its device lies in presenting an apparent congruence between real time and time in the **dramatic context**. The central temporal narrative device of a figurative painting is to appear to arrest the narrative and embody an essential narrative focus in a frozen moment of particular significance. The central temporal narrative device of an epic or a novel is to reduce the significance of the lack of congruence between the real-time act of reading or hearing, and the events themselves. Homer's *Odyssey* is a long poem, but not ten years in the listening; on the other hand James Joyce's *Ulysses* may take considerably longer to read than its events take Leopold Bloom to experience. However, the link between the participant/audience's attention span and the length of the narrative is not in the synchronous nor the diachronous time spent, but in the impedances, or breaks and extensions, in the *expected* time of the narrative.

The audience at a performance experience *virtual* time; this is a 'first order' of experiencing, as distinct from the 'second order' of narrative fiction.[55] The particular genre of drama in education imposes another dimension of temporal experience through its use of the participant mode. In a drama in education the participants may, according to the particular role-distance and stylistic convention being employed, experience the dramatic action in three quite distinct ways.

1 In experiential role-play the participants *are* the characters –

in the sense that the characters exist entirely as shared constructs of the participants' intentions in creating, defining and agreeing to accept their characteristics. Therefore they experience the dramatic action in *first-order* real time.

2 they may experience the action in *first-order virtual* time. The most common manifestation of this within a drama is where the audience function becomes primary for the participants, say as spectators at a ceremony, or where they watch other action going on, while their own is completed or frozen.

3 they may experience the action in *second-order virtual* time. Examples of this would include acting-out an accompanying narrative or listening to the teacher supplying a narrative continuity link; or being involved in a reflective discussion evoking the action already experienced, such as after a drama about a hijacking, where the children and leader sat together to 'write the last page of this story of our adventure'.[56] Another convention, the 'frozen effigy', freezes the synchronous action and re-places it in a diachronous mode, but with the participants still in role as characters within the **fictional context**.[57]

Time in the narrative

Narrative is also the expression of cause and effect through time, and this is a useful way of perceiving the construction and management of dramatic action. The dramatist takes a focussed event and characters, and moves forward through its consequences, backward through its causes, or backwards and forwards to show the causal network. Many drama in education leaders use this kind of structure.

Timing and tempo

Part of the link between real time and narrative time is the moment by moment selection of pace at which events move and characters act and react within those events, including the contrasts of pace dictated by the selection of particular narrative events and focus on particular characters. These qualities of pace are often known as *timing* and *tempo*. They are perceived by audiences mainly in the unconscious terms of the comfort levels provided by the drama, though they have impact on the construction of meaning too. This is very noticeable in drama in education, where management of timing and tempo has a direct bearing on the explicit learnings sought and the implicit under-standings which emerge – and often on the leader's control of the class.

7 Audience

One of the most simplistic notions of the relationship between artist and audience is that of an absolute distinction, embodied in the writings of the post-war New Critics, and a great body of the teaching of literature in schools, where the function of a con-struct called 'reader' is to come to *the* meaning of a construct called 'author' who is always a different person. This meaning is entire in itself, and must not be 'socialised'.[58]

The 'traditional' view of a playwright no doubt owes a lot to these scholars. It certainly carries some currency in contemporary life, particularly among those who ascribe a didactic purpose to drama. The belief that some drama – 'the best' – has something to say, and that the majority of us who are basically non-artistic should be given access to this, underlies the teaching of dramatic literature, particularly Shakespeare, within many English and drama classes in schools and tertiary education.

This tradition in schools is very much at variance with the drama in education movement. Such a static notion of the relationship between initiators and responders cannot be true of drama, partly by the very nature of the *direct* communication between them, and partly because the function of responding (or 'audience') is in at least three ways integrally bound up with that of initiating (or 'artists/interpreters'): (a) the meaning of the experience is negotiated and recreated as the audience perceive it (this is true of the novel too – its meaning can and will be 'socialised' by what the readers bring to it); (b) their response affects the nature of the initiative or 'artistic' behaviour, actively or by implication (this is peculiar to drama – the audience chemistry can hardly work on a printed book as it does on performers); (c) the role of responding has the potential to become partially but significantly that of initiating (in other words, the audience can become participants and help 'write the book').

This is particularly characteristic of several of the processual genres of drama which are being examined here. The book examines the psychological and sociological origins of dramatic activity to discover processual aspects of the audience function and the ways in which the notion of audience is being renegotiated in contemporary processual forms of theatre other than drama in education. Among the most enterprising of these renegotiators have been theatre in education companies, particularly in the UK, and particularly from 1965 to 1980. Audience participation in theatre is a contentious issue but an important one.[59]

As a halfway house between conventional performance drama and drama in education, TIE throws light on three important factors: (a) the expectations of an audience and how they must be renegotiated if they are to include a participant role; (b) what effects incorporating the audience has on the nature of the performance; (c) how the audience constructs meaning within what is now a first-order temporal experience through the management of tension. Accordingly, in chapter 4 both *time* and *audience* are dealt with jointly with *tension*, as, together, they embody one of the most significant areas of negotiability. Examples are taken from both theatre in education and drama in education.

8 Location

The drama space

Perhaps the element of drama which distinguishes it most immediately from literature is that it happens in space, and more or less in flesh and blood. All the genres under discussion have a significant immediacy of physical presence. This book is regretfully not big enough to consider the semiotic implications of withholding or modifying some components of that physical presence – for example both film and television do without the third dimension and each alters differently the relative size of the remaining two; nor can the drama be touched or smelt. Radio drama withholds all visual and visceral stimuli. In all live drama, the element of *location* operates, as do all the elements introduced so far, as a condition within the **real context** and as an element of the **dramatic context**.

Traditional expectations about the nature of the space used for drama vary from society to society. In the form most recognisable to most of us, it is a special building called a theatre built or chosen for the purpose of drama, sometimes with no other purpose or attachment. Sometimes the theatre is specially designated, but incorporated within a larger complex as part of the purposes of that complex, such as at some holiday developments – once on a pier, now more often in a casino – or as a stage in a shopping precinct, or in educational establishments, where the theatre may serve other functions, as an assembly hall or sports centre.

These different spaces, however, usually share a significant message, and fulfil a set of expectations in their users: at least to the degree that they are a 'theatre', they are a place of special appropriateness for this activity. These expectations usually embody sets of ritualised practices for the participants, different sets according to the participants' dominant functional role. For the audience, the set may be called 'going to the theatre'. The specialised behaviour this traditionally invokes in our society includes making social arrangements (going to the theatre is very much a 'social' activity, and few audience members voluntarily go alone); particular clothing (which will vary according to the class and age orientation of the audience and their perception of the expectations of the location); specialised eating and drinking behaviour, timing, movement and gestures. Sub-spaces of the theatre (e.g. 'booking office', 'cloakroom'), and attendant functionaries ('ushers') will cater to these expectations. For the actors, the theatre space invokes a quite different set of appropriate behaviours.

A flexible approach to the concept of theatre is a characteristic of recent processual genres of drama. This often includes a conscious renegotiation of the appropriateness of certain spaces. In its simplest form, it comprises transposing the drama to a space which will have messages unfamiliar to 'theatre', thus making the performance strange – Shakespeare in a circus tent complete with sawdust. An alternative to this is to make the theatre itself strange, by changing some of its messages, as for instance in a theatre in education performance which transformed the interior of the theatre into a 'town-planning seminar'. This particular programme also concealed the fact from the audience that the building was a theatre, by leading them into the 'seminar' by a back door.[60]

The next processual step is to use a space which is normally not a theatre, and incorporate this within the **fictional context**. Chapter 5 looks in detail at a celebrated piece of what the playwright calls 'location theatre', which took place on a tramcar. The author of this mobile experience perceived a number of spatial factors which theatres and trams shared. He renegotiated the particular messages of 'tram-ride', incorporating them in his fiction to make them appropriate to the expectations of the audience (the play was about people riding in a tramcar). The tram became a theatre by being made special.[61] Soon after seeing this, and directly influenced by it, I devised a piece of community theatre with its origins and its audience in the past and present pupils of a one-teacher country school. This was played in and around the school building itself.[62]

At both of these plays, the audience was prepared, and had come specially to a space which they expected to be transformed. Theatre workers take another processual step when they choose to work in a physical environment which is a normal real-life environment for participants, with strong messages that are unrelated to theatre – a **context of the setting**. Community theatre and theatre in education groups nowadays frequently perform in spaces like pubs, prisons and schools. As will be seen, these companies have to develop strategies for overcoming the 'normal' messages, or reducing their power sufficiently for the messages of the drama to be perceived as significant.

Two extreme forms of this are street theatre and drama in education. Street theatre often has the added problem of needing to distract the audience from other purposes properly belonging to that environment and to which the dramatic purposes are irrelevant, such as shopping. The case of drama in education is somewhat different, especially when it takes place, as it frequently does, in a classroom, where other behaviours, physical constraints and expectations are normal that may actually conflict in purpose with drama. Students may see a classroom primarily as a space where they sit in rows all facing one way attending 'serious' presentation of 'real-life' material in silence (*partially* like a theatre audience). Students may see another classroom as a place for purposeful activity, moving around and working in groups (quite *unlike* a theatre audience). These spatial messages and expectations need to be taken into account in choosing appropriate dramatic conventions and strategies.

Location within the fictional context

While dramatic participants in genres like drama and theatre in education often have little flexibility in their choice of real space, they do have control over the locations they choose within the **fictional context**. They are relatively free to set their dramas in any location appropriate to the subject matter. The location chosen carries its own set of messages which act upon the situation and the characters. For instance, a death notification may have a quite different impact on the behaviour of the characters (and on the experience for the audience) if it takes place in a queue waiting to hear the names of victims, at a Christmas party, or on a building site among chainsaws and pneumatic drills. Each of those locations has particular physical characteristics, especially in terms of the correlation of sound with mood: the silence of the first, the controlled musical jollity of the second, and the tense cacophony of the third will affect the characters' reactions to the same news, and probably its manner of being told.

Particular qualities of location include the dimension of *closure* or *openness*. A closed location is defined as one which carries a limited and inflexible set of messages, and a limited flexibility to introduce characters from outside – for instance, a prison cell. An open location is flexible in terms of the messages it may carry, and the characters who may be introduced. In *The Winter's Tale*, Shakespeare sets much of the first half in the claustrophobic atmosphere of a court, and the second in the fresh air of the countryside, signalling this clearly in the text, in order to make a thematic contrast. Sartre's *Huis Clos*, where Hell is depicted as an elegantly furnished, entirely closed room, is an extreme example of a closed location. Alternatively, the playwright may devolve part of the choice to the director, as I noticed in two productions of the same theatre in education programme *Year Nine are Animals*.[63] The playwright sets one scene merely 'in a museum', with children surreptitiously smoking. In one production the museum was shown to be crowded with exhibits, display cases and people; in the other it was depicted as empty and echoing. Both of these interpretations were equally appropriate to create the semiotic of 'museum' and to highlight the dramatic tension. A subtly different mood was created, however, and different tasks for the characters.

Though normally in drama in education the participants are as free as a playwright or director to choose their dramatic location, two factors are relevant here which can act as a constraint. Congruence of *space* with *location* needs to be considered. This is because the **context of the setting** is usually particularly dominant in this genre, and it may be necessary to help prevent the 'normal' messages of the space interfering in the messages of the internal dramatic location and perhaps overwhelming them.

9 The Participant Group

As drama is a *group* art, any group of participants may theoretically create a different negotiation of the terms of the art form. This may be seen in contrasting manifestation in the genres of (a) the traditional western play, (b) community theatre and theatre in education, and (c) drama in education.

In a play within the western tradition, there is a small group of people (sometimes as few as one) of 'primary producers' – playwright, producer, director, designer, composer – who make virtually all the major artistic decisions. A slightly larger group of intermediaries – the actors, crew, etc. – carry out these primary decisions and communicate them to the audience. This, the largest group of the percipients, is put in the position of *reception* and little else. They can have a small direct effect on the intermediaries, through what is often referred to as the 'chemistry' of performance. The effect they have on the primary producers is distant, indirect and generalised, manifested in terms of what subject matter, conventions and styles those primary producers deem the audience will find acceptable.

In some community theatre and theatre in education, the negotiative power relationships are somewhat differently devolved with the intermediaries of the first model becoming also the primary producers. A small company which produces both community theatre and theatre in education provides one typical example.[64] They function as a cooperative, with a common leadership and ideological orientation and no 'director', in the limited locality of one provincial city. They often seek a future audience's *direct* input of ideas in order to provide a drama specific to an interest group. The material is structured through discussion and improvisation. Sometimes they *then* call in a playwright with a compatible philosophy to shape their material to performance standard. They rarely work in conventional theatres, preferring the locales familiar to their audiences. Their own centre is a semi-converted dockside warehouse, where some performances are staged. This company is in a different and far more two-way communication with their potential audiences. That in turn imposes directions and constraints on the artistic product.

In drama in education, an even more specific situation exists. The audience is no longer limited to reception, but is expected to take a pro-active part in the creation of the art work. Purposes of leader and audience have to be matched. Together the leader and the audience form the whole participant group; there are no intermediaries. The participant group members normally know each other very well in contexts other than drama, and negotiation and renegotiation of many factors – power, status, comfort levels, peer group and sub-group loyalties, etc. – take place constantly. The leader is usually aware of this, and aware also of the educational needs, the social needs and the limitations of both the group as a group and the individuals in the group – its 'luggage'. The group itself is usually equally aware of these, and some groups have the capacity or experience to manage their own social dynamic to a considerable extent. In selecting the **fictional context**, the focus and in particular the dramatic roles for all participants including the leader are negotiable and they have to make personal choices and manage together all these needs and limitations as artistic constraints upon the drama. This is why the group needs to be highly motivated before a drama in education can even happen. This entails negotiating and accepting contracts, explicitly or implicitly.

10 Language and movement

The classical writers considered drama as a poetic way of storytelling essentially akin to epic. In Aristotle's words:

> epic poetry has been seen to agree with tragedy to this extent that it is an imitation of serious subjects in a grand kind of verse.[65]

That concentrates unduly *literarily* on the language in which tragedy is expressed as verse. However the same writer also emphasises:

> tragedy is essentially an imitation . . . of action and life – all human happiness and misery takes the form of action; the end aimed at is a certain kind of *activity*.

In this book, language and movement are considered together, along with the paralinguistic components of the gesture and the action. Language (i.e. utterance in *words*) is a very important kind of action, and movement is another aspect of that same action. A full analysis of dramatic language, and the negotiations of language from which meaning is derived, demands a multidimensional paradigm which cannot be condensed within one chapter. Accordingly, one particular dimension is chosen for analysis, a contextual dimension. Instead of primarily regarding language and movement as parts of the stylistic conventions for expressing the drama, for our purposes they form the natural operation in action of the drives, purposes and tasks of the characters within the drama. (A distinction does need to be made between 'natural', as used here, and 'naturalistic', which is in itself a self-concealing convention that is a part of the conventions of drama.)

Any dramatic action has at least three functions. What it denotes for the enactor, the *purposive* function, relates to the tasks that form the basis of the action. What it denotes for others, the *communicative* function, relates to the constructions to be put upon the action by others. The action is also necessarily *expressive*, where the action reveals aspects of the character's nature that modify or throw light on the purposes and may permit renegotiation of details of character and relationship within the drama. These main functions can incorporate others, such as *reflective, referential* and *poetic*.[66]

In the genre of drama in education, as outlined above, the functions of audience and participant group are significantly renegotiated from the conventions of western theatre. Accordingly the purposive and particularly the communicative functions of the dramatic action which those participants engage in are renegotiated. Language and action which they generate within the **fictional context** may simultaneously have functions within that context and within the **context of the medium**, operating either as primary text and subtext, or as two parallel texts. A clear example of this is the celebrated injunction 'Pick up your guns!'[67] to start a drama in education. Within the **fictional context**, the commander instructs the soldiers quite appropriately, stimulating further action from those characters. Within the **context of the medium** the teacher, assuming role as the commander, is signalling that the play has begun, and that the other participants are to take specific roles, that is as soldiers, and respond within the fiction.

In this framework, language and movement as forms of expression of the stylistic conventions of the drama express themselves in the linguistic genres and registers employed by the participants, and the effect that this has on the belief in and commitment to the drama. Participants in drama in education frequently have only a limited command or variety of registers of language and gesture available to them, and leaders often use drama in education to stretch and extend their range. In fact language acquisition, practice and development are commonly high among the purposes for drama in education in schools.

11 Mood, symbol and meaning

These elements are, in a sense, of a different order from the 'substantive' or structural elements discussed above. As the 'Dramawise' diagram (Figure 1) suggests, they are the products of those elements – except that the very word 'product' could imply a substance which mood at any rate does not possess (like tension it is immediately apprehended, but you can't pin it down or reproduce it), and a stasis which would be extremely misleading as we consider meaning. Meaning is often assumed to have this substantiality, but it is a negotiable dynamic, subject to its context or contexts and with a considerable social component.

Mood

Mood may most simply be dealt with here: I am using the word to denote the overall emotional climate created by the action and setting of the drama or a section or scene within it.[68] It thus forms the background for creating dramatic symbols and a constraint upon the 'free' and in Barthes's sense pleasurable construction of meaning.[69] Mood is most usually perceived in the moment. It is

not to be confused with 'empathy', although empathy is one of
the components of the mood.

Symbol

Symbol is of course crucial to drama – drama is a symbolising
activity, incorporating all the stages of symbolisation from
purely iconic imitation or 'mimesis', through the associative to
the metaphorical, the abstractly referential and thus fully
dramatic symbol.[70] The word 'symbol' is doubly important in the
case of drama in *education*. The development and management
of symbolic behaviour is a very important part of all education,
and as I have already suggested, play is a crucial factor in that
development. The symbolic processes known as language underlie most human thinking (some structuralists would say all),
though some formal 'education' systems actively inhibit both
explicit language development and symbolising behaviour:

> David, a student in Grade Eleven, was given a piece of Virgil
> to translate. He wrote a literal translation that he found
> unsatisfactory because it lacked the spirit of the poetry. He
> spent the rest of the evening turning that prosaic translation
> into poetic form, and next day submitted both pieces to the
> Latin teacher. His poem was returned, crossed through in red
> ink with the words 'This was not asked for'.[71]

This has particular reference to the problems faced by exponents
of drama in education in establishing themselves within those
very educational systems.

Chapter 8 explores dramatic symbols, how they are constructed
and their relationship to the drama's meaning outcomes within
the **real contexts** of schools. By symbols I do not mean merely the
use of associative signs with metaphorical reference, such as
significant properties – a walking stick denoting 'age', or a
particular use of a language register to indicate royalty. More
important is the creation of symbols *within the dramatic action*
and their subsequent meanings which can be generalised beyond
the **fictional context**. To explain my meaning, let me contrast
two kinds of symbol used in drama.

1 An immediately recognisable example of a dramatic symbol
which exists more or less solely *within* the **fictional context**
would be the kewpie dolls in Ray Lawler's *Summer of the*

Seventeenth Doll. These signify the importance of their annual meeting for the characters, who first cherish and finally destroy the dolls as the last assignation turns sour and is abandoned. It would be perilous for the audience to make any kind of generalisation from the fate of dolls into their own real world.

2 However, a piece of theatre in education opens with a sixteenth-century woodcutter raising his axe and bringing it down expertly on a log of wood, the gesture of a craftsman with his tool. In the final image of the play, the woodcutter, driven to desperation, raises the axe again, now a weapon against his oppression. The playwright, Geoff Gillham, expressly intended this symbol to be operative in the **real context** of the clients – to give them a rationale for opposing repression with whatever tools and weapons they can.[72] This particular extremely elegant symbol, though clear enough from the playwright's point of view, is problematic in terms of what meanings the audiences actually derive and use in their own **real contexts**, since in theatre in education the play's the thing, and the team do not have the luxury of the drama teacher to construe and reconstrue the meaning with their audiences.

Since drama in education, too, is concerned with making operative in the real world the implications, ideological discoveries and symbols that emerge within its fictions, this question of how symbols operate, and how they may be applied – and misconstrued – in schools is also dealt with in chapter 8.

Meaning

Dramatic meaning *emerges* – it is not laid down. It is a multiple and many-layered dynamic. It is to a degree always negotiable, and continually renegotiable – and more than this, it is not always controllable. Drama in education provides a particularly interesting framework in which to perceive and study the dynamic nature of the meanings which emerge from it. It is one of the most entirely evanescent of all dramatic genres. A significant proportion of the action is invariably improvised, so it has a spontaneous life and instant death. It is therefore not reproducible, and cannot even be replayed without a major transformation and changes to the messages, the mood and the meanings which are palpable to the participants. Unlike other, more performative genres, it is almost impossible to observe from outside, since the roles are only externalised far enough to allow the other participants to note and act upon the signals. Sometimes even, information must be concealed from one or more characters within the **dramatic context**, and so it is concealed from those participants. It is a particularly frustrating genre to catch at all on reproducing media such as film, video or sound tape. All of the participants are to some degree, according to differences of role, creating their own meanings which are partially shared and not fully externalised. The roles they create are temporary refractions of themselves as constrained by the demands of the role, and at this time only. In short, it is intended to be satisfying in itself. This makes, even for the participants and especially for the leader, observation and evaluation extremely difficult.

This evanescence also makes the element of dramatic meaning extremely difficult to *control*. This is both one of the attractions and one of the biggest problems for those exponents who are trying to establish the genre in schools as a teaching technique. To find the participants' meanings we must look at their *purposes*, and in particular those in control of the medium. The leaders or teachers normally appropriate the functions of playwright and director, and they may also take role as a player and devolve some aspects of 'playwright' or 'director' to the other participants.

To teachers and to their clients, the creation and negotiation of meaning is usually expressed in terms of the word 'learning'. The multiple constructions put upon the meaning of this word have created an industry almost as big as the education industry itself. We will restrict ourselves to some of those meanings of the word 'learning' which are understood and pursued by the exponents of drama and theatre in education.

At its simplest level of purpose, drama may set out to teach 'objective' facts, skills and processes – both drama and theatre in education have been used as a way of introducing concepts in maths, commerce and technical drawing, of acquainting students with new words in foreign languages and English syntax, and of training aspects of fine motor coordination or bushfire rescue drill.

A little more sophisticated definition of learning is evident in much functional role-play, however, when it seeks not only to acquaint students with 'surface', reproductive knowledge, but some 'deeper' implications, transformational knowledge – using identification with a **fictional context** as a way of assisting them to discover aspects of that situation, by 'putting children into others' shoes'. Many exponents believe that drama in education has the transformational capacity to assist students to develop skills which will aid them in the social contexts in which they find themselves. This manifestation of learning, often known as 'drama for capability' or 'drama for empowerment', is quite a savage political battleground of right and left, with one set of exponents using drama to socialise children into the society in which they find themselves, and the other using it to give them a critically active and activist orientation.[73]

The phrase 'drama for change of understanding' is one that has acquired almost entirely common currency. This study defines the term as it is used within the genre, and in particular investigates the strong influence of phenomenological thinking on two of the most influential exponents, Dorothy Heathcote, who frequently refers to 'the universals', and the less rhetorically flamboyant Gavin Bolton, whose writings gave this term 'drama for change of understanding' its widespread usage.[74]

Teachers are by the nature of their occupation concerned with the **social context** in which their teaching operates, at least at the micro level. This book takes as its basis for ideological investigation the commonly held view that, virtually by definition, state-provided or accredited educational institutions exist, among other things but most importantly, to maintain and reinforce the power structures, as well as the other traditions, attitudes, values and mores consistent with those power structures which exist within that state. That they are usually quite efficient at this maintenance, the whole 'deschooling society' movement of the early 1970s has noted.[75] They usually have the agreement of most of their clients at all levels: children, their parents, the local communities, and the eventual users of the children such as employers and the sellers of goods and services.

This is the context in which virtually all exponents of drama in education and theatre in education work. Promoting and evaluating the work in terms of its possible impact upon the ideological framework of schools, either in reinforcing or in challenging the ideology, and how that manifests itself in assumptions and action has been a major focus of practice and scholarship within both the drama and the theatre in education movements. TIE in particular has been intensely and explicitly political since the late 1960s, much more so than the bulk of drama in education. However, there has been a great deal of cross-referencing between the more influential figures in both genres. A key unresolved debate of the last few years centres upon the extent to which drama in education practice is as encouraging of social change as most of its exponents believe, or whether some of its practices actually achieve the opposite or at least something very different from what they intend.

12 Further elements

In addition to the key elements incorporated in the model, there are a number of other elements which relate specifically to the *performative* aspect of drama, rather than to the nature of the dramatic action itself, which is why they were not included in the original model. These may be labelled *the performance elements of theatre*. They include: acting styles and conventions of performance; stage design and settings; artificial lighting; the accessories of the characters, namely costume, make-up, masks and properties; sound effects; incidental music; dance, gymnastic or circus tricks and other physical spectacle.

To these might be added a number of subsets which have been dealt with in the pages above: focus within the moment, including *contrast, timing* and *tempo*. However, no static model of a dynamic event like drama can ever be complete, and there are many other ways in which all these elements could be re-combined, and other terminologies with which you may be more familiar.

Aristotle defined among his six basic elements two which are in fact performance elements – Spectacle and Melody. Aristotle regards both as peripheral:

> Melody is the greatest of the pleasurable *accessories* of tragedy . . . Spectacle, though an attraction, is the least artistic of all the parts. The tragic effect is quite possible without a public performance and actors; and besides, the getting-up of the Spectacle is more a matter for the costumier than the poet.[76]

Which puts the design and production team in its place. And the actors, for that matter.

Now it may be validly argued, particularly if you are a semiotician, that these performance elements are as much a part of the total event as the structural and processual elements in the main model, since they are just as much a part of the semantic network of signs which is the drama as perceived by its audience. Be that as it may, this book follows the model (and Aristotle) by being what might be labelled *context-centric*. Therefore those elements of the spectacle will be focussed on only as they are relevant to the contextual elements of the dramatic action. For example, a component of spectacle which accrues a special meaning in relation to the **fictional context** – such as the white colonists smashing a giant papier-mâché totem which the natives have with much careful labour constructed to represent their tribal identity[77] – is an intrinsically dramatic symbol. Such elements as incidental music or lighting effects, which reinforce the known messages, or only have a specific meaning at the moment of perception, are ignored as extrinsic or peripheral signs.

Chapter 1

The dramatic contexts

To recapitulate the Introduction, the word 'context' needs to be treated with care, as the word is used, and used frequently, with two entirely distinct connotations throughout the book: 'real' and 'fictional'. 'Purpose' and 'role', therefore, are two words which have two entirely different connotations according to which 'context' is being invoked. Furthermore, in any dramatic event, within the **real context** there is always at least one further contextual layer, and sometimes two, the **context of the medium** and the **context of the setting**.

THE REAL CONTEXT

The background to any drama experience is the percipients' own **real context**. This is taken to mean the real pattern of relationships and situations from which the whole text which is the dramatic event arises – all the people involved in making the dramatic event (with the functions of writers, teachers, actors, directors, interpreters, audience, participants, etc.) *and* the social, ideological and cultural context in which they are living.

THE CONTEXT OF THE MEDIUM

The coming together of people for the event itself creates an intermediary **context of the medium**. A somewhat equivocal truth about drama is that it is always 'an event of special significance . . . it generates meaning'.[1] It is a group art, whose action and meanings are collective. There has to be a coming together of people, who separately or simultaneously embody a number of distinct functions. This takes place in what is, or must become, a specialised location, where the art form is expressed and communicated through the medium of some of the percipients, augmented by performance elements.

In conventional genres of western theatre, this coming together happens in a theatre, which is basically a building or space which is designed to make it easy for the participants to create the **fictional context**, and for the audience to believe in it. That is why auditoria are usually darkened, with as few extraneous activities as possible going on, to keep the audience focussed on the fictional action and help them forget those elements of the real which are incongruent with it. The theatre is not just an external setting for the drama, like a randomly chosen picture frame, but germane to the social occasion that is a drama, which many of the participants are engaged in creating for the audience, who are not there by accident, but by contract. The makers of the drama, and where and when it happens, are therefore all part of the medium by which the elements of dramatic form are made manifest. I call this contextual layer the **context of the medium**. Some scholars prefer to use the term 'the performance context', but when dealing with processual genres where there may be little performance as such, like drama in education and TIE, this can be misleading. Even if there is no theatre building, if the drama takes place in a classroom, this **context of the medium** is present: there has to be an agreement to use the (often unyielding) space for the fiction; the group has to be united in agreeing to have a drama. This is one reason why some teachers are scared of using drama with their classes: you can't impose an agreement to do drama, it has to be negotiated with the children. If one child refuses to accept the group's fiction – who, when the rest of the class are tensely engaged in rescuing the orphans' gold from the dragon's cave, loudly states 'There isn't a dragon, it's just Philip', or in egotistical bravado creates his own fiction and zaps the dragon, cave and orphans with a raygun – the dramatic context disappears, and with it the drama. Both of those responses happened to me within the same drama, and I assure you it is so. In a theatre, this contract for drama is made easy: the people are there voluntarily, drama is what they expect will take place, and those who are audience accept that their path through the **fictional context** has been pre-set by those called playwright, director and actors, and that they have prescribed ways both to respond and not to respond.

Inexperienced audience members may be confused within this **context of the medium** and shatter it by incorporating inappropriate responses into the **fictional context** from their own **real context** – such as the legendary American cowboy at a nineteenth-century touring melodrama, who rescued the (fictional) heroine by shooting (really) dead the actor playing the villain. Less spectacularly, this phenomenon often happens in children's theatre, and even cinema, where children unused to theatre gratuitously supply their comments on and assistance to the action. This happens so frequently that encouraging loud but limited and peripheral audience participation long ago became incorporated into the **context of the medium** as a convention of children's theatre and Saturday matinée cinema: 'Hellooooo, Uncle Arthur!' and 'Look out behind you!'

THE CONTEXT OF THE SETTING

Sometimes, drama happens in places which are not specifically designed for drama, and where the participants may have different purposes from doing or watching a drama, places such as a shopping mall, or a pub . . . or a school. This may be said to form another layer of the whole context, the **context of the setting**, where the setting imposes very dominant messages which make drama difficult, and so the renegotiations have to be either very beguiling, in order to deflect the hoped-for percipients from their other purposes (like shopping), or very specific, in order to persuade them that the drama's purposes are in fact in line with their own. For instance, in Brisbane where I live, during the International Expo 1988 street theatre on site was one of the most popular attractions. For audience and performers alike it was far easier and more successful than in a normal shopping centre on a Saturday morning, since *entertainment* and *spectating* formed part of the purposes of the pedestrians at Expo.

Drama in education and theatre in education are two more such genres. They take place in settings which actively mediate against the ready suspension of disbelief; schools have very specialised purposes, and very strong messages of reinforcement for them – many of the practices of schooling are specifically designed as focussing devices for those purposes. In such cases, steps must be taken to ensure the transformation of the **context of the setting** into one congenial to the medium or art form.

In fact, an inadequate awareness of the potency of the **context of the setting** has been one of the major factors hindering the growth, effectiveness and recognition of drama in education in schools. For a class to take drama seriously it is necessary for the teacher to persuade the clients – and colleagues, usually – that drama will contribute to their learning; that is the students' expectation of what a school day is for. This is why drama teachers do not like drama being regarded (as it often is) as a reward subject, or one to fill up a wet end of term Friday; this automatically devalues the experience in the eyes of its participants because it has nothing to do with their real purposes.

THE FICTIONAL CONTEXT

Within these layers of the real world, a **fictional context** is created, consisting of a situation and characters – the selected and focussed pattern of fictional or fictionalised human beings, their location and their relationships which are the subject matter of the dramatic narrative. Figure 2 indicates a few of the internal frames which may exist within the fiction. In terms of the elements of dramatic form, only the **fictional context** is an element of the drama itself, the primary one in terms of where this book starts.

CONTEXTUAL FRAMES

In other words, the whole context incorporates numerous contextual layers or concentric frames, three of which are external to the drama itself, which forms the fourth, and which may itself contain several more. It is little wonder that conventional literary theory has tended to find drama too hard to analyse in linear terms. This may be depicted as shown in Figure 2, equally for a conventional play (*Hamlet*) and for a drama in education (*The Fields of Orange and the Float of Ignorance*, described in detail in chapter 7).

In one very important sense, **fictional context** is a derivative from **real context**. It is a particular *framing* of aspects of the real, for purposes which relate very directly to the real, and the real network is never fully or deeply suspended. This is particularly true in the genre of drama in education. In a genre like this,

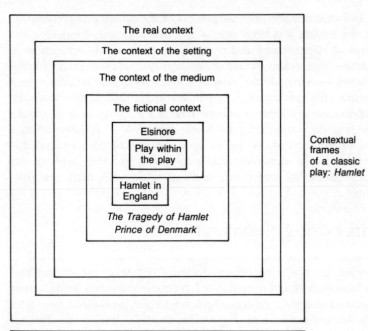

Contextual frames of a classic play: *Hamlet*

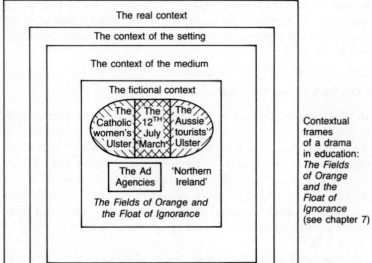

Contextual frames of a drama in education: *The Fields of Orange and the Float of Ignorance* (see chapter 7)

Figure 2 Contextual frames in drama

where the audience are also simultaneously pro-active participants, it is very hard totally to separate the messages and meanings belonging to the **real context**, the **setting** and the **medium** from those of the dramatic fiction. The **real context** and the **context of the setting** are virtually unchangeable within or by a drama, though that cowboy in the melodrama audience certainly crudely altered one actor's reality. Short of such drastic action, the real context cannot be renegotiated within the active life of a drama, though the whole polemical theatre movement, and drama in education, are predicated on the belief that some change in the **real context**, however minute, is possible as a result of the drama. However, the **context of the medium** is more negotiable – as we have seen, a theatre can be replaced by a shopping mall, a schoolroom or even a tramcar – though not without effort. The **fictional context**, the subject matter of the drama, is entirely negotiable. All four layers are interdependent.

In drama there must always be some congruence between the **real context** and the **fictional context**, and the ideological purposes within that context, whether subversive or reinforcing of the contextual values and attitudes, cannot be achieved without the control and management of this congruence.

DRAMA IN EDUCATION: CHOOSING A CONTEXT

The notion of allowing the clients to select their subject matter has been a vital factor in the development of drama in education from the time of the pioneer practitioner Peter Slade (the 1950s). This, according to Slade, was a concomitant of harnessing the natural instinct towards dramatic play inherent in children. Slade and his followers respected (to a point of encouraging random ideas, sometimes) the offerings of children, trusting them to reach 'significance', which for him lay in the natural patterns of the art form, and in particular the patterns of archetypal symbolic movement, which emerged automatically from children's play.

> Whilst young, the Person has ideas already. The ideas are shown to us by words and action . . . where the right conditions prevail we begin to see the now unmistakable signs of an *intended* [Slade's italics] art form . . . it is the dawn of a certain seriousness . . . Their language contains moral and

philosophic references, a new poetic flow and views which often surprise. The period is one of . . . great enchantment, and the extra sensitivity that is developed brings the Child to the threshold of the most wonderful years of Dramatic fulfilment.[2]

Though many later practitioners would not subscribe to the unrestrained romanticism of the thought and the language, Slade's willingness to negotiate the subject matter of the drama with the clients has led to one of the most characteristic conventions of drama in education: 'What shall we make a play about?' This convention seeks to assist the participants to arrive as a group at a central focus which can be both sustained and modified by further questions as the drama proceeds, eventually creating a fluid but clear contract which holds the action together. This is dealt with in detail later in this chapter and in chapters 6 and 8.

While the language and romanticism of Slade are clearly Rousseauan (though Slade does not explicitly acknowledge Rousseau), the 'deep soul experiences . . . and ice cold logic' to which he is referring are derived from Jung (whom he does acknowledge[3]). For Jung, the collective unconscious may be revealed through forms of action, such as religious ritual, which are in fact dramatisation: 'organised religious ritual expresses . . . the living process of the unconscious, in the form of the drama of repentance, sacrifice, redemption'.[4] These revelations through symbol, myth and ritual will 'naturally' evolve in any community *given time*.

Time is usually the problem. The succeeding generations of drama teachers found that these natural processes, if indeed they exist in the lyrical forms of Jungian psychology invoked by Slade, are usually severely inhibited by the **contexts of setting** in which they happen. Schooling is neither automatically educational liberation nor cultural enrichment, as three drama educators from different genres, Bertolt Brecht, Albert Hunt and Brendan Butler,[5] combine to make eloquently clear. Books much read by drama teachers have included *How Children Fail, Deschooling Society, Teaching as a Subversive Activity, School is Dead* and *Pedagogy of the Oppressed.*[6] At the very least, the drama teachers have discovered that 'Schooling is but a small part of education . . .,'[7] and the negotiability of the art form in pragmatic terms as well as philosophical/ideological ones is bounded by the messages of that schooling which forms the intermediate **context of setting**.

A theatre is a physical environment designed to assist the creation of drama, by neutralising the messages of the **real context** – in a standard theatre, by the concentration of focus upon a specially recreated location, while the rest of the space is temporarily suspended in silence and darkness. A schoolroom, which is where the vast majority of drama in education and TIE events take place, is entirely different. The expectations of the participants are that non-fictional events are what normally take place, that the 'learning' which goes on in a classroom is part of the 'real world'. *Objectivity* holds sway. The physical environment obtrusively reinforces this: the physical setting of the furniture, the concomitant sounds of bells, the properties like blackboards and pens, reinforce the normal activities, which are the outcomes of the status relationships and purposes of the participants – namely, that the room is where this 'learning' happens, through the medium of a teacher teaching children 'subjects'. Therefore, far from being an easy or appropriate environment for Slade's 'natural forms', the classroom discourages the kind of 'absorption' which is for him a prerequisite for the automatic elevation of children's ideas into significance. In other words, the dynamics of drama are actively at odds with the environment. This is dealt with in detail in chapters 5 and 6.

There are two ways in which drama teachers have coped with this incongruence, and these two approaches have formed the foundations of the two major strands in drama in education (and the base of one of the two major dichotomies that have bedevilled the movement):[8] (a) drama as 'service'; (b) drama as 'subject'.

DRAMA AS SERVICE

Teachers have attempted to play down this conflict between the environment and the art form, by seeking congruence, firstly of expectation, then of subject matter. This movement has often typified itself as 'drama as a service' within the curriculum. School is where certain subjects are 'normally' taught, so drama makes it its business to fit in with those subjects, to be a teaching method. The **fictional contexts** are taken directly or indirectly from these subjects, and the allied explicit purposes of classroom discourse. Drama in education becomes functional role-play.

Subject matter and situations relate directly to the curriculum as it is being studied, through factors which are unrelated to the drama, such as syllabuses and standardised units of work. *The Industrial Revolution, The Nativity, Computer Studies, Goldilocks, Italy, Cruelty to Animals, Antarctica, The Pitjatjantjara people of Central Australia* and *The Vietnam War* are some of the topics providing the **fictional contexts** of a recent publication compiled to assist primary teachers to use drama in this fashion.[9] The book consists largely of schematic descriptions of these dramas, which mostly are taken from units of work in Social Studies or Language Arts, as they were taught by local teachers. None was originally taught in a lesson called 'drama'. The emphasis throughout is on pedagogy. In most cases the purposes of the teachers only transcended the curricular parameters of these subjects in order to fulfil allied, approved aims of the official curriculum – such as giving the children the opportunity to gain self-confidence, make public speeches, practise interviews, or create related art and craft work.

Functional role-play is frequently assumed[10] to be of a lower artistic order than 'drama as an art form'. It may indeed often be so, if the purposes of the functional role-play go no further than simple interactions for short-term pedagogic ends. However, study of these particular functional dramas is revealing: several use quite complex and elegant artistic structures. The drama on Aboriginal traditional life involved the children taking two roles, where they had to take decisions in each role consistent with the action taken in the other role, which also involved concealing from one role what they discovered in the other.[11] This is a sophisticated task for ten-year-olds, but one which adults might find more difficult, as children's spontaneous dramatic play frequently contains such cruxes. The drama on Vietnam returnees[12] interfaced with the **real context** in a very Brechtian and sophisticated way: firstly the teacher used a real-life visitor, a social worker engaged in rehabilitation with war veterans, *in role* as one of his own clients; several sessions later, the drama climaxed with an Armistice Service and a two-minute silence, which was timed actually to happen at 11 a.m. on 11 November, Armistice Day, as the whole school held a two-minute silence.

In other words, the **fictional context** is only minimally negotiable in this sub-genre of functional role-play which comprises drama as service; far less so, in fact, than in a normal theatre. A playwright is frequently constrained only by the preoccupations and interests of his or her generation and him/herself, tempered by the awareness of what will be acceptable to whatever audience is in mind. The drama teacher, on the other hand, is in the position of the commissioned writer, given a range of specifics, or even one subject, and a specific audience. That audience is almost unique among audiences in that it is virtually entirely captive. Negotiability must be left to the focussing and the management of the subject matter – to the internal elements of the drama.

SERVICE AS SUBVERSION

Most drama teachers use functional role-play as part of their normal teaching duties. However, not all drama teachers are fully in sympathy with the aims of the establishment which provides their income. The notions of schooling and education being distinct or even contradictory terms have been very influential. In such a case, the teacher as educator may see a duty to subvert the schooling processes. This has not been confined to drama teaching – these ideas have been current in tertiary education studies departments for twenty years; arts teachers, particularly, have sought to implement them in schools. Very recently, science teachers have been demonstrating serious concern over the dislocation of science from the lives of most people, and in particular the alienation of many school students from it.[13]

A strong current of ideological investigation and scepticism about the purposes of schooling has emerged within the genre of drama in education during the 1970s, no doubt fuelled by the aforementioned 'deschooling' texts, and intensified into the mainstream of philosophical discourse during the 1980s.[14] It is appropriate and should be expected that a clear critique and standpoint should have emerged in South Africa, of all the countries currently engaged in drama in education. In a very elegant article written in 1983,[15] Brendan Butler, a young South African drama teacher, questions the use of the word 'process' for what normally happens in schooling. South Africa during this period had four education systems, each established on explicitly racial lines, with differentials of funding and expertise along the same lines. In this context, as I witnessed in 1982, the implications are every day evident of what Brecht defines, with a stridency attractive to teachers seeing themselves trapped within a system with which they were not in accord, as 'the Barbarian in unforgettable form . . . [and] limitless power. Equipped with pedagogical skills and many years of experience he trains the pupil to become a prototype of himself.' Butler quotes Albert Hunt's gloss on this trenchant critique:

> The sense of other people, with mysterious knowledge, controlling your life is what our education system is structured to communicate . . . The lining up in the playground when somebody blows a whistle; the morning assembly, where power is displayed, often decorated with theatrical emblems, such as gowns; the rituals of moving from room to room when the bell rings; all these are theatrical in their effect . . . The organisation is about organisation.

He then takes this metaphor of the theatricality of schooling further, to state that 'our schooling system . . . serves to perpetuate existing power structures through specifically theatrical devices'. The elegance of the argument is in the way Butler takes the contentious issue within the genre, between 'product' (theatre) and 'process' (drama in education), and applies it to the whole of schooling, which he refers to as a 'theatrical given', contra drama in education 'which serves to remind us that reality is a dramatic process'.

> Of all the anti-educational feelings and attitudes instilled in us by the theatricality of schooling, the most damaging is the feeling of theatricality itself. Once pupils and teachers begin to perceive their classroom interactions as taking place on a plane 'one step removed from reality', the possibilities of any real education taking place are nil.

Butler sees the processuality of drama in education as giving teachers the opportunity to 'subvert this theatricality (in a way that rational argument never can) because it is able to meet the enemy on its own terms – the affective, feeling level of experience'. Butler does not suggest that alternative subject matter should be smuggled into the schoolroom, but that, on the contrary, it is imperative to start with the 'official reality' of the subject matter of schooling, the curriculum, and deconstruct this to show its artificiality, and thereby understand its workings sufficiently to transcend it or oppose it.

This proposes another purpose for functional role-play. The **dramatic contexts** are not, need not be negotiable – they remain as the *text* of the dramatic encounter. The purpose of the drama therefore becomes for the teacher and students to renegotiate the contextual *subtexts*: what the essential features of the situation are, how the characters do or may operate in this situation, and what constraints and taboos they face . . . and which of those constraints and taboos are given and immutable, and which, maybe surprisingly, are not.

In the primary school dramas referred to above, there were elements of this visible in some of the dramas. While the drama on *Antarctica* concentrated purely on acquainting the children with the physical facts and associated human problems of its subject, the *Vietnam War* drama left the students with probably less factual information but, instead, a very strong affective and intellectual response to the problems faced by war returnees, not just of Vietnam but of any war, and a range of articulate opinions and proposals for action (these are explicit in the children's writing, some of which is included in the document).

DRAMA AS SUBJECT

Drama is not always bound to the subject matter prescribed by the school curriculum. Where drama is perceived as a curricular 'subject' in its own right, or where the leader has more freedom than is otherwise available within the school curriculum – such as in a tertiary course, a youth theatre group or an adult group – more negotiability of subject matter is possible. It may occur in subjects like English or Citizenship Education, where the notion of expressive language may be acceptable within the standard curriculum, and where the available **dramatic contexts** for exploration are less circumscribed. Since Slade, drama teachers have been expressly willing, where they have not been bound to the specific subject matter of the curriculum, to negotiate the subject matter of the drama with the clients.

This willingness has led to the characteristic starting point of drama in education referred to earlier: 'What shall we make a drama about?' This convention has been extensively used by a generation of drama teachers, initially led from the UK by the examples of the pioneers Gavin Bolton and Dorothy Heathcote, who altered the carte blanche offered by Slade to a very different notion. The students' chosen subjects are starting points which are indicators of their concerns, but not necessarily directly and explicitly. The difference may be perceived clearly by a comparison with Slade's starting point of 'the ideas game', where the students are invited to supply, quickly, a number of unrelated ideas, which the teacher takes and weaves into a story that forms the basis for the drama. In the Sladean game, a number of (perhaps significant, perhaps random) ideas are accepted, then further randomised by being fitted together by the teacher into a narrative whose only logic is that of plot.

The 'What shall we make a drama about?' convention demands a process of negotiation and consensus, which involves the teacher and the students in beginning to perceive the possible dramatic subtexts. In the simplest form of the convention the teacher, with chalk poised, asks the students for a subject, which may be an *issue* of social or personal concern ('Insanity', 'Northern Ireland'), or a suggestion for a topic to form the basis of the **fictional context** ('Climbing Mount Everest', 'Road Accident'). The students' ideas are usually phrased in a single noun phrase, and in students of secondary age or above most consist of abstract nouns ('Fame', 'Euthanasia', 'Homelessness'). A number of possible topics are canvassed, and each is briefly discussed. This discussion is crucial for the playwriting function in both teachers and students, for it allows the first glimpse of the dramatic possibilities of the word. It assumes that whether for an explicit reason, or for one more deeply embedded, there is a significance about the choice of subject which may be explored and explicated in a drama. This is a necessary part of the contract of expectation between teacher and students, and if it is not accepted by both parties, this kind of discussion quickly breaks down and other agendas become dominant – expressed for instance in students deliberately choosing 'funny' or 'impossible' phrases.

This convention permits a number of interpretations of the starting points:

1 The subject may be a matter of immediate concern for the students (e.g. in the week following news reports of a mass trampling to death at a football stadium, a request for a drama on

this topic), so the teacher who is interventionist/playwright will be concerned that the **fictional context** representing this subject will be explored beyond the students' textual knowledge to uncover or discover subtextual elements or extensions of the context of which the students were previously unaware.

2 The subject may obliquely be of personal concern, and it is incumbent upon the teacher to discover during this brief interchange whether this is so, and what is the concern that is being simultaneously concealed and revealed by the students' offer of the subject. In a celebrated piece of teaching,[16] Heathcote asked a group of delinquent children in a high-security residential school for a topic, and was offered 'Prisoners of War', with an accompanying request for an escape. Recognising the implicit connection with the reality of the children's own lives, Heathcote was able to formulate a **fictional context** with an appropriate subtext concerning loyalty and betrayal, which kept the drama at just enough distance to generate a strongly empathetic response that did not spill over into the **context of the setting**. In many cases the embedded motive is more concealed than this, and the teacher may either need to explicate it further, or be ready to deal with the motive when it emerges in the drama.

3 The subject may in fact be just a matter of passing interest, such as the suggestions by a group of inexperienced tertiary students for 'The Titanic' and 'The Beach' as subjects. If the discussion does not reveal any particular motive beyond that, the teacher's role is to find a way of maintaining the interest while constructing a sufficiently engaging **fictional context** with substantial subtexts.

4 A trivial topic of passing interest may indeed be chosen, if for some reason the students do not wish to become involved in a 'deep' or intense experience (this was in fact true of some of the tertiary students above, who had heard that a parallel group had been involved in a drama which had become 'too heavy'). The job of the teacher/playwright is further modified by the need to allow the students to maintain their levels of comfort, while extending the dramatic possibilities of the subject matter into a context which will provide a significant experience and outcomes of meaning.

Concern about those properties of the art form which could result in drama 'too heavy' for the - remember, captive - participant group, has led a number of practitioners to eschew interventionist teacher-as-playwright forms. The critique is worth examining, and the ideas still persist in management of preschool and infant play, where there has been a movement to cut down or even forbid any intervention in the dramatic play of infants, certainly in their choice of subject matter.[17] Slade himself encouraged freedom of play in the young child, but insisted that 'the adult is vital to the best in this form of activity'.[18] Observers of Slade's own teaching note that it was characterised less by creative liberation of the children than by close control and the systematic management use of his own considerable charisma.

The last major movement in Australia to maintain this position was constructed as a deliberate attack, with an explicit ideological basis, on the strongly interventionistic mainstream of drama in education. It was led by Garth Boomer, a senior educator with many of the same deep concerns about the manipulative nature and purposes of schooling as the interventionists whom he was attacking:

> This drama teacher, allegedly committed to the empowerment of her students, critical of existing power relationships in society and in the school . . . is out of habit and some delusion teaching dependence and powerlessness because she has not confronted the fact that in addition to experience and status she holds secrets which constitute power and could constitute power for others if shared, particularly with those who live in schools.[19]

This particular attack led to a bizarre and short-lived manifestation in South Australia known as the 'apricot jam' method, where the children's expressive ideas were given primacy, and the teacher was there to offer the 'ingredients' of drama skills, and 'take the pot off when it was ready'. In practice, as witnessed by this writer, it was indistinguishable from the discredited 'get into groups and make up a play to show us' convention: the students spent a great deal of time engaged with the teacher in developing sufficient presentational drama skills to recreate the original idea, untouched by much intellectual transformation or dramatic process.

However, Boomer's article was a salutary warning of a danger just becoming clear to many of the teachers ideologically committed to using drama to assist in changing attitudes, that of replacing one set of concealed power constraints with another. In fact the cogency of the argument has led to several of the principal practitioners whom Boomer was criticising looking for a resolution in terms of empowering the students through giving them access to the negotiations of the playwriting process, and in fact to the elements of the art form itself. In this way it has served to re-emphasise the artistic nature of drama in education, through pedagogical concerns.[20]

ISSUES AND CONTEXTS

The same debate has been very articulately carried on in the UK, crystallising predictably into the 'process versus product' arguments[21] and less obviously but perhaps more productively into a discussion about 'issues' and the connections between **real** and **fictional contexts**.

Those students who requested a drama on 'The Beach' were very inexperienced in drama in education, which partially accounts for the defensive and tentative nature of their initiatives. Most participants in drama in education, who have gone beyond the initial stage of familiarity with the genre, choose subjects that are clearly 'issues', which they can identify as of social or moral import to themselves. This is particularly true of secondary school children.

The ways in which these issues are treated, in order for them to *serve as* appropriate **fictional contexts**, is a key element of the genre, and in fact is itself a controversial issue among the workers, especially in the UK. In a way, this is a sophisticated and concealed form of the 'subject and service' debate. There are those, particularly teachers committed to ideological change, who would prefer the notion of the issues being *served by* appropriate **fictional contexts** rather than as defined above. These teachers would privilege the issues, rather than the use of drama, as the primary factor.

This debate is both accentuated and clouded by the quality of the work itself. Teachers who focus upon the *issue* by directly recreating it do not in general produce good drama, because drama is not just a mimetic reflection of life, but essentially both an oblique and a transcendent medium.[22] This obliqueness will be dealt with more fully below in terms of drama in education. It is as true of adult theatre, as Brecht and his followers well understood: 'All art is abstracted from life, with considerable subtraction and distortion on the way ... One may be a pessimist, but to sing one's pessimism is to transcend it.'[23]

The debate in drama in education has been intelligently resolved by the recognition of the nature of the relationship between the **real** and the **fictional contexts**. The educational linguist Harold Rosen, whose work has been influential in both the UK and Australia, clarifies thus the relationship of issues to context in education and life:

> What people say derives from praxis. The social context ... is not an arena in which we perform our dramas. [NB: Here Rosen helpfully uses the normally obfuscating meaning of 'drama' as actions in real life which have dramatic qualities.] It is the dramas themselves: people in action with each other and against each other improvising the text as they proceed.[24]

Implicit in this is that 'issues' are abstractions from contexts. In order to understand the issues, the clients need to understand the social contexts which generate the issues. Elsewhere, Rosen notes that drama provides 'a particularly efficient laboratory for the analysis of social contexts [through] its conventions of form that allow us to break the context down so that its constituent elements can be recognised and understood'.[25] This breaking down and transforming through conventions of form is what is meant by **fictional context**, the model-building process referred to earlier. To Butler, there is no problem. Working in South Africa, the **real context** is explicit and inescapable, the issues are apparent, and inevitably the fabric from which the **fictional contexts** of drama in education are tailored.

FLEXIBILITY OF FICTIONAL CONTEXT

The starting point and initiation of the **fictional context** can be variously negotiable between the leader and the participant group. In addition, one of the characteristic features of the genre is that it can be renegotiated as it goes along, either by stopping the drama and jointly replanning, or even by intervention from within the drama. This frequently happens, often on account of the external givens of the **context of the setting**. If students who have been absent for parts of a drama return in the middle, they need to be incorporated, as in one secondary classroom drama where I had the students cast (or enrolled, as it is usually termed) in a mental institution and some potentially disruptive students returned from absence. They were initially disposed not to take the **fictional context** seriously, and certainly had no intention of being put cold into the roles of the insane. However, they had to be incorporated, so I enrolled them as visiting medical students, and their keen participation, combined with a piece of individual opportunism by one of the other participants, created an entirely different central crisis from what I had expected and been planning. This drama is explored in detail in chapter 2.

The reverse can also happen, of course. Since many drama participant groups are captive, they frequently display different levels of commitment to the drama, and if the drama is not working, it may have to be stopped and renegotiated. An example is 'there was not much tension – why, and what can we do about it?' (where the renegotiation is likely to lead to a replay, or an alternative scene true to the demands of the original **fictional context**). Sometimes the problem lies in that context itself, in which case the situation and roles have to be renegotiated if the drama is not to be abandoned. This may even be achieved within the drama, without stopping it. A frequent manifestation of the teacher-in-role convention is 'the messenger', who intervenes to bring an entirely new constraint, perhaps in the form of 'a command from my mistress, the Queen', in order to reintroduce tension into a sagging situation. The participants themselves in role may introduce it. I had focussed an upper primary school drama about Lewis and Clark's exploration of the Oregon Trail on the logistical difficulties of mounting and supplying a nineteenth-century expedition. The children were beginning to show their not unreasonable boredom, but were persisting desultorily in role. Two 'scouts' who had been sent out to look for Indians returned shouting that they had just found Eldorado. I had to decide quickly if this geographically suspect and historically untrue new situation was appropriate, decided that in terms of learning possibilities – and in the spirit of Sir Philip Sidney's 'framing the history to the most tragicall conveniencie' – it was, and so I accepted it without breaking the role-play. The drama then became centred round the looting of this city of gold, which provided me with a quite different pedagogical opportunity to focus the participants on the moral questions implicit in discovering treasure which might be others' precious artefacts.

Afterwards, we all felt that the change of direction was valid and created both a richer drama and different but stronger learning than the original **fictional context** which was virtually abandoned, only used as a very loose framework ('When we get this lot back to New York . . .'). I imagine those children still know very little about Lewis and Clark and the logistics of expeditions.

Within a drama, as well as the **fictional context** itself, the basic model, being renegotiable, so are the thematic subtexts. In a drama I led in South Africa, the initial intention, which I negotiated in advance with the participants, was to investigate 'how appropriately do we deal with those who are involved with drugs?' There were about seventy mainly white observers of this black class's drama. One student's suggestion sparked off the impulse for me to use them peripherally within the dramatic exercise work leading up to the main **fictional context**. The students at a break then bravely agreed to incorporate this mass of observers from the **real context** into the **fictional** – to include them integrally in the drama. As you can imagine, their presence modified the drama considerably. Although the central theme remained the consideration of methods of dealing with drug offenders, another very strong subtext was added to that, the racial components of those methods in the society of the participants. This subtext was never made explicit within the drama, but it certainly affected the dramatic action, and it formed the major part of the reflective discussions which followed the drama, both immediately after the drama, with all the participants, and the following day, with the 'observers' only. This drama was for me at any rate a very significant experience, and it is referred to later, in chapter 4.

ANALOGIES

Earlier in this chapter drama was referred to as an *oblique* medium. This is perhaps best shown in the use of analogy as a major convention. Dialectical playwrights demonstrate their contextual examinations through situations whose similarity to real life they may leave implicit and indirect, as for instance Caryl Churchill in *Top Girls* and *Cloud Nine*, or may choose to make explicit, like Brecht through his balladic continuity in for example *Arturo Ui*, a play written with a very specific analogy as its base that Brecht had no intention of hiding or mystifying.

In drama in education, as in TIE, how much analogy the leader needs to use relates directly to the negotiability of the participants, and the learning outcomes which might emerge. A drama teacher in an inner-city school wishing to engage with the issue of racism with a group of Grade 12 students felt she could not confront the issue directly, since there were some very real tensions within the class between the main traditional ethnic groups of Anglo-Saxon and Greek, and the Vietnamese, who had recently formed a major group of new residents within the catchment area. She felt that the attitudes of all the students needed to be respected, and while it was imperative for her to bring up the subject and attempt to use drama to 'challenge the group's initial perceptions' (especially those which were of a racially aggressive nature), she did not wish to bring the drama into conflict with strongly held prejudices and risk aggravating those prejudices. Accordingly she set the **fictional context** for the drama in seventeenth-century England, among a group of Flemish Huguenot weavers and the residents of the area where they settled.[26]

This particular drama had structural problems, which prevented it from fully realising its potential for examining this subject in the relative protection of drama – not least, the students' unfamiliarity with that period of overseas history. However, the technique is widely used, particularly for dealing obliquely with themes like racism. A TIE team with whom I worked wished to examine the theme of unemployment and its causes. We were working in an area markedly polarised on the subject, with some of the client schools full of the children of the unemployed, but others where most of the children and teachers believed that unemployment was largely the fault of the inadequacies of the unemployed. Rather than create two separate programmes, we took our subject matter from the Industrial Revolution, whose distance would give safety in examining the causes of unemployment. This programme[27] is described in more detail in chapter 4. The team left the responsibility or choice of making explicit the issue and causes of modern-day unemployment to the teachers in the school, some of whom used the programme to examine the issue, some of whom preferred not to. In at least one school, the issue became a raging debate within the staffroom, more so than in the classes.

Chapter 2

Role

ROLE IN REAL LIFE

In the genre of drama in education, role is the most extremely processual element. Out of all the elements of drama being analysed in this survey, the metaxis between the **real** and **fictional contexts** is most evident in the word 'role'. It has already been noted in the Introduction that role-theorists – a branch of mainly phenomenological analysts of real-life behaviour – have utilised *teatro mundi* ideas in their codifications of how people behave.[1] It may also be seen more mundanely in the language of everyday life, that of all the *teatro mundi* words which are in everyday currency, 'role' is the one most unselfconsciously and accurately used. Newspapers are full of 'tragic' accidents or mistakes which are in Aristotelian terms not tragic at all, though they are disastrous, and 'dramatic' rescues, by which is usually meant 'suspenseful'. The self-consciousness of this usage may be commonly seen in the educational world: frequently when a drama colleague or I go into a school – particularly one where little formal drama is happening – we are greeted by the Principal or classroom teacher with the defensive quip: 'There's no shortage of drama goes on in this school, I can tell you' (meaning 'crises'). Following this witticism up, an individual child is likely to be pointed out with 'Oh, he's a real comedian' (usually meaning 'individualistic' or 'naughty').

On the other hand, in such phrases as 'what's your role in this?' and 'my role is . . .', used in a wide variety of applications and situations, there is rarely any conscious sense of the etymologically buried metaphor. Admittedly there is a touch of self-conscious reference to the theatre in Banton's definition of roles as 'the clusters of rights . . . and obligations within a social unit . . . the parts that every member has to play',[2] but this was understandable as he was explicitly charting the territory between **real** and **dramatic context**.

The role-theorist Erving Goffman uses a very complex application of theatrical metaphors.[3] In order to manage within the 'roles' with which each human is endowed throughout each day, 'mask'-like 'personae' are put on. However, he then goes on to deny that *teatro mundi* is a valid way of seeing the world *per se*. A critique of Goffman's theory of role-playing in real life, revealingly entitled *Role and Identity*, actually reinforces Goffman both in theorising from a *teatro mundi* starting point –

> *Part One, Theatre and the Appearance of Reality* . . . This is a book about art, particularly theatrical art. But since art is a part of life, it is also about life

and then rejecting the notion as an all-encompassing worldview:

> Although theatre is an *essential*, central and powerful metaphor, it is not an all-powerful one applicable without limit to the world. Its power over actuality derives from its fictionality.[4]

In fact, in the terms of this book, these perceptions are problematic, for the very reason that the theatrical understanding and references which underlie both writers' theories are entirely based on the notion of theatre as *product*. The *essence* referred to in the above quotation is based on a static view of performance – both writers take their examples from dramatic script, and from description of particular finished productions, perceived as if they have an 'essential', reproducible, shared and non-negotiable meaning. The usefulness and limitation of this understanding of reality, and of a purely phenomenological approach to drama itself, is further explored in chapter 8.

ROLE-PLAY AND TRAINING

The categorisations of real-life behaviour implicit in the word 'role' have been neatly defined with no such theatrical inference at all by a quite different writer, who is a practitioner of role-play:

> Roles . . . may be allocated by *social position* such as teacher, husband, juvenile delinquent . . . a role is then a way of expressing group norms and the social pressures acting on an individual. Sometimes role is defined in terms of the *context* in which people find themselves, such as a church . . . or a football match. The role behaviour of an individual changes in accordance with his surroundings . . . the role behaviour of a congregation is different from a football crowd. Role may also be defined in terms of *function* or *purpose*. The people who are to be found in a hospital may be carrying out the tasks of doctor, administrator, patient, visitor or chaplain.
>
> The process of role-taking is a natural and continuous one for anyone who is socialised within their community.[5]

The very lack of any theatricality of reference in this definition is both useful and significant. It forms the introduction to a teacher's handbook on the use of role-play as a *training* technique. Although the writer, van Ments, does acknowledge briefly the theatrical derivation of the word, there is a clear emphasis on the functional application of role-play as a form of behaviour modification, not an art form. In fact, he leaves all further reference to the art form of drama to page 158, where he very briefly refers to 'creative drama', as the last of a number of uses of role-play as 'experiential methods' – methods in his words 'which are occasionally confused with role-play . . . [of] . . . enabling the student to express himself using body, voice and instruments'. This, according to van Ments, results in 'the development of more self-confidence, a release of innate creativity, and an increased awareness of the value of the arts in general'. The placement of these words is interesting: one generalised reference to creativity and one to the arts provide absolutely the last purpose for role-play that the author considers worth mentioning. Furthermore, van Ments's definitions would not be acceptable in this form to most arts educators, and certainly not to drama in education practitioners. He goes on to note that 'a casual visitor looking at creative drama sessions . . . could well *mistake* them for a role-play simulation in progress. A close inspection would show that the emphasis is on free expression and not so much on a constrained situation.' This last phrase contrasts interestingly with Bolton's widely accepted definition of drama in education as 'the *art of constraint*'.[6]

This particular handbook has been looked at so closely because it highlights some interesting schisms within the educational application of role-play, and raises the question of whether role-play has an innate or even necessary artistic aspect – a question frequently raised by some philosophical defenders of art form in education, who are made nervous by the extensive use of role-play, particularly in its more functional or 'service' applications, fearing that the aesthetic elements of drama education are being devalued or overlooked.[7]

The use made of role-play by practitioners such as van Ments also highlights the issue of negotiability of role. There are many handbooks of this type, and a whole movement of educators engaged in devising structured role-play and simulation activities for learning, who are entirely divorced from the genre of drama in education, though the uses they make of role-play are almost identical, except for the matter of negotiability. Drama in education practitioners would have no problems at all with van Ments's definition of role in real life, from which both sets of activities take their origins. Many of the activities and events created by exponents of simulation and those of drama in education are in fact entirely identical, and not just to the casual observer. The difference is in perspective and in underlying philosophy. Simulation exponents see their work as absolutely functional, and though they may use structures which are dramatic, and consciously employ tension, focus, space and time as would a drama teacher, they believe that it may be conceived of in purely functional cognitive terms. They conceptualise 'drama' as something else.

The educational philosophy underlying the simulation movement is rigorously behaviouristic, as is the methodology. The widely used *Instructional Design Library: Roleplaying*[8] manages to make not a single mention of drama. Its form reinforces its determinedly mechanistic title, with the central chapters labelled 'i. Use, ii. Operational Description, iii. Design Format, iv. Outcomes, v. Developmental Guide'. Its preface claims to

identify the sequence necessary to conduct role-playing sessions: 1. determination of training objectives; 2. outlining of the three phases of role-playing . . .

. . . the book includes information on how to 1. create steps related to method centred role-plays; 2. write roles for role-playing cases; and 3. develop and use observer guides for use during role-playing enactments.

The word 'drama' does not appear in the book. You may have noticed the number of nominalisations (making actions into nouns) the authors use, in title, chapter headings and preface. These provide a clear clue towards identifying the book's educational tradition. Even the publishers call themselves Educational Technology Publications. This book offers a rationale for role-playing:

> Role-playing is used to broaden people's repertoire of behaviours and to help them gain insight into their present behaviour and possibly to modify it. Role-playing gives people an opportunity to try out behaviour before mistakes are made in a real life situation.

The second sentence has been used, almost word for word, by many drama teachers. What they would have difficulty with would be the first sentence, with the plural use of 'behaviours', and the attached verb 'modify'. Objective-centred behaviour analysis and modification is not art. Drama as an art is holistic, even in its application to learning.

As a result, between exponents of drama and exponents of simulation there is considerable confusion and misunderstanding of what each does, and the differences between them:

> Unlike some informal dramas or role-play exercises where the participants are told 'You are angry', 'You are obstinate', 'You are weak', a genuine simulation does not try to control behaviour – behaviour depends on the participant and is real, not assumed.[9]

These 'examples' of drama come from another handbook of simulation which is explicitly hostile to drama, and are meretricious, quite apart from the loaded word 'genuine'. Such practices have in fact been obsolete and discouraged in drama in education for almost two decades, and are only to be found among teachers who have no knowledge of drama in education. These practices belong not to modern drama in education but to its precursors, notably E.J. (later Bishop) Burton, whose little handbooks of the 1950s were directly or indirectly responsible for the thousands of teachers who in the name of creativity adjured their classes to be trees and melting ice blocks, and to explore strong emotions by mimicking them faithfully and out of context, just as described above.[10]

Moreover, many drama exponents note that the tight and behaviouristic rule-based structures of simulations are designed for the express purpose of controlling behaviour (the Instructional Design Library handbook makes no bones about it), and claim that they significantly lack the natural negotiability of 'real' drama. Both simulation and drama exponents believe that the behaviour of their participants is real, not assumed.

ROLE-PLAY AND GAMES

An element of genuine difference between simulations and drama is the individual competitiveness which is at the core of many simulations. This derives from the games which underlie both simulations and drama. Drama and all art are playful behaviour and very purposeful (this idea is further explored in chapter 3).[11] One aspect of play is the rule-based structures of interaction known as games. The developmental purposes which games play in the education of a child have been thoroughly explored by educators, with for instance Piaget investigating the particular importance of rules in his classic essay on Marbles. The development of self-control and discipline through negotiation and maintenance of rules in a competitive situation is central to this analysis. However, the sensitive documentation of children's games by the Opies in the UK and Turner and Spatchcock in Australia shows that this reading of games, though plainly evident, is not the whole story.[12] Drama educators have taken up the notion of drama as a game, but demote the role of competition, for 'neither the social interactions of real life nor of drama are necessarily competitive'.[13]

It may be helpful to consider why games *are* competitive, by reversing this analogy and looking at how games are like drama. A drama frames a particular set of interactive behaviours between people, each of whom has purposes and motivation towards goals. These goals of the characters, like the drama, are expressed in representational terms, imitative of the goals of equivalent people in real life; these goals are subject to *constraints* caused by the situation and by the actions of the other characters – that is, dilemma and conflict. In a game, all these elements still exist, but simplified, stylised and, through the rigid rule-base, ritualised and reproducible. The characters become 'players'; characters with common interests become 'teams'. Players and teams retain the word 'goal' (literally or metaphorically) to define their purposes.

The constraints may be within the situation (the dilemma, physical obstacle to be mastered, or problem to be solved as a direct creation of the rules themselves) or between characters and teams in direct conflict. If so, the goal or goals manifest themselves in *competition*. Because the complexities of representational behaviour have been edited out, virtually the whole purpose of the interaction, the game, is to achieve the competitive goal. In football, for instance, there may well be an aesthetic dimension, say in the effective management of the elements of space and movement, but even in a public performance such as a Cup Final this is subordinated to the simple resolution of tension through achieving (scoring) goals. In figure skating, the very aesthetic dimension is itself traduced into the competition and points given for artistic merit.

In drama, though conflict of individuals and team interests are still a crucial part of the action and the tension, they are no longer exclusively so. Other aspects of the interactions which are being represented become worthy of concentration in themselves. The dilemmas which the dramatic situation proposes reveal a wider range of behaviours from the characters than simple confrontations. Unlike the players in a game, who are limited to the behaviours dictated by the rules, the characters are constrained only by their human characteristics – social, relationship and personal – modified by the particular focus of the representation. These are, if you like, the playwright's rules.

ROLE-PLAY AND CONTRACTS

There is a related and perhaps even more important difference between games and dramas, in the nature of the tension – and so the nature of the emotions generated, and therefore the affective component of the whole experience. In a game the tension is a simple one between the motivation and the resolution, existing in the action and its constraints. However, as O'Neill[14] points out, there is a deception underlying all dramas: the action is never what it seems; it is never merely representative of its surface meaning. It can even be suggested that the essential tension of drama consists of the disjunction between the surface text and the subtext(s).

This depends on two shared understandings, which together form an unspoken contract, the dramatic ellipsis,[15] among all the percipients of a drama: (1) that this is a selected and ordered representation of an interaction, a model where some of the underlying structure is being made explicit and finite; (2) that the actions and language of the characters represent to the audience – or the audience function – both what they want the other characters to perceive (the surface text), and what they want the audience to perceive about their motivations, which will be hidden from the other characters (the simple subtext). There may be a double deception, as the character 'unwittingly' reveals to the audience aspects of his/her nature unknown to him/herself (in the form of more deeply embedded subtexts). Further subtexts may exist in the area of metaxis where fiction meets the reality it is representing, where the ellipsis includes a shared and private knowledge, say in a satirical portrayal or role-play not essential to the narrative function of the character. In simple form this may be a child, who is role-playing an authority figure in a drama, parodying the gestures and language of the Head teacher, or even the drama teacher in the classroom. What is important about this dramatic ellipsis is that it is understood that *the deepest subtexts are the truest*, as the example below will demonstrate.

I had the privilege, as a young teacher, of unwittingly creating and witnessing this spectacular example of metaxis, and of the tension between text and subtexts, fused into a brief moment of climax and significance, consisting of nothing more than a single answer to a half-facetious question.[16] The theme of the drama was *Madness* and the **fictional context** was a mental institution. Most of the class were enrolled as patients, with a variety of disorders, and taking the drama seriously. A group of boys who had been absent at the beginning of the drama I enrolled as medical students gathering information. Without the same commitment to the dramatic fiction, they were looking for laughs. They turned their questioning on to a very unpopular girl, rather ugly and of restricted growth – virtually a dwarf – playing a patient. Their questioning ran as follows:

'What's your name?'
'Mary.' (Laughter.)
'Who do you think *you* are, Mary?'

Phrased with some contempt, this questioning only partially belonged to the characters in the drama – it brought with it a component of these participants' real dislike of the girl, and of their gender competitiveness. I was tempted to intervene to protect her, but did not need to. After a very dramatic pause, she quietly and slowly said, her eyes first fixed on the group then controlledly taking in the rest of the participants:

'I'm a giant. I'm ten foot tall. I'm taller than all of you.'

No laughter, but a stifled gasp from another 'patient', followed by a long silence, broken eventually by me. I now construe this silence to be the explicit manifestation of the dramatic ellipsis.

If this was in fact so, the interaction may be deconstructed as follows:

1 The surface text, clearly, was literally untrue, and meant by the character to deceive the other characters (simple subtext).

2 It was, however, understood by all the other characters to be the words of a madwoman and therefore to represent a (deeper) subtext of that character's self-deception.

3 At the even deeper level of metaxis there was another, parallel text, and subtexts whose understood meanings were the *exact opposite* of the subtexts of the drama itself. The dramatic 'madness' of the character allowed the actor to speak personally and truthfully to the group. Significantly, this girl was the only one of those role-playing 'patients' who retained her own name, Mary, for her character, a decision which had just previously caused a laugh.

4 The surface text was demonstrably untrue of the *participant* as well as of her character but she did not seek to delude the other participants into believing it.

5 The simple subtext was in fact telling the other participants that the statement was false. The unexpected statement, and its juxtaposition with the **dramatic context** of madness, was to shock them into an explicit awareness of its falseness.

6 The actor herself was not mad, and therefore the deeper subtext could not be read as self-deception. If the statement was not literally true, it must be representative of a metaphorical truth – that she was as figuratively tall, that is worthy of respect,

as any of the others (in her eyes at any rate, and using the hyperbole defiantly to counteract their low opinion of her).

7 Her manner of delivery, in contrast to the boys', bespoke its own subtext, reinforcing the above, again by contradiction. Neither was at the level of naturalistic, unselfconscious role-play usual in this mode. The boys betrayed their lack of commitment to the dramatic moment by a casual presentation, with paralanguage like smirks and giggles underlining the real message they were conveying. Mary countered this by taking on a stylised and equally self-conscious *acting* posture. In normal life she responded to such taunts swiftly and gracelessly, with an awkward truculence. Here, she was gracefully taking on, exaggerating, the falseness of the actor. This simultaneously gave her protection (if challenged, she could have said 'it wasn't me, it was just the drama') and allowed her to drive home the sincerity of the message through the inversion – the falseness bespeaking truth. If she had said this outside the drama the others would have laughed at it as fantasising, or ignored it as self-pitying, because the real context was dominated by their *lack* of respect for her. However, the drama both suspended this and validated the fantasy, and the 'madness' of the character acted as a reversing, refractive mirror of reality.

In recognising this incident as characteristic of drama rather than simulation, there are three key components:

1 It was *voluntary*. It was unplanned by the group or the teacher in advance, although it was quite within the 'rules of the game', quite within the constraints of the situation, and of the character that Mary was playing.
2 Its shared meaning emerged through deep levels of *subtext* which in fact contradicted the surface text.
3 The tension generated by the disjunction of text and subtexts expressed itself in a strong *emotional* impact upon all the percipients, emotions which were highly relevant to the message which Mary was communicating, which her character was communicating, and therefore to the meanings which the other percipients derived from the experience.

What *drama* exponents maintain is that the purely cognitive approach favoured by simulation exponents ignores entirely, or tries to minimise, the affective dimension, even though emotions run high in simulation, and the affective element of tension is an essential ingredient. Some go further, and suggest that there is an aesthetic dimension in effective simulation work, whether the exponents acknowledge it or not: that the structures *are* essentially dramatic, that the role-players *do* become characters in a drama, and that the fusion of emotion and purpose in those characters realising their goals and resolving the tension is a form of the art.[17] *Starpower*[18] is an example of a simulation game where the emotional commitment of the players is used to ambush their expectations.

Though the creation of dramatic symbols is never part of the agenda of simulations, looking at simulations with a dramatic eye often reveals them. Similarly, the geography teacher using a simulation on Hindu marriage would hope not just for a set of facts to be instilled, but for a holistic and sympathetic understanding of the subject, akin to dramatic meaning, to emerge. This is clearly perceptible in the structured reflective discussion which followed a simulation on this topic:

> 'We had nearly impossible jobs to do. They were interesting and challenging.'
> 'Was it necessary to hold the debriefing?'
> 'Yes, because some people were pretty frustrated.'[19]

If this perception of the hidden and unacknowledged affective dimension of simulation is right, then it seems likely that the difference is more in the eye of the beholder than in the practice of the beheld – or at least in the experience of the client. There are, as always, bridges. Dorothy Heathcote was quite a critic of the behaviouristic uses of simulation and gaming as being mechanistic, denying the negotiation implicit in drama in education, and therefore destructive of the client's own input. However, in an early essay, addressing the very question of 'How does role-taking help in the processes of coping and creating?', she answers the question by asserting that teachers, as 'creators of learning situations for others . . . are concerned in arranging their material in such a way that by meeting the material the pupils are . . . *modified* in some way'.[20]

ROLE-PLAY IN THEATRE IN EDUCATION

Theatre in education teams have from early days been ready to incorporate not only role-play, but the tight participatory structures of simulations, into their programmes. More than one programme has even constructed the children's participation into a life-size board game.[21]

The Coventry Belgrade programme *Rare Earth*,[22] regarded as a classic and many times performed by other companies, interspersed two performance segments or acts with a complete simulation game. The three parts, performed on successive weeks, were virtually entirely separate, linked only by theme (and one character between parts 1 and 2). The theme for learning of the whole programme was the care or otherwise of the environment. In Act 1, a stereotypical British emigrant family, the Ramsbottoms, represented humorously the careless use of resources; they were juxtaposed with Wakatanka, an American Indian spirit, the more serious embodiment of caring for the environment. The thematic link between Act 1 and the simulation game which formed the whole of Act 2 was not revealed to the children until halfway through the simulation, in a strong (if ethically questionable) *coup de théâtre*.

This the team set up apparently unconnected to what they had done the previous week. The children were invited to play a game where groups of players representing 'developing nations', were given varying amounts of 'resources' and encouraged to try and win the game by being the first nation developed enough to build a jumbo jet. The organisation of the game actually quickly left some of the children without resources, whereupon they were unceremoniously removed from the room, often very angry and frustrated at having been, as they thought, left out of the *game* itself (for them this was real, not the willing suspension of disbelief).

Outside in the corridor they were met by a 'school cleaner' (again the character was ostensibly a real person) and consoled. The cleaner turned out to be the character Wakatanka from the previous week, now like the children reduced to powerlessness. She heard their story and observed how greedy the game was. She had little difficulty persuading the newly dispossessed children that she would join them in gatecrashing the game, in order to try and dissuade the remaining participants from continuing this game of greed. That purpose then hijacked the simulation, and the rest of the game became a proto-dramatic debate that was really a concealed dramatic analogy, superficially about the desirability of continuing the simulation game, but subtextually about the environmental issues. The outcome was left very much in the children's hands, and varied from day to day: sometimes the other children were persuaded by the exiles and Wakatanka, sometimes they ignored them and continued their competition, and sometimes they devised compromise goals for the game which maintained the competition but were less ecologically unsound.

This programme raises crucial questions about the nature of the processual art form, the contracts which are essential for either art or learning to take place, and the links between negotiability and art, and negotiability and learning.

ROLE-PLAY AND SELF-IN-ROLE

At this point the question needs to be raised as to what extent the children and actors were 'in role' – using the term within the **fictional context**.

1 The actors who the previous week had been the Ramsbottoms were being 'themselves', that is, the members of the Coventry TIE Team. However, as organisers and approving managers of the competitive game they were consciously taking a fictional perspectival position – embodying a specific subtextual ideological stance (which was the opposite of their real-life ideology and teaching purposes, though they did not reveal this till the end of the simulation).

2 The actor playing Wakatanka was in fictional role and character, but this was subsumed in another fictional role posing as a real role, as 'school cleaner'. This was intended to dupe the children to begin with, and was in fact a *dual* role existing within two frames – the dramatic logic of one frame was that she was 'a person expected to be around schools who shared with the dispossessed children the fact of being low status, but who could provide adult consolation and advice'. The dramatic logic of the deeper frame was that, having been personally dispossessed and disempowered (just like the children), Wakatanka had 'in fact' been forced to take residence in the embodiment of a school cleaner.

3 The bulk of the children were working as *players* with what were roles in relation to the goal of the game, as *group* members of the fictional nations competing. The defining characteristics

of the role were that they identify with the shared goal and the group 'nation' identity which they had developed in striving for that goal.

4 The focus group of children had originally had these *player* roles, then they were placed quite involuntarily in another participant role as 'dispossessed' – the characteristic of which was a complete powerlessness both within and apparently beyond the game. New roles were then negotiated, where they were asked to work sophisticatedly, firstly to respond to a sympathetic adult (real for them), then to the character of Wakatanka (they were re-entering a fiction, but remaining as themselves), and then to take the revised role of players with a new goal of renegotiating the rules of the game.

The interwoven web of real-life role and dramatic role is even harder to separate, and more problematic, in the sub-genre of TIE known as 'adventure programmes'. In one example, *Ifan's Valley* – another Coventry Belgrade piece – the children are taken by a 'Water Board official' on a real coach tour to the site of a 'proposed dam', where the official teaches them about the need for water, before they meet an 'angry Welsh farmer' and become embroiled in a battle between Coventry's need for water and the rights of the Welsh hill farmers who are about to lose their land for the dam. All this time, the children believe that the characters are real, not fictional. They are reacting in real life. The deviser of this programme, team director David Pammenter, expressed his rationale for this deception as follows: 'if the situation is real then that accepted reality becomes a springboard for using the imagination for a much more specific and demanding purpose'.[23] In the light of deep concern about the ethics of presenting fiction as truth, this sub-genre has been savagely attacked as not art, but a confidence trick. Recent scholarship has revealed more about the nature of a person's commitment to the fiction in drama in education – what Vygotsky calls 'dual affect' – and the important part that distancing the **fictional context** has to play, and so the genre has virtually faded out. Artistically (though not ethically) this may be a pity, for the best of these programmes contained some very elegant devices for harnessing the real motivations of the children towards fictional goals, in manipulating their roles, and in presenting the denouement in such a way that it carried the excitement of theatrical ambush, rather than the sense of being cheated by a cheap trick.[24]

SIMPLE ROLE-PLAY

Traces remain, however, in drama in education as well as TIE. To inexperienced teachers and leaders, who do not trust the dramatic contract, it often seems attractive to ambush the children with a surprise. I recently watched a teacher and her Principal prepare her class for a visit by two old people, describing them as 'friends of ours needing assistance' – the children had been studying old age and had already visited a retirement home. On a pretext the teachers withdrew, and then returned a moment later, (over)dressed as the two old people. The children, unused to the teacher-in-role convention, firstly thought that this was very funny, then rather uncertainly joined in the teachers' game and did what their teachers had asked. The whole event was over within twenty minutes.

As a strategy for improving the learning environment this was probably very effective. The children appreciated and reacted warmly to their teachers suspending their (real-life) teacher roles and unbending from the high-status authority positions which they normally adopted. I observed, however, a strong feeling among the children, and even shared by the teachers, that this was not really serious – it seemed to me that its unintended impact was to trivialise the subject matter, and make the two 'old people' the subject of good-humoured patronage.

Although the teachers involved believed they were 'doing drama', this activity should probably be classified as proto-drama, for as an engagement with the art form of drama it was really rather odd. The children were given a role-function, which was not explicitly fictional, in that they were asked to help the old people. They were not in any way enrolled as people other than themselves. This was left to the teachers, the people in the room least accustomed to explicit dramatic role-playing. (I base this judgment on the assumption that the children, being normal, would be quite used to using role in their own games *outside* the classroom.) I could see that the teachers clearly felt themselves to be *acting*, because their role-taking was characterised by many stereotypic signs of 'old age' such as shaking voices and hands, as well as by equally stereotypic behaviour, such as forgetfulness and lack of confidence. The resulting interaction was somewhat self-conscious on both sides, unsurprisingly. It had the hallmarks of an approach to drama which was based on the notion of public performance – children's theatre, in fact. Essentially the teachers had assumed the real-life roles of actors, taking fictional *role* as old people to give the children a show. The children were in the real-life roles of an audience, there to watch the actors, albeit an audience which had been invited to help. This has the same characteristics as the *peripheral* participation common to children's theatre, where the audience is urged to help by warning characters of the approach of the villain, or more boldly for one or two to come on stage to help. The move from the 'audience' frame to the 'helper of old people' frame was one which the children could manage quite easily, since it did not demand any specific behaviour uncharacteristic of 'themselves'. The whole transaction lacked depth of belief and its purpose was trivialised because there was a confusion of contextual frames. The slightly perplexed teachers admitted later that the children had behaved with much more sophisticated, understanding and caring behaviour on their real trip to the retirement home the previous day.[25]

In contrast, working with children the same age in a nearby school, on a similar theme of caring for the environment, instead of twenty minutes *in toto* I found I needed three and three-quarter hours, spread over three sessions, to enrol the participants strongly enough. By this I mean for the dramatic crisis to provide a challenge which in my judgment would provide significant meaning outcomes. From crisis to resolution took a further three-quarters of an hour.[26]

There are, in fact, a number of levels of enrolment available within a processual drama, between the two extremes of 'leaving the children as themselves' and a deeply empathetic engagement. It needs to be examined whether, if the teacher chooses to 'leave the children as themselves', this is in fact what happens. The idea is usually presented to the children that some action 'is going to happen to us'. To use a very simple drama as an example, similar to the 'old people' drama above but structurally much less suspect, a class of infants had been studying farms, and paid a visit to a model farm. After preparing the children for a drama (not a piece of real life), the teacher, Miss Thompson, started by introducing 'Miss Jones, a friend of mine who has a problem, which I thought this class might help her with'. Miss Thompson then, in front of the class, took role as Miss Jones – merely by nominating a seat where Miss Jones would sit, and putting on a shawl to indicate the move into the **fictional context**. Miss Jones explained that her problem was that she had been left a farm in a will, but that she was a townsperson and did not know anything about farming, in fact she was so ignorant that she could not tell a cow from a horse. She had heard from her friend Lesley Thompson that Lesley's class had been studying farms, and were very clever and very knowledgeable children. Could they help? The drama progressed from there as the children advised and instructed the inept Miss Jones, even setting up a farm simulation in the classroom, with themselves 'acting as the animals', so that she could get some practice.

At first sight it may appear that this example lacks the deception implicit in the dramatic ellipsis. Apart from their brief excursion into animal caricature, the children seem be literally left as themselves, although the situation is quite clearly fictional. Closer examination shows that this is not in fact so. The convention which Miss Thompson used, of endowing the children with a sufficient specialised expertise to solve a dramatic problem, is generally known as giving them 'the mantle of the expert'.[27] The metaphor in this phrase is very accurate in pointing to the artificiality of the device. The expertise is thrown over the children, to cover them like a cloak, a disguise. In the farming drama described above, the group of children know perfectly well that they do not in fact know enough about farms actually to help an adult manage one, just as they know that no adult is actually going to be so ignorant as not to recognise a cow, nor so stupid as to ask infants for advice on farm management and economics. There was no hesitation in participating in the drama. They were, then, participating within the **fictional context** in role not as themselves, but as 'a group of children just like themselves but with the power to help an adult'. The device empowers them, but only in the drama. It may also give them added self-confidence by letting them take control of a situation within the classroom but from beyond the classroom, and succeed. In that sense it may be empowering beyond the drama, which is often used for that very extraneous purpose, particularly with young or disabled children. This metaxis does not, however, empower Miss Thompson's children actually to take charge of a farm.[28]

A rather more sophisticated piece of infant drama in education shows this kind of enrolment very clearly, juxtaposed with an enrolment at a level even more embryonic, in a very elegant artistic device, which was devised to explore this very dimension. The introduction indicates the parameters:

> Kathy Kiernan was intrigued by the way her class of 6-year-olds loved to recount blow-by-blow descriptions of what had just happened as soon as she stepped out of role – as if she knew nothing about it at all. The children were spontaneously bringing the drama into the world of the classroom and creating a new frame outside and around the original drama.[29]

The drama was very complex, and in this same rather odd sub-genre where the teacher does all the identifiable fictional role-taking (in this case the teacher played three different people including Goldilocks, and incorporated the teacher-aide, a parent and the Deputy Principal, while the children just remained 'themselves'). The drama incorporated several aspects of the real world. The school Secretary, as herself, made several interventions within the **fictional context**, such as bringing a letter apparently unknown to the teacher (though the children realised that the real Miss Kiernan must have written it). After many vicissitudes, the 'children' agreed to help Goldilocks to mend Baby Bear's chair in secret. She specially asked them 'not to let their teacher know'. After the drama session was over, Miss Kiernan tripped over the chair and asked what it was doing in the classroom. The children spontaneously nearly gave the game away, then quickly covered up, and even resisted Miss Kiernan's attempts to have the chair thrown away. They then surreptitiously mended, washed and painted the chair. They maintained this fiction for two days, while the drama was not taking place. In fact, of course, they knew that Miss Kiernan had devised the secret that as Goldilocks she had adjured them not to tell Miss Kiernan, and provided the chair. What they created together was the inversion of a 'play within a play' convention, namely a 'play outside the play'. As Stevenson's introduction observes, they had placed another dramatic frame around the outer frame of the drama. Instead of role-playing [themselves helping Goldilocks] they were taking role as a new 'duality of themselves in the classroom' composed simultaneously of 'themselves and [themselves helping Goldilocks]'.

Stevenson and Kiernan both further observed that the 6-year-olds had no difficulty in holding and managing this Pirandellian interaction without any confusion over a very long period. They derived great pleasure from the complexity of the artifice. This drama also shows the game-like structure of drama, in the way the children respond to it as a game. As well as the other levels of role, they are a team of players, and the teacher is the opposing player. The task is scoring the goal of helping Goldilocks without being tackled by Miss Kiernan (who of course is also Goldilocks).

Role-taking in drama in education may be distinguished from the characterisation work of actors in a theatre by the role-taker being permitted to behave in ways entirely normal to him or her, which will then be appropriate to the role. This is thus much more negotiable than a part in a scripted play, and can affect the very narrative of the drama. In pursuit of authenticity when exploring situations through experiential role-play, leaders actively discourage acting, and anything more than a minimal signalling of the condition of the role sufficient for the other participants to identify it. As we have seen, a participant 'steps into the shoes of another' in order to experience *subjectively* some aspect of that other, or the situation in which that other is found. To do that the subject must implicitly identify the humanness of that other, acknowledging that he or she is capable of that other's actions, and so identify with the character in the situation.

INDIVIDUALISING ROLE-PLAY

If the gap between self and other is wide, considerable skill and practice may be needed to step into other shoes. The requirements of the role may also need to be simplified judiciously. Suppose the role of an autocratic dictator is required, even, specifically in a period improvisation, Adolf Hitler, and a female is assigned to play the role. Initially, the convention must be established (as it invariably is) that the role-players can speak and act naturally, not try to mimic Hitler. In terms of the three categories of characteristics of role (see chapter 1), the *social* and status characteristics of the role need to be signalled, of course, for the *relationships* with other characters in the role-play and the narrative line to operate acceptably. Then, an experienced woman, with a wide command of language and paralinguistic registers, and of the history of the period, is capable of finding the internal *personal* identification and has the necessary

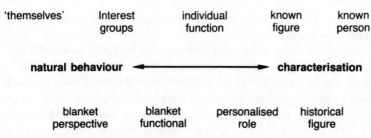

Figure 3 Scale of individualisation of role

repetoire of appropriate signals to take role as Adolf Hitler. She can be entirely convincing internally and to the other participants, because the content of what she says and the motivation are both appropriate. On the other hand, an inexperienced adolescent, cast in that role with little knowledge of the history or of Hitler, would probably need a frame of action limited to simple statements and postures of warlike rhetoric and dictatorial authority, and only need to identify with the pleasure of being the automatic centre of attention, and having commands instantly obeyed. She might also need a physical property, a *sign* both to represent the character to others and to give her reassurance.

The extent to which role-players need to individualise their roles, or merely operate from generalised attitudes or perspectives, may be conceived of in the form of a diagrammatic continuum (Figure 3).

The example of the woman playing Hitler would be at the opposite end of the scale to the infant children engaged in *Goldilocks* or *Miss Jones's Farm*. For them, behaving naturally was not a problem, since their roles merely demanded that they behave like themselves. In terms of the three categories of characteristics, the role itself contained the special *social* characteristics of their class group identity, which were important modifiers of the event. The teacher kept the *relationship* characteristics at a simple enough level of interaction for the children to manage – 'Miss Jones' was a friendly character within their range of experience, who approached the 'children/experts' with a problem that was possible for them to solve. As far as *personal* characteristics are concerned, the role was generalised and shared, and did not require specially delineated drives, motivations or attitudes, beyond an orientation to be helpful and a pride in their specialist knowledge.

In fact, another dimension in practice needs to be considered when working along this continuum – the dimension of stylisation. At this point we must admit that the continuum is not simply linear. On the left side of the continuum, at least as far as 'personalised role', experiential role-play – apparently naturalistic – is normally appropriate. In this process, negotiability is at a premium, and leaders employ progressively more complex forms of enrolment, or 'building belief' as they are often called.[30] These in fact become tasks that are often considered structurally as part of the drama, and may to some extent be incorporated in, or combined with, the narrative structure. This is further analysed in chapter 3. These very enrolling structures, in so far as they *are* considered as organic to the drama, actually subvert the convention of naturalism, because they are special tasks which are ordered not chronologically nor necessarily in narrative sequence. Naturalism, in the form of empathetic experiential role-play, is the end point to be aimed at by the enrolment.

In a fully developed drama, experiential role-play is rarely the only convention which the leader uses. Various conventions of *distancing*, *refracting* and *fixing* the experience are almost invariably juxtaposed with the directly experiential. Beyond the personalised role, purely naturalistic role-play is rarely feasible anyway. It is a Stanislavskian task to master the social, relationship and personal characteristics of known figures, demanding great skill and more time than is usually available to drama in education. Instead, the leader, as playwright, negotiates the form of the role with the role-player to take account of the necessary limitations. They will selectively focus on certain embodiments of particular characteristics; these the role-player will express in schematically appropriate language and gesture. Within the action, the role will only be required to make a severely limited range of action, initiatives and responses. The role will be given a position in the narrative structure which will permit these limitations on the action as appropriate.

ROLE-PLAY, NEGOTIATION AND LEARNING

Underlying the notion of characterisation is a deeper one of the *dramatis persona*. If the *drama* is fixed, as it is in a scripted play, the *persona* has very little room for negotiation. The actor has to make the character authentic in a given narrative line, within a given sequence of actions, words and sometimes even gestures. However, the structures of role-play are often more fluid. The persons within the **fictional context** are in fact not static and subservient to the dramatic narrative, they are embodiments of the conditions of the whole dramatic situation, and can be invented, reinvented and rearranged within the situation, which itself is thus responsive to these rearrangements. The constraints which role-play offers may in fact just be those of role and situation – those social, relationship and personal characteristics operating within the specific fictional situation which is invariably the first given condition: 'here are these characters in this situation – let's see what they do'. They may indeed also be constrained by a given narrative: we know that Red Riding Hood went through the wolf-infested forest to visit her Grandmother, but what was her mother thinking of to let her? Was Red frightened, headstrong, sulky? There's a rich scene to be role-played between the two. It will be constrained by: (1) the given outcome – Red Riding Hood takes the butter and griddle-cakes to Grandma; (2) the given *social* characteristics – mother and daughter status levels, and family expectations. All the other characteristics are still negotiable: the *relationship* might, for instance, be that Red is a step-daughter, resentful of her new 'mother'. The *personal* characteristics could create an entirely different scene, too: how old is Red, six or sixteen, and would it make a difference? Suppose Red is wilful, or complaisant?

Within these constraints, role takes primacy over, and is the precursor of, narrative and dialogue. The leader and participants may then provide further constraints according to their particular purposes.[31]

In the end, perhaps the main feature that distinguishes drama in education from simulation, or, come to that, from Greek Tragedy, is that it is an *a posteriori* genre of learning discourse. This is apparent in the use made of role. In a Greek tragedy and in a simulation game, the social, spiritual or historical processes have been mapped and the conclusions to be drawn by the learners already defined *a priori*; the *process* has been arrested. Tragedy and simulation have clearly defined learning objectives, which are also defined within the aegis of the occasion – a quasi-religious festival and a geography classroom. The **fictional**

contexts specific to those learning objectives and that occasion embody functional *personae* who behave appropriately according to the given narrative and the exact lesson to be derived which the *a priori* playwright/simulation deviser has prescribed. Philoctetes, Neoptolemus and Odysseus[32] behave with a predictability suggesting they might well have been given the role-cards which are a standard feature of simulation games, but which are becoming rarer nowadays in drama in education.

What makes role the most 'extremely processual element', besides the overall negotiability that role-play permits, are the areas of very specific negotiability. In the terms of the 'Individualisation of Role' continuum (Figure 3), this flexibility and negotiability is most pronounced in the middle, and least available at the two ends. The reasons why this is true at the *characterisation* end of the continuum have already been dealt with. It is equally true at the other end.

When the children are enrolled as 'themselves', they are expected to behave as themselves, free only to do that. Behaving as 'other' is inappropriate to the terms of the dramatic structure which the playwright/teacher has set up. The child who produces a raygun to shoot dead the dragon is killing the drama too, because he is introducing a personal characteristic of 'superhero' that does not fit in with the much more modest characteristics of 'a group of children dragon-hunters'.

The next categories permit gradually more variation of personal input from the role-players. *Blanket perspective* requires no more than jointly accepting a point of view, usually responding to a use of the teacher-in-role convention or to materials, archives, etc. They are loosely enrolled, for instance, as 'historians engaged in revising the History of England', interviewing the 'Sheriff of Nottingham' who is asking for a re-evaluation. Their role demands merely the reactive perspective of a good historian, a willingness not to be prejudiced, but to weigh up evidence. In fact, they will bring their own perspectives to bear in the dialogue as well, mediated by this 'professional' demand. What they hear may well determine the future action to be taken – that is, the ensuing dramatic narrative. The historians having heard the Sheriff decide to travel back in time to the thirteenth century to investigate further, and have a wide choice of relevant situations in which to participate: the Sheriff's castle, planning strategies for capturing Robin Hood; a village meeting discussing how to deal with the imposition of further taxes; Robin Hood's gang planning a raid; King Richard overruling pleas not to raise another financially crippling Crusade.

Blanket functional role is really an extension of this, where the participants are asked to deal pro-actively with a situation. Having taken a blanket perspective as, for instance, 'social workers listening to a case briefing concerning a suspected child-battering', they may be asked to work individually interviewing the 'parent'. Their blanket perspective will still operate as a constraint; how they tackle that parent is very much in their own hands, with a range of possible strategies, and a range of personal feelings involved. There is likely to be quite a range of results, as some manage it more deftly than others.

This kind of role is often used by leaders as a way of drawing participants' attention to their own interpersonal manner, and to some of their preconceptions. For instance, in a human relation-ships training course for police recruits, some role-play per-sonalised roles as distressed persons, crime victims or suspects, citizens receiving death notifications, etc. Others, enrolled as 'police' with the blanket functional roles they will shortly be adopting in real life, have to use their knowledge of procedure and their own personal skills to uncover information or other-wise deal with the situation.[33]

When the role is individualised, *personal* characteristics become central to the negotiations that will provide the drama. They provide the source of the tension, but, being individual, are less controllable and predictable than negotiations made jointly as a group. I once led a class of adults in a drama on the theme of *Utopia*[34] which this feature turned into a rollercoaster ride for me as much as the other participants. Perhaps there is something about the subject – on two other occasions I have led dramas on this topic, chosen by the participants, which also nearly led to real bloodshed! This drama involved two separate enrolment procedures. The basic conflict which I prescribed for the group was that a piece of Crown land was being made available for Utopian experiment (this the class knew), and a Canberra error had granted the land simultaneously to two incompatible groups (this they did not). The first was a 'committee to set up a Pestalozzi International Children's Village'. The roles were pre-scribed, but needed to be individualised, so the participants were asked to select among themselves a number of fixed roles –

paediatrician, child psychologist, architect, etc. Time was then allocated for the participants to background these roles to find a personal identification and self-esteem, in this case based on the expertise of the role and the 'professional experience'. Then, together, they started to draw up plans on the given map, for the design and management of their village. The second group were 'individuals who wished to drop out of normal society' who had responded to a Utopian society's call for volunteers to establish an alternative community. Enrolment exercises followed for these participants to background themselves with strong personal motivations for wishing to drop out of society, and with specific skills which would be useful. Then, on site, they set about building their Utopia and laying down rules. My original plan for this drama was a simple conflict model of dramatic action, to bring the two groups together and let their incompatible dreams clash in reality.

This dramatic set-up has been described in some detail because that purpose was in fact subverted by a bizarre renegotiation of role that turned it into an entirely different drama from what I had intended or the class expected. The participants were experienced drama teachers taking part in a three-day workshop course. Among the 'drop-out' group was a participant who, it became clear in retrospect, had his own agenda, which included a scepticism about the use of role-play, and a definition of improvisation quite at variance with that shared by the rest of the group. He set out, in fact, to prove that role-play was a sham. This did not emerge in the original discussion, nor in the preliminary enrolment exercises, which were internalising and personalising. However, as soon as his group, the 'drop-outs', started to work jointly and with commitment, he began to disrupt their task, at first facetiously, and then, as the group coped with this quite adequately within the **fictional context** itself, more obtrusively and aggressively. Where a sub-group were building a fire, he 'nonchalantly' kept walking across the space, denying that there was a fire. A very interesting phenomenon then happened. The group, quite tacitly, set about remaining in role as stubbornly as he was intending to make them break it. Real aggression set in as he was driven to more and more extreme behaviour to try to get them to break role, smashing down their constructions of tables and chairs and butcher's paper. There is an elegant comparison to be made with the *Madness* drama referred to earlier, where the girl Mary elected to reveal an aspect of the **real** within the **fictional context** in the guise of being mad. Conversely, the *Utopia* drama contained a participant in the **real context** who was actually refusing to be a character in the **fictional** – who was refusing to acknowledge everybody else's 'reality'. Clearly he could only be mad, and must be dealt with as such. The situation escalated, the Pestalozzi group arrived and were quickly diverted both from their purpose and from the original focus of the drama, as this participant's behaviour became more and more extreme – in his terms emphatic, in their terms insane. The metaxis manifested itself in the rising anger of all the others at his out-of-role provocations, which was channelled into the drama. Finally, as he would not be contained, he was taken by four men strong enough actually to restrain him, and 'killed', with the eager concurrence of almost all these pacific utopians. At this point, he could for the first time have successfully broken their fiction of his madness, and the fictional framework, whose parameters clearly did not include the dead walking. Instead, for the first time in the session, he accepted the fiction and 'stayed dead' (he later admitted that he had at last read the reality of their anger and was too scared to take the risk).

A very intense reflective discussion followed. The next stage of the drama which I had planned was entirely abandoned in order to deal with the strong and very real emotional residues which remained after the session – these included anger with the 'madman', and such emotions as shock as individuals realised their own unexpected potential for violence. I was forced to negotiate with the group a complete restructuring of the drama. This began immediately with a complex series of exercises to de-role the group. Then I could re-enrol them only by focussing the drama in an entirely different frame. The way the frames were then gradually superimposed on each other is dealt with in chapter 3.

This one participant, the 'madman', had alone not recognised and accepted the dramatic ellipsis. It later turned out that he was artistically committed to the notion of drama in education being about 'acting', and teaching children acting skills. Part of the **real context** he brought to the drama was his hostility to the notion of role-play providing either dramatic art or significant learning. It is doubtful whether he had given much thought to the question of the contexts that actors act out, or the personae which they take on. In this drama, he was himself, not even 'himself', and certainly not in either fictional role or character. He alone had not signed the contract.

Chapter 3

Purpose and focus

GENERAL PURPOSES OUTSIDE THE CONTEXT

In the Introduction I proposed that all art is *playful* behaviour. Like all play, art operates between two polarities, the urge to explore and the urge to control – between freedom and the testing or breaking of rules, and confinement and the making of rules. Both are always operative, and part of the source of the pleasure which is found in play is the tension which exists between the two. These polarities are not unrelated to the continuum that exists between process and product in drama.

As a general rule, in art and play, children move along the scale from exploring towards fixing as they grow up, and their play changes. The play of the very young child manifests a large proportion of exploratory behaviour. However, mastery of rules, the syntax of games, exists even in the game of Peekaboo, generally taken to be the earliest manifestation of projected or dramatic play.[1] As the child becomes older, a greater proportion of interest in rules appears, and eventually play-forms like sports, skipping games, group dramatic play and so forth emerge as well as what are more recognisably 'art forms'.

The element of spontaneity (or at least apparent spontaneity, in the form of the unexpected) always exists in the most rule-dominated games, and accounts for their tension. The seeds of the process and the product are always present in their opposite. If this dialectical representation of play holds true for art, then the kinship may be clearly seen between a 3-year-old child 'singing lolly nolly, nolly lolly, nilly lolly, sillie billie, nolly lolly . . . as he was being undressed'[2] and *Façade*, the choral suite by Edith Sitwell and William Walton. The first may be more spontaneous than the second, with its complex rule-base of written versification, harmonic and melodic forms. However, it is easy to perceive in both a similar delight in the haphazard *discovery* of meaning emerging out of exploration in sound and rhythm, and in the *fixing* of form and symmetry.

Some thinkers would widen this significance of play further to incorporate play-behaviour and motivation into the matter of all behaviour. Koestler for example suggests that 'All coherent thinking is equivalent to playing a game according to a set of rules.'[3] The nineteenth-century Utilitarian Jeremy Bentham saw with horror, not pleasure, what he called 'deep play' where 'the stakes are so high that it is irrational for men to engage in it at all'.[4] He saw it as irrational and sought to make it illegal. Dickens graphically conjures up a society ruled by Bentham's values in *Hard Times*, and begins this with Mr Gradgrind the schoolteacher ironing out of his charges any possibility of independent thought or art.

The anthropologist Geertz took up Bentham's notion of 'deep play' in the spirit of enquiry, rather than political moralising. Analysing an example of such activity, a cockfight in Bali, he concluded that at an individual level it may have been irrational, but it was deeply significant in terms of social identity and status management. Very perceptively he identified the *aesthetic* component of the activity. He concluded that

> [for the Balinese] the imposition of meaning in life is the major end and primary condition of human existence, [so] the access of significance more than compensates for the economic costs involved.[5]

In other words beneath the apparent lack of purpose there were deeper purposes operating.

There is a considerable canon of work on the nature and development of play. Apart from Geertz, quoted above, most of it is concerned with the play of very young children, and little with the play of adolescents and adults. Virtually all the literature contradicts the Benthamite notion which still pervades western schooling systems that play is what you do in the 'playground' outside the school, which is where you do something else, called work; where work is still seen to be purposeful, play trivial. Analysts of play have always asserted explicitly its purposeful nature, none more trenchantly than Groos almost a century ago:

Perhaps the very existence of youth is largely for the sake of play. The animals do not play because they are young, but they have their youth because they must play.[6]

Lev Vygotsky, probably the play analyst most influential to drama in education in the last decade, declares:

It is incorrect to conceive of play as activity without purpose; play is purposeful activity for a child . . . the purpose decides the game. It justifies all the rest.[7]

That is an internal purpose which Vygotsky is describing, rather than the objectivised purpose which an observer, parent or teacher might see for the activity, in contributing to that child's development. (The distinction between these – the play for the child and the play for the adult – is very significant to drama in education, with the word 'play' taking on some of its theatrical meaning.)

The educator Jerome Bruner begins his categorisation of the functions of play with 'minimising the consequences of one's actions and learning' and 'providing an excellent opportunity to try combinations of behaviour that would, under functional pressure, never be tried'.[8] This provides a context for play activity which might be said to do very well for the art of drama. The behaviour within that context which many analysts see as most basic is that of imitation, and the development from imitation into symbolisation, which is also the basis of drama. This has been charted in terms of dramatic play by Vygotsky, who shows the changing equations among *action*, *object* and *meaning*, and the connection between symbolisation and rule management in 'a movement towards the conscious realisation of . . . purpose'. The increasing independence of meaning through action from the signifying objects provides 'the negative of a child's general everyday behaviour'.[9]

Writers on drama in education have recognised this as the embryo of drama in education, and explored it in terms of the continuing dialectic which exists between the concrete and the abstract, the particular and the universal. They note, too, that the meanings which emerge are to some extent collective.[10] Drama being a group art, the process of making drama involves the creation of group meanings. These in turn depend on the shared purposes of the participants, and the contracts which make those possible (see also chapter 6).

There is another side to the imitation which underlies children's play and the art of drama, connected with the 'negative to . . . everyday behaviour'. Rosen elegantly sums it up as 'For drama to be effective, we must know it for what it is'.[11] Rosen is here concerned not with the links between play and drama and children's play, but between drama and the embryonic dramatic dialogue and narrative in real contexts which are both playful in function and concerned with aesthetic form.

> Imitation becomes representation, in which objects are no longer received in their finished structure, but built up by the consciousness according to their constitutive traits.

This affirms imitation as an active and creative process. Rosen notes that dramatic behaviour, as distinct from *affectation*, 'which we must not know for what it is', is always embedded in other behaviour – the **fictional context** in the **real** – to affect its meaning. It proclaims its fictionality, at the very moment of appearing to represent actuality.

This brings us very close to Vygotsky's key concept of 'the dual affect – the child weeps in play as a patient, but revels as a player'.[12] This has been immensely influential in developing the genre of drama in education. It provides a rationale for using empathetic role-play, which is a direct derivative from children's group dramatic play, as the centre of the genre. Simultaneously the participant can stand in another's shoes, unconsciously feeling 'This is happening to me' (the first affect), and simultaneously conscious of the form 'I am making it happen' (the second affect). The sensuous internalisation of meaning which is happening in the first can be observed, externalised and made cognitively explicit in the second. Knowledge which emerges as dramatic meaning is neither just propositional comprehension nor sensuous apprehension, it is a fusion of both. Put thus in academic language, this concept can seem either profound or pretentious. Yet very young children both know and exploit it: in the outer frame of the *Goldilocks* drama described in chapter 2, the 6-year-old children were revelling in exploiting the duality which they were sharing with their teacher. She disingenuously enquired what Baby Bear's chair was doing in the classroom. One child immediately gave the equally disingenuous excuse:

'Oh, we've just been imagining a lot lately' – an answer equally apt within the drama and without. The dual affect is not just elegantly encapsulated in this exchange, it is actually made explicit.

THE TEACHER'S SPECIFIC PURPOSES

The question of the propositional nature of art or otherwise is at the centre of the 'subject and service' debate, previously charted, between drama in education as an art form and functional role-play. In pragmatic terms, this often means advancing specific curricular purposes for drama, while actually being more deeply concerned with the art form. Drama teachers in the UK and Australia have become adept at smuggling drama into the classroom under the noses of disapproving colleagues or Head teachers in the guise of 'language arts' or 'experiential approaches to history'. However, it disconcertingly appears[13] that those very educational leaders and Principals who appear to devalue the arts, in fact often find it easier to accept a demand for a not-very-well-justified theatre course which appears to have little to do with the standard curriculum, than to accept the attempts of the drama teachers to align the subject alongside or within the respectability of the standard curriculum. In their concern to justify and provide an acceptable rationale for their subject in the terms of the schooling systems, these drama teachers have often overlooked the fact that with subjects like music, classics and religious education, these same Principals have been living comfortably with the same double standards and lack of clarity for all their teaching lives. These subjects may be awkward, demanding and impossible to justify in utilitarian terms, but, like Everest, they are there. Not only that, many of these Principals have their own purpose for encouraging drama, which may not be congruent with that of their drama teachers – namely to use drama through the school musical or play festival, or other public theatrical forms, to enhance the cultural reputation of the school, or provide a major collective celebration.

Most Principals would probably share with their drama teachers 'the final inadequacy of any instrumental view'. As a warden of a Drama Advisory Centre, from day to day concerned with all aspects of drama in schools, very much including its instrumental use, puts it:

If we don't attempt to place drama [and here he is talking specifically about the genre of drama in education] squarely in its aesthetic field then narrow and partial influences will determine its nature, recasting it as a recreation or simulation activity for the young, and not as a potent artistic medium and a great arts discipline.[14]

In the territory of Purpose, then, there are normally two sets of specific purposes operating for the leader:

1 Instrumental

As Heathcote reminds us, drama is always about something, it 'depicts matters of significance'.[15] The instrumental purposes are by no means confined to low utilitarian ones. A London drama teacher nails her flag firmly to this mast, 'first and foremost committed to drama as a method of learning'. She is concerned with artistic form, but for that purpose, and appropriates control of it to herself: 'I like to structure the drama from within but I am flexible. I will try any method that I think will give the pupils a deeper and richer drama experience.' And this experience, she makes clear, is concerned not with art, but with being black and female and growing up in Britain during the 1980s: 'It is through drama that I hope my pupils will feel more aware of their own worth, power and potential, and thus more visible.' The descriptions of work which accompany these assertions show a sophisticated dramatic artist at work, offering a large amount of control over the subject matter to the participants, and crafting it into complex drama in education. Deeply embedded is the accompanying hope that 'by the end of the fifth year my pupils are capable of making that statement with authority and autonomy'.[16]

2 Aesthetic

Not only do 'characters and events become resonant with a cluster of meanings and feelings which not only unify the action but also universalise it',[17] but the experience involves 'the discovery of what was not there before – the insights the artist experiences during the act of art-making'.[18] In other words, for there to be aesthetic understanding of the drama, part of the

meaning which emerges is mediated by a corresponding awareness of the form.

CHILDREN'S PURPOSES

There are some purposes which belong more to the participants
than to the leader. In a useful phrase that is cant among drama
teachers, there are always two plays: 'the play for the teacher and
the play for the children'.[19] For the contractual 'dramatic ellipsis'
to occur, the children must believe that their purposes will be
fulfilled, too.

In other words, whether the class is embarking on a drama
about 'the Industrial Revolution' chosen by the teacher, or on a
drama about 'murder' chosen by the children, the beginning
must be a negotiation of the purposes, in order to provide a focus
and a starting point from which the contractual obligation for all
the participants to commit themselves to the drama and its
constraints can be ratified.

Given the relationships between pupils and teacher and their
perceptions of roles which normally obtain in classrooms, where
most drama in education currently takes place and where the
context of the setting asserts itself, there is likely to be an initial
disjunction between the teacher's purposes and the children's.
The teacher is being paid for pedagogy, and some didactic
purpose is inevitably uppermost, for example to demonstrate the
connection between the Industrial Revolution and the settlement
of Australia, or to help them understand the Industrial Revolution's analogies with their own lives, such as the connection
between technological advance, unemployment and social
change. This will be the (primarily instrumental) 'teacher's
play'.

A group of adults educated in history might conceivably select
this topic as the starting point for a drama, and decide on the
above objectives themselves. However, a group of 12-year-old
children are very unlikely to do so, even unconsciously. For a
start, few of them have even heard the phrase 'Industrial Revolution'. First and foremost they will be hoping to get some pleasure
out of their dramatic play. In fact, if we consider play and art as
at least closely related, their purposes will be closer to the
aesthetic than their teacher's will. They will want the drama to

give them pleasure through the operation of tension, while they are projected into roles in which they are interested, and with which they can identify closely enough to maintain the dramatic fiction. Moreover, limits to the time available for negotiative discussion, and the tolerance of a group of thirty children, usually entail the teacher taking responsibility for the children's play too.

If they are to be engaged enough to sign the dramatic contract the teacher has to gauge what will 'arrest their attention – make them say "What's up?" '[20] Acting on their behalf, and on his or her knowledge of the group's interests, the teacher might thus decide to focus the drama on child labour and set the action in a sweatshop making toys for rich children.[21] Though they have no experience of factory labour, they know what it is like to be twelve, and powerless.

When the children themselves make the choice, and choose 'murder', they will be anticipating an exciting narrative. In fact, this does not fit comfortably and automatically into drama. As is shown in chapter 4, narrative and dramatic structures are different, particularly in terms of focus and time, and also in terms of managing that structure to satisfy a group of thirty participants. However, that is 'the children's play'. Therefore in fact the topic already makes a considerable demand on the playwriting skills of the teacher to achieve *their* play and satisfy their purposes. The children want to enjoy the frisson of a subject full of potential for horror and fear and violence – and the romantic glamour of these vicarious emotions, untouched by any reality in their perception of the subject (if any participant did have any direct personal knowledge of this subject, most teachers would in fact avoid it). Such a dramatic game is unlikely to satisfy a pedagogue, so the teacher must also formulate 'the teacher's play'. Murder is unlikely to figure in the school curriculum, so refuge in the simply instrumental is not available. Confronted with this subject, Dorothy Heathcote solved her problem by simply asking the initial question 'Now what could *drive* anybody to commit that kind of crime, I wonder?'[22] This already points clearly towards 'the teacher's play', allowing the teacher the general instrumental objective of making the universal visible in the particular. It is also still in aesthetic territory, exploring both narrative and character motivation. It does not, however, destroy 'the children's play'. The discussion which would normally follow this kind of question would then negotiate the details of the action.

All this points to the element absolutely crucial to the operation of any drama in education, that of *trust*. In a subject of the teacher's choosing, in order to select an appropriate children's play for them he or she must know them well – the teacher is usurping their rights, after all. In a drama of their choosing, the children must know that their play will be respected. This is a precondition of the contract. There are pragmatic elements of the classroom relationship which can actually aid this delicate negotiative process. The children know that they are supposed to be learning important things, and, once they have got over the novelty of the use of dramatic play within the work environment, they will tend to look for a rationale that will justify the continuance of this activity, which is almost by definition more pleasurable than many other classroom activities and (for them) passive passages of time. On the other hand, the teacher is constrained by the need or expectation that this work will contribute to the process of evaluation and assessment of the individual children's progress within the school. Sheer pleasure can rarely dominate the teacher's agenda, though many drama teachers have read or would subscribe to the words of Brecht: 'The contrast between learning and amusing oneself is not laid down by divine rule . . . there is such a thing as pleasurable learning, cheerful and militant learning.'[23]

FOCUSSING: TRANSLATING PURPOSES INTO DRAMATIC ACTION

Those probably mismatched initial purposes of leader and participants must be coalesced and focussed into an agreed 'our play'. It may entail some explicit negotiation, a preliminary discussion where the students give the teacher input about possible lines of interest in the subject, possible plot opportunities and conflict. This may even be extended into exercise work where the teacher finds out by such techniques as inviting group freeze-frames, establishing simple role-plays between characters within the context, or laying out butcher's paper for the students to write or draw their responses to the potential subject matter.

The extent to which the teacher at this point proposes, reveals or discusses with the students his or her purposes in relation to the subject matter is of some contention within the practice. The Canadian drama educators Morgan and Saxton, approaching the medium with primarily instrumental purposes, propose that 'The teacher does not necessarily reveal "her play" to the students, as this tends to prohibit, rather than promote, learning.'[24]

Ken Byron, a noted proponent of a highly negotiative – that is, processual – approach, implies the opposite: 'Agreement needs to be reached in order that everyone understands the nature of the activity they are about to engage in, its rules and boundaries, and its central core – the predicament the drama is examining . . . Contract is a two-way affair: the play is built collaboratively.'[25] The leader can rely on the ability of the participants to suspend their disbelief more willingly and with more control over the nature of the experience, if they are fully informed – and particularly if they have previously been able to negotiate the particular narrative or purpose of the scene. To take an example which certainly backs up Byron's contention, I watched a group of 8-year-old children and their teacher spend ten minutes drawing out a climactic moment of role-play where they tricked, then overpowered a hijacker (the teacher).[26] That they were totally engrossed was testified to by the delighted screams and laughter of released tension which followed the end of the scene. What was significant about this was that the scene had been twice planned out in advance – firstly at the beginning of the lesson, which was the third session of this particular drama. When the narrative initially reached that point, the children had lacked self-control, had rushed the hijacker with intemperate and illogical bravado, quite lost the plot and the tension, and discovered that they had created an anti-climax. In one sense this had fulfilled 'their play' by providing them with a victory, but a victory that was so easy that they themselves could see it was emptier than they had hoped. It certainly had not fulfilled 'the teacher's play'. Accordingly, he had stopped the drama at that point, and a discussion had ensued where the children and teacher together had analysed the reasons for the scene's failure, and how it might be improved dramatically. They then re-enacted the scene, completely empathising in-role – in spite of the presence of three dozen adult observers seated around – but also in control of their actions in and out of role. The suspense was palpable – a clear example of Vygotsky's 'dual affect'.

This whole session also clearly shows the aesthetic dimension in play, of the very young participants making explicit, both within the dramatic action and in discussion, their developing understanding of the form of the art.

As Byron suggests, this has to do with the nature of the contract. The drama depends to a large extent on the trust existing within the classroom. The drama happens within the larger **context of the setting**, and its mutual expectations. In a primary school classroom the children will normally share a high degree of trust with their teacher, whom they see all day, and who manages the rest of their learning. The subjects may or may not be pleasant, but can normally be related back to purposes of their own that the children are likely to accept as 'normal'. This trust is less predictable in the secondary school, where the drama teacher may be an infrequent visitor, and the level of trust is less a socialised part of classroom behaviour. Primary or secondary, one expectation which children do not have of a teacher in a timetabled class is that just facilitating pleasure is their job. 'They are paid to teach us, not play with us' commented a critical 14-year-old, after a student teacher had endeavoured to manage a drama in education over several lessons by entirely deferring to the students' wishes throughout.[27] The children had, predictably, responded by interpreting the teacher's stance as abdicating authority, and used the session to flout expectations by misbehaving. They were dissatisfied with the experience, and resentful of the waste of time. Schoolchildren expect the teacher to be aiming to teach, and are often mystified if there do not appear to be any teaching purposes. They accordingly spend much of the drama wondering what the teacher's purpose is, or trying to fit in with what they imagine it might be.

Certain areas of knowledge, or exploration, will be outside the boundaries of dramatic exploration, because they are outside particular tolerances of the school system, or of the teacher, or of the children. Clear delineation of these boundaries and their restricting effect on the drama is essential for participants to operate comfortably. In a classroom, the whole negotiative process is in any case constrained by the children themselves. Particularly if they are very young, they will want to get into the dramatic action as quickly as possible, to give themselves what we might call the proto-aesthetic gratification. Whether an elaborated and explicit negotiation takes place with the participants or not, the leader must be aware of the students' interests and concerns, in order to select a 'specific setting in time, place and action'[28] which is appropriate and to which the participants will respond. In this, what must be borne in mind is the crucial *dimension of familiarity*.

Particularly for inexperienced leaders, finding an appropriate **fictional context** and starting point is the hardest and most daunting task in creating and managing this genre. A common initial response is for the teacher to describe herself as unimaginative, or, less excusably, to rationalise her own planning shortcomings with the depressingly common phrase 'oh, these children have no imagination'. It is certainly true that teachers are trained for kinds of lesson planning which involve a convergent approach to achieving given skill or content objectives through logically sequenced activities and resources. Quite apart from this, the negotiative process that must take place in order for a drama to begin successfully is very complex. Morgan and Saxton[29] draw attention to the 'substructure' of considerations which the teacher must take into account before focussing a drama, including the social health of the class, and the 'teacher's and students' personal luggage'. This luggage consists of imperatives and taboos which may be ascribed to the school or classroom ethos, or which may reflect wider social norms. A colleague and I were called in to work with a class of year 4 children, where a social problem had arisen which was distressing the children.[30] A rather isolated child, Sonja, was strongly suspected by both teacher and class of being responsible for an outbreak of pilfering. The teacher suspected that its main motive was attention-seeking. The other children were beginning to exact their own punishments, so the teacher brought drama to her aid. She wished the subject to be raised and explored in a fictional setting, but was not prepared to take the risk of enacting an instance of classroom pilfering. Accordingly we focussed this purpose through a far-distant analogy of a city preparing for a regular celebration, where the populace threw coins for the poor into a fountain. The king (myself in role) was willing and friendly, but so incompetently destructive of the preparations that the children 'townspeople' became exasperated and unceremoniously threw him out. After the ceremony, the people found the coins missing, and with great ado traced the crime to the king, who first truculently then remorsefully admitted the crime, and submitted to the sentence of the townspeople. The mayor (my colleague) demanded punitive revenge, but after a spirited debate the children plumped for leniency. As soon as the drama finished, the class teacher initiated a reflective discussion where immediately Sonja aligned herself with the king and without any prompting or pressure chose to confess her real-life pilfering. By explicit consent of all participants, this session then became socially and personally therapeutic. The *dramatic focus* had provided an *educational focus* for action in the **real context**. It might not have done. It was up to Sonja whether she chose to build back the dramatic analogy to real life, explicitly or implicitly; she could have kept silent.

Deepest within the substructure is the network of permission and prohibition which needs to be dealt with and if necessary renegotiated in terms of focussing decisions. When a class of 12-year-olds chose to do a drama about 'violence in schools', Gavin Bolton was faced immediately with problems. In some schools, this very subject would be entirely taboo. In any classroom, the anarchic – or at least subversive – possibilities of the subject matter, and the dangers inherent in the closeness of the *drama* subject to the children's *actual* experience, enjoined cautious focussing. The teacher decided that in this case more information from the children was essential before he could begin. 'As teacher, I need to find out what they mean or I cannot do anything about extending that meaning.'[31]

Had he been in a school where this whole subject was taboo, this would have been necessary in order to find an analogous but safe situation which would allow the children to explore whatever it was which had made them interested in the topic, and *start* from there. That might have been: (a) the children wanting to make a statement about how institutions validate violence against children: in this case an appropriate focus might have been to set the drama in a nineteenth-century orphanage; (b) a prurient interest in bullyings and beatings: in this case he might have set the drama in a torturer's academy in Central America; (c) wanting to indulge their power fantasies about being strong and violent, or violently upsetting the order of schools. In that case an even more distant analogy might have been necessary, where a kind of violence acceptable to the real school authorities could be explored that would still allow the children to explore their excitement in the subject and its implications: for example, within a strongly Christian school, to set the drama among the martyrs and lions of Nero's Rome.

As it happened, these conditions did not apply in Bolton's class, so the above examples of focussing through analogy are speculative. In order to find out what the children's agenda actually was, he started the drama with 'a staff meeting discussing the recent shocking behaviour of the 5th Form' (NB *older* children). He left it open as to what that shocking behaviour was. The children chose to relate anecdotes about the fifth-formers' anarchic and *illegal* behaviour. He construed this as a request to indulge fantasies of irresponsible power – that was their 'children's play'. This eventually found a focus in the setting of a school classroom at one remove only from reality, a situation which would allow them to indulge those fantasies, to be transformed through the operation of metaphor and dramatic symbol into an aesthetic meaning. In his own commentary on it, Bolton implicitly distinguishes between the two forms of 'teacher's play': instrumental learning, which he acknowledges was lacking in this particular product, and aesthetic learning, which he claims was present.

Besides this network of validation and prohibition which constitutes the school ethos and their own personal luggage, the luggage also includes all that the children bring into the classroom: 'knowledge of the subject, general knowledge, skills, [social] health, values, experiences, feelings.'[32]

The subject matter itself imposes the first focussing choice, in the dimension of familiarity: 'making the unfamiliar familiar, and the familiar unfamiliar'. It is a truism of drama in education that the leader must 'start where the children are at'. This means that if the material of the subject matter is unfamiliar, or unlikely to be of immediate interest to the children, the teacher must find a focus with which they are familiar – for *The Industrial Revolution* toys and child labour. If the subject is one familiar to the participants, especially if the familiarity is likely to result in stereotypic responses, then it must be approached through unfamiliarity. *The Nativity* is a subject I find hard to escape from in schools, around Christmas time; the test is to find anything new for the subject to say to one's clients. Working with upper secondary students, a sympathetic re-evaluation of Herod the Great and the Massacre of the Innocents proved provocative and productive. Working with infants, I chose to concentrate on the

Journey of the Magi. However, my entry point was a mystery in a department store at Christmas time.

FRAMING

The second step, deciding upon an overall structure for the selected **fictional context** and an entry point, is potentially most daunting of all to the inexperienced. Many drama leaders follow successfully an early technique of Heathcote's, *segmenting*, brainstorming within a series of segmented circles. This technique may be reduced to classifying possible key issues within the subject matter, then contextualising these issues through certain kinds of questions, oscillating between generalising and concretising.[33]

More recent work of Heathcote and others exploring the notion of *framing* the action is proving extremely helpful in discriminating within the possibilities of the dramatic context. Drama's use of framing may be said to relate back to the play theorists such as Bateson, and equally, more recently, to the use of the notion of framing action in semiotics and the study of film and television. 'A drama is like a picture frame with a range of interesting pictures that fit inside it. Once you have the frame you can keep swapping the pictures around until you have the one which suits your purpose.'[34] This metaphor of framing is not unconnected with the concept familiar in literary theory of 'narrative viewpoint'. Framing techniques have a very basic advantage with young participants who are likely to tend towards privileging narrative as the means towards gratification in that 'the overall frame within which the re-enactment takes place gives it an orientation such that narrative drive does not predominate.'[35]

This may be seen in Figure 4. The first Diagram is derived jointly by Heathcote and her collaborator Dr John Carroll,[36] the second is a simplification of that, devised for use in schools alongside the *Zola Budd* drama described below.[37]

The playwright and the leader in a drama in education both manage their narratives through their selection of frame and picture, and this selection delineates the dramatic meanings which are available for the participants to construct. Heathcote and Carroll have actually sustained the metaphor and expanded the 'picture frame' to incorporate the dimension of what they call

Figure 4 Role-distance

depth. The frame is seen to be three-dimensional, embodying two qualities: surface and depth. 'Surface' is the particular dramatic convention or style which is being employed. In drama in education, this is normally role-play of various kinds, which can sometimes incorporate conventions of acting and theatrical performance, and apparently non-dramatic activities which are none the less dramatic tasks. 'Depth' is the *role-distance*, that is, the distance, and also the angle of viewpoint, of the role assumed by the participant or participants from the centre of what Carroll calls the 'focus event', the event which is the centre of the dramatic situation.

Though explained thus it may seem rather complicated, it actually simplifies a leader's focussing, giving a range of practicable options beyond framing the action *at the centre of the event*. A colleague and I were leading a drama about a notorious incident from the 1984 Olympic Games. In the Women's 3,000 metres race, a South African teenager named Zola Budd, running for Great Britain, tripped up the race and crowd favourite Mary Decker, pushing her out of the race, perhaps accidentally. Budd finished seventh. This event was certainly dramatic, in both the literal and the cant meaning of the word, potentially a rich focus event for a drama. However, while it might make good cinema, it was quite impossible to recreate the event itself dramatically within the dominant **context of the setting** of a school classroom – the dramatic colour of a classic race and the tension, which depended on running round and round a very large track. Accordingly, we reframed the action *on the edge of the event*, in other words altering one or more (but not all) of the elements of time, place or role. Using the 'surface' convention of experiential role-play, we set two scenes with the students enacting different roles, firstly as 'the athletes in the dressing room after the race' then as 'Zola Budd's family listening to the race from South Africa'. We then reframed it *outside the event* in terms of time, place *and* role, with the participants enrolled as radio or TV journalists with a given range of attitudes to the issues embodied in the event, studying footage of the event and making a feature programme about it.[38]

In fact this is a common narrative device of performance drama. The dramatist selects the entry point and the relationship of the characters to the 'focus event' from the set of possible dramatic frames, and invites the audience to perceive it thus. In

The Winter's Tale Shakespeare uses several different depths and surfaces. He chooses for the audience to *see* at first hand Leontes's jealous banishment of Perdita (the dramatist setting the dramatic action in the centre of the focus event). The audience *hears* of Leontes's subsequent long penitence from those close to him at the conclusion of that penitence (setting the action on the edge of the event). We only *overhear* the news of Perdita' s restoration to court by the distant third hand of a street conversation by characters unrelated to that event (setting the action outside the event). In the same play he daringly plays with both 'surface' and 'depth', as he switches viewpoints and styles right in the middle of what is clearly a focus event, Perdita's abandonment and Antigonus's immediate death. The scene starts with the first-hand poetic realism of Antigonus grieving over the child as he selects a place to fulfil his sad task of abandoning it; it lurches quite unexpectedly into first-hand grotesquerie as a bear lumbers on and sets about the unfortunates. It then switches straight to the second-hand mix of comedy and philosophy as two rustics swap stories of his death and her discovery:

Clown: . . . the men are not yet cold under water, nor the bear half dined on the gentleman – he's at it now
. . .

Shepherd: Thou mettest with things dying, I with things newborn – here's a sight for thee!'

Hard upon that, Shakespeare brings on a third-hand narrator to provide a device common in drama in education work, a time-jump of sixteen years.

Heathcote and Carroll follow Aristotle and Horace in perceiving a protective function for the audience/participants in the use of role-distance. Aristotle implied that for aesthetic reasons there were certain kinds of violent action better reported about than seen:

the plot should be so framed that even without seeing the things take place, he who simply hears of them shall be filled with horror and pity . . . to produce this same effect by means of the spectacle is less artistic.[39]

Horace went further and invoked the need to protect the audience: 'You must not, however, bring upon the stage things fit only to be acted behind the scenes.'[40] Byron puts it syno-nymously in modern terms:

> by framing the participants appropriately, i.e. endowing them with a specific viewpoint on, or relationship to, events in the drama, which offer protection because it enables them to deal more indirectly with emotive subject matter.[41]

A good example of this is the *Hijack* drama mentioned earlier. Before the characters' successful overthrow of the hijacker (first-order experience right in the centre of the focus event), the teacher started the drama on the edge, in the future, with himself role-playing a journalist interviewing 'the survivors of the terrible hijacking'. His purpose here was to allay the very real fears of some of the children, who were a bit apprehensive about this dangerous subject, which had been chosen by the majority of the class. Starting by showing that 'you all survived unharmed' had no effect on the tension of the ensuing drama, but it was necessary to establish a **context of the medium** where all the young participants could feel safe – to establish a trustworthy contract.

Such forms of distancing in drama in education have a further important function. The greater the distance which the participants adopt from experiencing the focus event as a character within it, the more detachment about the event will be natural to the role. This means that levels of externalisation and alienation of understanding about the subject matter can occur within the **fictional context**, that is, the drama itself. Children involved in a drama about Inca civilisation were first enrolled not as Incas but outside the event as modern historians, investigating some newly discovered artefacts – which raised their interest and focussed what they decided they needed to find out about Inca life. They were then re-enrolled within the event as Incas, making those very artefacts for a ceremony. They moved backwards and forwards a number of times, with the 'historian' role giving them the opportunity each time to reflect from without on their experiences within.[42] This is much the same as the experience of the audience in *The Winter's Tale* as they move from empathy to objectivity and ironic comment, and back.

PURPOSES AND TASKS WITHIN THE FICTIONAL CONTEXT

The purposes within the drama itself are those of the characters, and are realised by the tasks which they carry out in pursuit of their goals. As the above examples show, drama in education is a very Brechtian medium. Percipients constantly oscillate between the **fictional context**, the **context of the medium** and the **context of the setting**. The real networks of signs and meanings are never suspended very deeply. The **context of the setting** rears its head every time a student slips disruptively out of role or otherwise breaks the contract, say by bursting into tears and retiring to the teacher-aide's lap; the frequent external interruptions which beset classrooms can also cause breaks or suspensions in the drama. A notice over the school public address that the girls all have to go to have their rubella injections at the end of the lesson will put paid to the most robust drama – though I am still often surprised how easily the participants of an absorbing drama can screen out more run-of-the-mill interruptions. Throughout a drama the **context of the medium** is frequently asserted – and not always by the teacher – as the play stops for renegotiation, or changes from one frame to another, one style to another and one mode of participation – especially between experiential role-play and performative action. A fairly common convention among groups who are experienced in drama in education is the 'talk chair' where the teacher or any other participant may sit in order to suspend the drama, to suggest a new tack or renegotiate the characters' tasks within the action.

It may be helpful to categorise the tasks of the characters as one of three kinds, each with a different basic relationship both to the purposes of the participants and to the centre of the **fictional context**: *enrolment* tasks, *experiential* tasks and *reflective* tasks. The experiential tasks are internal to the **fictional context**, the enrolment and reflective tasks are at least partly outside, part of the **contexts of the medium** and the **setting**. Within these three categories there are also variable degrees of experiential engagement. *Enrolment* tasks and *reflective* tasks are in fact also key aspects of dramatic focussing.

Experiential tasks

The *experiential* tasks refer to those actions taken by the characters in pursuit of their goals in the drama – the way, as it were, they live out moment by moment their fictional lives: tasks which form the centre of the narrative, but which they do not perceive in this way, any more than real humans perceive themselves moment by moment as enacting a narrative.

Here role-play operates quite differently from theatrical performance, in the manner of its representation. In a play, actors go through actions which are intended to represent the activities of their characters. They may do this relatively close to, or far from, naturalistically. If the action consists of talking, or performing actions confined enough to be performed on a stage, like kissing, or making a cup of tea, they may actually perform them. The resources of the camera allow a wider scope for naturalism in film and television. A tree may actually be felled, or a car may crash. On the other hand, there is a limit to the contract for the audience as well: if the action is love-making, the audience will normally expect the act to be simulated, whether it is on stage or screen; if the action is tree-felling, they will know that, on a stage, it must be simulated. Cornwall's task in *King Lear* is to put out Gloucester's eyes. Not only would an audience not expect the act to be really performed, they would be horrified if it were. Accordingly, the act must in some way be simulated. This may be done naturalistically, in such a way as to appear real – sleight of hand or lighting effect creating the illusion of blinding, which the audience know to be illusion. It must still, however, horrify them vicariously – through the dual affect. Nowadays a simple illusion is unlikely to be effective, even if it were in Shakespeare's time – the apparent reality of an act so grotesque can seem just funny, not brutal; besides, this particular scene has been done so often that any form of naturalism has lost its power to shock. To interpret this moment successfully it may be necessary for directors to utilise what has been called in literature the 'theory of intermittence' – that the pleasure lies in the gap between the reality and what can be imagined.[43] Therefore some other, non-naturalistic convention may be invoked. The necessary intermittence, together with the shock of the unexpected, may happen through suggestion – as in Peter Brook's film version, where the act itself is hidden, but the camera lingers on torturers' instruments being picked up. Alternatively the horror may be invoked through analogy, as in one English production where, as Cornwall merely passed a hand across Gloucester's eyes, a jackbooted guard dropped a tangerine on the floor and stamped on it, so that the pulp spurted into the audience.[44]

Such distancing conventions cannot be employed in those sections of a drama in education where experiential role-play is the *modus operandi*, though more will be said on this shortly. The participants' external purpose is for them to experience the events of the fiction, not vicariously but personally and unselfconsciously. Usually, as far as possible, the leader constructs genuine tasks which can be performed within the time and space constraints. As in theatre, the tasks of the characters are often expressed and completed through talk.

A further set of constraints relate to the expectations of the classroom. The classroom, school hall or drama studio is not as negotiable a space as a drama stage. Spatial constraints are not the only ones. Love-making, simulated or otherwise, is certainly off the curriculum, and both leader and participants know this.

These constraints are not all negative; in fact the participative nature of the drama permits a range of tasks which cannot be performed by actors to an audience. A group role-playing prisoners of war can spend an hour excitedly designing their escape plan in great detail, then tracing their path to Switzerland through a map of Germany, before writing a letter to throw the guards off the scent. A group of geriatric workers designing a new and appropriate institution for their clients can absorb themselves in studying transcripts of old people talking.

This allows the teacher/leader to bring into the drama tasks which are part of the activities normal to the classroom, such as art and craft, and writing activities. A detailed example from infant drama in education may serve to show the wide variety of the 'experiential' tasks which can be used.[45] Back at *The Nativity* my specific purpose as teacher was for them to come to understand through the drama the link between the modern giving of presents and the traditional story. I enrolled them as department store assistants at Christmas time and let them choose what departments they served in. Their first experiential task was to help me, role-playing a baffled stranger, a time traveller named Caspar, to decode the cryptic pictures that were jumbled images from an important dream Caspar had had. They decoded the pictures as images from the story of the Nativity – which was unknown to Caspar – and explained to him that he must be one of the Wise Men, and what his duty must be. He then invited the shop assistants to take the journey to Bethlehem with him, after acquiring presents from their own departments of the store and making an appropriate one for him. Then followed an art and craft session as the children made gifts – in the case of 'jewellery' or 'toy' departments making a close approximation of the real with the aid of coloured macaroni, crepe paper and so on; in the case of the children who had eccentrically chosen to be lawn mower salesmen they made a more distant representation by way of a painting of a mower worthy of presenting to the baby Jesus.

It may be seen here that some of the tasks were real enough: deciphering the scrawls and explaining the nativity to Caspar entailed no more than the simple first suspension of disbelief to accept the fiction – the 'first order of abstraction'.[46] Other tasks took one step further into suspending the disbelief. Even if macaroni might be a first-order substitution for reality, the painting of a mower was at one remove, not to a second order of narrative, but with literally one dimension of the reality of the first order of abstraction removed. Moreover, the children knew that shop assistants do not normally make the products they sell; yet this task was carried out entirely seriously, and their ownership of the products they had genuinely made with care had an extra 'enrolment' effect of further committing them to the importance of the climax, when it came, of meeting the baby Jesus.

This on its own would not be enough to give the climactic presentation the sense of importance and achievement which was one of the purposes of my 'play for the teacher' – which would also fit in with their 'children's play'. They did not want an anti-climax, either, though their understanding of dramatic form would be unlikely at this age to dominate their urge for immediate gratification. Constraints and tensions had to be provided, and in terms of the narrative these would have to be during the journey.

I chose to negotiate this with the children, and an out-of-role discussion resulted in three salient narrative constraints proposed and selected by the children, in order 'to make the journey hard and the adventure exciting': a perilous path across a snake-filled swamp (geographically suspect, but the children wanted it); an encounter with Herod's guards at the gate of Bethlehem; and a mistaken encounter with an impoverished family. The classroom was then set up into four areas where the events, including the presentation to the Holy Family, would take place. Each of the four 'adventures' was taken as a separate scene, with a cut after each one. In fact three of the scenes entailed a few children changing roles to become, temporarily, Herod's guards and the members of the two families. The first scene, the swamp, was the task least real in its representation. I chose to narrate the children through the scene while we all simulated the actions being narrated. This very stylised convention was one of the earliest used in drama in education.[47] Now generally known as 'occupational mime', although it does not usually connote silent participation, it has somewhat fallen into disuse, partly because of the range of more real tasks which have tended to supersede it. We all added our own narrative embroideries, such as Caspar's terror of snakes, and several children being bitten by poisonous snakes and having to be nursed swiftly back to health.

The encounter with Herod's guards caused a very interesting renegotiation, owing to a confusion of internal and external agendas which led to one set of characters' task-purposes dominating the dramatic action to such an extent that the drama came to a halt and had to be suspended while the purposes were renegotiated. Two boys had eagerly volunteered to be Herod's guards and 'make it difficult' for Caspar and the shop assistants to enter Bethlehem, which they saw as something of a fortress. They so enjoyed the power of this temporary role that they did not just make it difficult, they made it quite impossible, so that eventually Caspar had to drop role, become the teacher again and, through a class discussion, remind the 'guards' that their roles were subservient to the narrative and could not entirely subvert it: after all, the real Caspar *did* reach Bethlehem. Reluctantly the 'guards' agreed, and the scene was re-enacted, with a degree of control very similar to the *Hijack* scene referred to earlier.

The third task demonstrates that the narrative itself was to a degree negotiable, as long as it allowed the primary purpose of the dramatic action to be fulfilled and the tension resolved. The visit of the travellers to the 'poor family' was quite a realistic task, consisting mainly of greeting talk and the presentation of presents in error. After the error was 'discovered' – the children were using a considerable communal control over the art form here, with a little help from Caspar – the family startlingly refused to hand the presents back, an action I had not expected. An impassioned debate ensued, on relative need. Since the messages of the Nativity were still strongly enough embedded in the children to preclude the holy travellers falling upon the family and beating them up or retaking the presents forcibly, this was allowed to stand, and the group, now including several truculent travellers with no presents to give, continued towards the stable. The 'family' rejoined the group in their former roles, and the final, very ritualised presentation was made to Mary and Joseph.

There was still a residue of tension, however, even after these purposes had been fulfilled. I interpolated a final task, with the news that Herod's guards were searching the district, and would be bound to find all these presents, which would give away Jesus' whereabouts. In an aesthetically elegant final resolution, the children decided unanimously to take back their presents to the twentieth century and give them to the Children's Hospital Christmas Appeal, leaving hidden only the box of frankincense which they had made for Caspar. Part of their decision included deliberately not telling the 'poor family', who still had a number of stolen presents, that Herod's guards were looking for just that kind of evidence. In this they resisted strong pressure from me as Caspar. It was not very Christian, but it was satisfying to the purposes of the dispossessed and still vengeful travellers, and effectively rounded off the drama.

Enrolment tasks

Enrolment tasks are more problematic in terms of whether they can be said to exist inside or outside the drama. This is because the functions of the participants as actors, as protagonists and as audience are being fulfilled simultaneously. In practice, no participants, however willing, can step into the **fictional context** to engage with a character empathetically at a moment's notice. We start tentatively, still literally self-conscious, and conscious of the **medium** and **setting**. To help, we usually put on ('assume' in both senses) what we already know of the role, and *model* what is effectively a stereotype. This 'fixed statement'[48] of the role may in any case be all that is required of the role, and it can therefore be constructed quite speedily. As the fictional tasks and narrative become more absorbing, we start to *manage* the role more instinctively.[49]

If the role-play is to be genuinely part of the dramatic process of personal and social discovery, then the participants must make it their own, and find whatever they can about the role to relate to their own experience and feelings. This complex *managing* of the role entails experiment, and a trusting and not over-demanding environment. The first phase of this is visibly tentative, and in the case of children often entails apparently irrelevant activity. Eventually, if the tasks of the characters are appropriate, and the drama is properly focussed towards the resolution of goals, the role will be internalised. This kind of enrolment may or may not be deeply empathetic, but it must be dually affective and dually active – the character must be behaving naturally within the situation, and must simultaneously be monitoring this operation for the sake of managing it within the **fictional context**.

Enrolment activities may themselves be phased. If the role is no more than the generalised point of view of 'blanket perspective' (see chapter 2), then little preparation will be necessary, other than a straightforward preparation for the first task. If the role is 'personalised', then a series of preliminary tasks may be necessary, and these tasks may in fact take up more time than the experiential section of the drama. In a series of lessons with primary children[50] the class had to be separately enrolled into two Stone Age peoples with different orientations, one with the use of language, one without. I asked the group who had not discovered language to discover and record their history on to a long roll of butcher's paper, all without talking. Meanwhile, the speaking people were decorating their cave in preparation for whatever religious ceremony they thought would be appropriate. The products of both of these tasks – the history painting and the ceremony – were in fact utilised later on within the drama, providing a need to engender talk between the two peoples when they eventually met. The primary purpose of the tasks, however, was to commit the children to their enrolment within each group. Both tasks helped the groups background themselves, and discover what belief systems they operated. As they themselves enriched the **fictional context**, so the children became more confident in 'managing' their roles in the drama.

Reflective tasks

The simplest reflective task is to hold a discussion immediately after the drama, out of role and entirely out of the **fictional context**. Something like this is virtually automatic anyway: as an experiential section of a drama is concluded, often by the leader stepping in quite suddenly and cutting it, there is typically a short silence, then a burst of laughter and chatter – this applies to children and adults equally. The release of residual tension (which may be quite considerable if there is no final resolution of the tension within the drama, which is often the case) releases a flow of language and energy. These are far from random. For the participants in a drama in education, just as for the audience emerging from a theatre after a strong experience, they usually consist of expressive reiteration, fragments of the experience retold in language: ' . . . did you see when I . . . what about that moment when she . . . ' If encouraged, and allowed to run their course, these exchanges are actually quite systematic, the first steps in decoding the experience for the participants in order to make it explicit, part of a coherent understanding.[51]

Reflective tasks of a more sophisticated kind may also occur within the drama itself. Very frequently, the phase of fixed statement is invoked as a strategy: to help to clarify the nature of the experience, participants may be asked in some way other than just verbally to make it explicit, in or out of role.

The participants may be asked to remain in the character, but to move from role-play to some form of acting and adopt a performance mode. A simple and much-used technique is to ask the participants, out of role, to decide what were three or four salient and crucial moments of the drama, and to regroup to show those as 'still photographs' or tableaux, perhaps naturalistic, perhaps stylised. This may be contextualised into 'suppose that a newspaper photographer was present, taking pictures of the whole scene; what photos would appear in the paper tomorrow morning?' Alternatively there may be a change of role, with the participants turning into a 'newsreel crew making a documentary about the event' or some similar loosely contextualised refractive device. This kind of 'fixing' activity allows leader and participants to reflect on what were the key moments, and to begin to draw out their particular meaning. Because they are what the group agrees to be key moments, dramatic symbols often emerge or become explicit in this task.

Byron notes that 'more specific opportunities for reflection and reflective talk may be built into a drama. This can be achieved by framing the pupils in a way that demands such reflection.'[52] Perhaps Byron does not go far enough. Throughout any drama the particular frames selected will always be dependent upon the *enrolment, experiential* and *reflective* phases within the overall purpose of the drama. The drama on *Utopia* referred to in chapter 2 is a clear instance of this. For all but the maverick participant, my initial quite standard enrolment tasks paled into insignificance as enrolling devices besides the challenge of dealing with his disbelief. The ensuing experiential fracas, and the significant residual anger transcending the drama, dictated a completely different framing of the *reflective* phase from what I had initially planned. The experiential tasks ended with the extreme emotions of the murder in which the Utopians had just participated very strong and quite unresolved. As a first step towards de-roling the group, I asked them to write a letter, still *within* the role, to an appropriate person or body, giving their perspective on what had happened. This cooled them off, pouring some spectacular bile into print, rather than into the discussion with which we finished that first day's session. It also gave me time to reframe the next phase of the drama to be refractive rather than directly emotional again. The letters themselves played a vital part in that next phase.

I chose maximum 'depth' of frame, to distance the event as far as possible. The action was moved forward some hundreds of years, and we envisaged a future Utopian world society 'existing in harmony' – the whole group negotiated the mores of this society. A new frame was created, with the group re-enrolled as combined archaeologist/actors (in the words of Heathcote and Carroll's diagram in Figure 4: *'researcher/ artists'*), whose mission was to construct a dramatic reconstruction of a pre-Utopian conflict which had happened in the twentieth century. The evidence of this conflict was vestigial and so far a mystery: merely a ravaged site (the room left as it was after the murder) and a bunch of unposted letters (the very letters which the participants had themselves written the day before in their previous roles). The participants took this opportunity to 'play' with humour and detachment at what had caused them much discomfort in their other roles. Significantly, many participants chose to stay as far away as possible from their own roles of the previous day, avoiding their own letters, and proffering fantastical 'theories' as to what might have happened on the archival site.

As the team began to reconstruct the events, from my role as the 'Producer' I gradually encouraged them to move closer to what had actually happened. I was unsure myself what would happen. With great discipline, the participants gradually stopped withholding their memory of the events, and in four tentative reconstruction scenes gradually came closer to the 'truth'. The depth of frame was shortening to *'demonstrator/guide'*. By the end of the fourth, it became tacitly evident to all participants what needed to happen (quite unplanned in advance). Those participants who were still resisting re-enacting their previous roles dropped their resistance, and took up their positions as characters of the previous day (still protected by the enveloping role of being 'actors from the future'). In a spontaneous approach to the centre of the event, the whole confrontation and murder scene was meticulously re-enacted, with control and clarity. The palpable tension of this final scene, which was confirmed in post-drama discussion, clearly showed that at this moment *two* fictional frames were operating simultaneously, superimposed upon each other – in the terms of Figure 4: *'I am in the event* and *I am re-enacting it so you can understand.'* Both those 'I's were within the **fictional context**, but in fact, in the **context of the medium** there was another 'I' operating – the real participant of the dual affect. There were three frames operating simultaneously: and the participants were conscious of all three.

PURPOSE AND FOCUS IN THEATRE IN EDUCATION

When considering processuality of purpose and focus in drama, it is revealing to compare drama in education with the neighbouring genre of theatre in education.

Theatre in education shares with drama in education the constraint upon its aesthetic dimension that there are always instrumental purposes which normally take precedence. These do not work quite identically, however, and the differences have to do with the *expectations* aroused by the event.

First, to reiterate the position of drama in education: for the students as much as the leader it needs to fulfil the expectation that it will be concerned with recognisable school learning patterns and activities. If drama is taking place within, say, social studies time, teacher and students privilege the instrumentality. The subsidiary role of the drama to the dominant subject is ratified, and this usually imposes ancillary tasks which the students accept as part and parcel of the social studies work – such as written work for assessment following the drama. As noted earlier, in many schools drama is confined to the periphery of the timetable, disparagingly known as the 'wet Friday afternoon' approach. Since the students at such times are motivated towards *play*, it might be thought that the aesthetic dimension could be strongest. In practice, the students' urge to play is itself incoherent, as much motivated by the desire not to be focussed into structured activity as to get away from instrumental learning. As a result, focussing into the coherent structures of drama in education becomes difficult for the teacher, which is why drama teachers invariably resent and resist this kind of provision.

The expectations of clients towards a piece of theatre in education are subtly different, and part of its appeal as well as a danger to be faced is the very 'wet Friday afternoon' syndrome. Teachers' evaluations of TIE programmes in Tyneside, England, and in Queensland, Australia, taken a decade apart, show remarkable similarity of response, even though the English programmes were by one locally based team, mainly to single classes entailing integral participation, while the Queensland teachers were responding to a range of touring offerings, all entailing performance work aimed at large audiences, with no audience participation during the show.[53]

The key to the similarity of response is that the teachers invariably privilege the aesthetic power and entertainment value of the programme over any instrumental objectives. More than that, they refer to their students' responses primarily in this way:

'This electrifying play really had the children on their seats throughout.'

'Some of the children came in not expecting much; thank you for sending them out breathless after such an exciting and enriching experience.'

'Frankly, the children were bored – they started out very

excited, as we do not get much theatre out here, but as the play dragged on they got more and more restless, and so did I.'

Specific educational objectives draw some mention, but often in fairly generalised terms:

'My children will certainly appreciate history more after this.'

'I hope my children will have a clearer idea of the importance of language and the power of poetry.'

'I still do not know what this play was supposed to teach, but I can make history much more interesting in my own classroom.'

In other words, unlike a drama lesson, teachers and students start out expecting an aesthetic experience – though with varying expectations concerning how palatable it will be. For a start, a TIE performance is not a normal part of the school day, but an abnormal interruption. It invariably takes some reorganisation of the normal schedules, and so is likely to be promoted as a special event; it usually happens in a place of special importance – the school hall or activities space (in many cases the students make a special journey to the theatre itself); it may involve the children in expense, with a levy or charge. This means that the TIE team *must* satisfy the aesthetic demands of the audience, if the instrumental aims are to be considered. One of the reasons why TIE caused a considerable amount of opposition in its early days, in both the UK and Australia, was the fear of many educators who were also theatre lovers that the power of the theatrical experience was likely to be lost to the instrumental purposes. Early TIE manifestos gave little reassurance:

We do not aim to create the social habit of theatre . . . a group of people define an aim, devise material to communicate that aim, then present the project using drama and theatre skills . . . to relate to the moment of commitment not the technical intricacies of production.[54]

The President of the British Children's Theatre Association, who was an influential Drama Adviser, expressed this fear:

It does seem a pity if children are to be everlastingly educated, in the name of theatre, through documentaries whether situated in the mills or the mines or out on the open sea without being brought into contact with the art of theatre.[55]

Within the genre itself, there was agreement about the primacy of educational aims, but some workers moved to protect the traditional aesthetic of theatre – expressed succinctly by the founder of the first specific theatre in education company in Australia, Salamanca TIE in Tasmania: 'Theatre in Education means education through theatre, and theatre means performance.'[56]

Teams have found that there is a fine line to be drawn between the aesthetic and the entertaining. Many TIE teams attempt to lock their educational purposes into the curriculum of the schools, most frequently in the form of teachers' notes and preliminary workshops. Many teams maintain contact with local educational authorities, and either solicit or respond to their ideas for programme material. Some teams make preliminary visits to schools, in order to workshop ideas, or even elicit them, from the clients themselves. Others take half-completed programmes into 'tame' classes, to try out the material. The Tyneside team, for which I was working, made strong schools contact a particular part of its brief. The team's touring range was within a small locality. For one of the programmes which provided the evaluation data above, *Labour for the Lord*, we firstly contacted schools and drama advisers in advance, to isolate material which would be of direct curricular value to teachers on the subject of the programme, which was about local history and the Industrial Revolution.[57] We ran workshops for all the class teachers being visited (the programme involved one class in integral participation over a half-day), attended by over 50 per cent, during which we outlined both preliminary and follow-up work possibilities. The team made clear to the teachers that the preliminary work would need to be done for the programme to proceed properly. We also produced a 30-page follow-up work-shop pack, intended to offer teachers a complete unit of work. The visit of the team itself was intended to be the centrepiece of a much larger drama-based experience, envisaged as a whole unit of work. Finally, as the team's education officer I made follow-up visits to over 50 per cent of the classes which had received the programme. The way we conceived of it would fit in with the three phases of the drama in education model outlined earlier:

- *enrolment*: the preliminary work
- *experiential*: the visit of the team
- *reflective*: the follow-up work package

In fact, as the team discovered, this was not how the teachers regarded it. In almost every case the preliminary work *had* been done, mainly so that the children would not be penalised. Virtually all the teachers commented how excited the children were, but only about half related this to the specific enrolling activities. The follow-up visits and the evaluation forms for this programme confirmed that the teachers had appreciated the visit as beneficial and entirely absorbing to the children. In spite of this success of the preliminary work and main visit –

- 30 per cent had not even discussed the experience with the children after the visit – and this was a single-class programme, with the teacher being the regular primary class teacher.
- Less than 50 per cent had asked the children to undertake a simple recording task based upon the programme, such as writing an account of the team's visit or recounting the narrative, or painting a picture connected with it.
- Less than 30 per cent had used the teachers' resource package; of those who had, less than 50 per cent (i.e. 15 per cent of the total) had followed through more than one activity.
- 4 per cent had followed up the resource pack completely.
- Under 10 per cent had devised their own coherent follow-up programme of work.

This survey reveals results very typical and familiar to many TIE companies, in both the UK and Australia. That would suggest that the teachers quoted above are neither untypical nor uncaring nor lazy. The teachers were assiduous in preparing the preliminary work; they were appreciative of the visit. Rather, it suggests that they regarded the actors' visit most importantly and essentially as an end in itself. A substantial minority of the teachers used the opportunities afforded by the visit to do something else; however, the majority felt that the stimulus of the visit was a strong enough learning experience, and was complete. Remarks like

'I didn't want to spoil it for them by bringing it down to an ordinary classroom level.'

'I wanted to leave it fresh in their minds.'

'I didn't think I could live up to the actors.'

were common. Common too were comments like

'We'd spent quite long enough on this topic – including a whole morning on the show.'

In spite of the efforts expended by the company in promoting the instrumental purposes of the programme, for the teachers the aesthetic impact that they could not provide themselves remained the most important element. The last-quoted comment would also seem to indicate that the teachers clearly had their own instrumental agendas, and a proportion of them were not prepared to be dictated to, and have those agendas modified, by a theatre company whose business was art and entertainment.

We can further illuminate the comparative processuality of the two genres by comparing the major functionaries – the drama teacher and the TIE team – each of which carries advantages and disadvantages in both instrumental and aesthetic terms, with key implications in terms of both purpose and focus. The comparison holds whether the team's visit is providing performance work or integral participation.

1 The teacher is a known figure, the team are strangers; their advantage is impact and novelty, but they cannot take into account the personal luggage of the audience. Processually, one up to the teacher.

2 The teacher is (usually) one person, the team is multiple. The teacher can only provide one simple dramatic reference point. One to the team.

3 The teacher has only one head in planning. The team has more heads, more research, more ideas – but also more opinions on where, when and how to focus the programme. Companies which generate their material collectively often find the focussing of the programme inordinately time-consuming, and sometimes productive of bad feeling that quite outweighs the benefits of negotiation. It is often for this reason, rather than solely dramatic expertise, that a writer, dramaturge or strong artistic director is called in to provide a single overview of the dramatic material which the team is generating. A draw – one all, still.

4 The team has time (more than the teacher) to research, plan, carefully structure, rehearse and modify. This means that the

programme will be more negotiable for them, but less so for the children, than a drama lesson – the team will be tied essentially to what they have produced over the rehearsal period.

> This programme is quite tightly structured. There are certain points – it's like a trail – you are aiming for those points of the story, and you can't go very far off the trail or you start on another story. So it's a matter of trying to pull everyone along the same trail, but leaving it open enough so that kids are suggesting and adding to the thing all the time.[58]

They certainly cannot stop and renegotiate the terms and structures of the drama, except under the rarest and most processual of circumstances, when such renegotiation has been structured into the programme. One example of that was a cleverly disingenuous programme where the performance was stopped to let the audience of shy and maladjusted girls discuss the central domestic dilemma; the actors 'volunteered to act out the girls' solutions' – and did this so clumsily that members of the audience took over and acted out their own solutions.[59] Such looseness of structure and negotiability is rare. Two–one to the teacher.

5 The team can bring in complex effects and properties beyond the scope of the class teacher: *Labour for the Lord* turned the school hall into a nineteenth-century chemical factory filled with smoke, and *Spacemen Have Landed in Leeds* (see chapter 4) incorporated a space-ship large enough for two people and several contraptions emitting weird noises and objects. Two all.

6 The team has performing skills beyond the range of the teacher. Even the teacher who can act will be limited by the students' familiarity with his or her 'normal' teacher role, and it is a commonplace observation of drama teaching that the theatricality appropriate to a theatre or an actor is quite inappropriate in the classroom unless wielded by a stranger. The reason for this is once again the students' expectations. There are dangers here for both teacher and actor, however. It is a thin line between inspiring and daunting, and a thinner one between the theatrical *tour de force* and the actor's ego-trip. I recall when acting in a TIE 'adventure programme', *Out of the Casebook*, making an entrance as an unpredictable father, angry, roughly dressed and with a fierce manner. Ineptly I crashed through the door with far more theatricality than was called for or than the

smallish classroom could hold, and the students, believing the occasion to be real life, were terrified and froze. I was supposed to engage them in conversation to find out where the 'social worker' who was lecturing them had gone. Nobody was game to move, let alone speak or risk catching my eye, and I retired ignominiously.[60] As an experienced teacher, I should have known better; unsurprisingly, actors without teacher-training often find it difficult to scale their performance down to the classroom. Penalty goal – two–three.

7 The team normally repeats the programme many times. For the drama teacher, the drama is usually a 'one-off', although the sequence may under some circumstances be used with a range of similar classes. During the run of a TIE programme, the team can sort out, modify, alter or clarify what is weak or unclear, as well as get to know and develop the strongest areas in the programme, both in terms of impact and of learning. Three all.

8 The main difference between TIE and drama in education, in terms of negotiability of purpose and focus, is that it is uncommon for an audience to have input into the focussing and structuring of a piece of theatre, which is already the product of a number of negotiations from genesis to production. As we have seen, this is a process in which the teacher is constantly engaged. Processually, then, the teacher wins.

Most often, the purposes of TIE companies do not include those of children in the decision-making which leads to a final programme. More than the drama teacher, they serve a number of masters, all of whose agendas have to be addressed. It must be in their minds to devise a programme which is aesthetically acceptable to the children, and ideologically acceptable to themselves, but these underlying constraints are overlaid with more immediate ones. The primary audience may be children, but there is a powerful secondary one of the teachers, who expect something both aesthetic and educational. Behind them are the authority systems of Principal and Education Department, which at the least make an evaluative input and whose reaction the team must predict in advance. Few education systems allow theatre in education to enter their schools unchecked, and their system of checks range from a comprehensive post-programme evaluation,[61] to a formal assessment preview amounting to a censor's panel,[62] to a Drama Adviser with executive power,[63] to some kind of Advisory Committee or Board.[64]

Two examples, successive programmes from Tynewear TIE, may serve to illustrate how negotiations with these secondary clients define purposes in theatre in education, which then dictate programme focus. For TIE teams, as for the drama teacher, the non-negotiable **real context** provides constraints within which the **fictional context** emerges and is shaped.

The first, *Time Please*,[65] was an Upper Sixth form programme requested by the Education Authority's unit on drug information and abuse. The given purpose was to warn the students about the dangers of alcohol misuse. The imposed audience size, 50–100, suggested the focus and the action was set in a raucous nineteenth-century temperance meeting. The participation was peripheral, and the frame – *I re-enact so you can understand* – distanced from the participants.

The second, *Play Shadows*,[66] followed a request from a Special Education Adviser for a programme on sensory perception for disabled infants, with the particular injunction that the programme should try and give the children what for them would be an uncommon experience of having power and being in control. A Special Education grant of extra financial assistance meant that *Play Shadows* was able to dictate its audience size of twenty maximum (an unusual bit of negotiability within the **real context**). This permitted the use of integral participation – the team had the flexibility to allow each member of that audience to contribute to solving the dramatic problem, framed in the centre of the focus event. A troubled shadow came to life through a *coup de théâtre* unachievable in a normal classroom, then the children had to take charge of it and teach it to understand colour, sound and texture, three sensual dimensions alien to shadows, before it could reveal to them the root of its problem, which they then solved.

Chapter 4

Tension, time and audience

DEFINING TENSION

The word 'tension' is not one which most schoolteachers are likely to regard positively as a key element of their teaching, rather than as something to avoid. The definition which we are using would probably be even less popular: that the source of tension is the gap between people and the fulfilment of their internal purposes, a gap created by deliberately imposing constraints in order to create an emotional disturbance (the tension itself) in the participants. Recently, to test this out informally, I asked two classes of teacher-training students, one pre-service and one in-service, whether they saw it as an objective of their teaching for their students to attain their goals as easily as possible. Overwhelmingly they did, and they reacted with disagreement and even hostility to my counter-proposal that one purpose of the teacher should be to create motivation and then deliberately place frustrations in the children's way. Part of the problem is semantic; the word 'challenge' might have been more acceptable to teachers than 'tension' and 'frustration'. Similarly, of the key words and phrases to be used in this section, they might find the word 'tasks' quite acceptable in the classroom, but not 'conflict', 'dilemma', 'secrecy', 'ritual', 'surprise' and 'deception' – all among the terms I shall be using to denote manifestations of the source of tensions in drama. While teachers are flattered to use the term 'the art of teaching' for what we do, we usually consciously perceive our operation in cognitive and behaviouristic terms – the systems we work in see to that. On the other hand, effective teachers may be seen to use retardation devices like 'wait and see' very frequently in all types of lesson

lesson context, and so the distinction may be more in the perception than in the practice. This, however, is a matter for a study of art in the process of education, rather than of process in art in education.

On the other hand, 'tension' is a word used entirely comfortably within all aesthetic fields, particularly drama, and so it may be said to belong to the aesthetic dimension.[1] Educators who work specifically in drama have tended in the last decade to concentrate on tension as a key element, not only of the art form, but of the resultant learning. As an experienced Drama Adviser puts it: 'Tension is the spring of drama. Not the action, it is what impels the action.'[2]

Tension, rather than being a substantive element of dramatic form, is a construct to define the emotional reactions of a group of percipients. To this extent tension may be said to be, or to be a part of, the *feeling* component of the aesthetic dimension. This is another reason why non-drama teachers, who are more comfortable when they can perceive their classrooms as places of cognitive action, distrust as uncontrollable, unmeasurable and out of place both the aesthetic and the emotional domains of action and thought. Teachers traditionally do not explicitly incorporate the 'affective dimension'[3] within their practice.[4]

TENSION AND TIME

At first sight, if the emotional domain is unmeasurable and apparently uncontrollable, then tension must be the least negotiable of the elements, the most resultant from other factors. However, emotions, even obsessive emotions, are far from uncontrollable, and children have a capacity to manage them which is frequently underrated by their adult teachers:

> One essential requirement for creative action is the capacity for tolerating tension . . . We can see this obsession in children's play . . . 'This is the gift that the artist is allowed to give himself if he is prepared to take the risks of survival'. Our system of education is structured so that this rarely happens. The further up the educational scale you go, the more the obsession is not accommodated.[5]

In the first place, the emotional effect that is tension is relatively easy to define. For this purpose, Gilbert Ryle's metaphor is helpful. Ryle, denoting an emotion as implying some kind of change of psychological state, describes it being like an 'eddy' in a stream, caused by the convergence of two opposing currents, or by a boulder interrupting its natural flow – where the ' flow' he speaks of is that of an individual's natural inclinations or dispositions.[6] A psychological investigation of tension in visual art comes to essentially the same conclusion, labelling the 'flow' as a 'homeostasis' or stable state.[7] Translated to narrative and dramatic theory, the audience's dispositional flow may be seen naturally to follow the narrative towards its conclusion and ordered resolution. In that order, effect succeeds cause as the events flow through time; the characters proceed towards their goals.

Very young children, lacking intervention in their dramatic narratives, seek swift resolution to a state of order – problems are solved quickly, by magic if necessary. In fact magic is often preferable to a logical solution – it confirms the solubility of problems. The function of the adult, the playwright or teacher, is usually to provide as much of a stay or retardation of this urge towards swift gratification as is not beyond the slim tolerance level of infants. Their desire for artistic satisfaction is subordinated to their need for confirmation and reassurance of an ordered world where the key elements of the order are sequence, causality and selectivity. The child experiences a series of events and can see that they have been specially chosen, and are linked together in a model which spells out not only *that b* follows *a*, but *why* it does and should.[8]

As the child grows older, and in adult drama, satisfaction is not present without challenge, so the characters in the narrative must experience vicissitudes, in order for the audience to feel sufficient frustrations for the resolution to accrue significance as an event. These frustrations provide the eddies in the dispositional flow, and both of Ryle's images – the converging currents and the boulders in the stream – are apposite for drama. It is worth briefly examining the vocabulary of narrative theory here. The Russian Formalist critics normally used the word *zamedleniye* or 'slowing down' – now usually retranslated as 'retardation' – as the source of narrative tension. Shklovsky also used the phrase *zatrudnyennaya forma* or 'form made difficult', and this may be whence came the occasionally used 'impedance', probably an image inherited from electrical technology.[9] Though 'retardation' is more current usage within literary theory, the difference is not insignificant to practice in drama in education, and both are applicable.

Typically, central to the structuring of a piece of drama in education are *retarding* devices – the characters have to accomplish a number of tasks, of both mundane and ritual nature, solve a number of problems which have been structured into the drama, and face dilemmas, before they can reach the resolution of their goals. These have frequently been negotiated by the teacher and students at the beginning of the drama, or even during it. In an experiment designed to test secondary students' implicit understanding of the importance of tension, the teacher set up a drama about sport and drugs, with students role-playing characters accused of illicit drug-taking. Immediately before entering in role as the 'Coach' bearing a letter, he suspended the **fictional context** to invite the students to decide what would be the contents of the letter. There were three options:

1 The letter would prove that all the 'athletes' were innocent of taking steroids (the simplest resolution of the drama).
2 The letter would prove that they were all guilty (which would provide a kind of resolution, too; in order to prolong the drama, it would be necessary to turn it into a simplistic 'us against them' confrontation involving group loyalty and justification).
3 The letter would imply that some of the athletes were involved, but not specify which ones (which would leave the drama entirely unresolved, and the likelihood of resolution considerably further off).

The class opted unanimously and emphatically for the third option, the most dramatic of the three in terms of potential for tension and dilemma.[10]

The leader or participants can intervene within the drama, particularly if the action is flowing too dispositionally smoothly for them, and the structural tension of retardation is sagging. These interventions often introduce an element of surprise or shock, a new mystery, or they may point out a previously unexplored implication of the plot. This provides an *impedance* – in Ryle's rather easier image, a 'boulder in the stream'. The intervention may come as an entire ambush to the other participants – in which case it is crucial to ensure that it does not leave them uncertain of how to react as characters, as we have seen with the ill-fated TIE programme *Out of the Casebook* (see chapter 3). The impedance may be something which had been expected or feared by the characters. It can impose a more significant hiatus than this, however, a hiatus of the **fictional context** itself; the action may be frozen, the convention altered or the frame switched.

This is the way in which the element of *time* works within drama, as distinct from other narrative forms, through the expectations of the audience mediated in direct interaction by those of the characters. In experiential role-play, which is the dominant specific convention of form used in drama in education, the characters are living through the narrative synchronously, just as they *appear to the audience to be* in most theatre forms and styles.

Workers in drama in education have difficulties with the notion of story not encountered by many professional theatre workers and formal scholars of performance drama. This is because in theatre practice and theatre scholarship the primary function is normally perceived to be the audience, and receptive – the play exists to be received by an audience.[11] The narrative can be revealed through 'second order abstraction'.[12] One of the dimensions which distinguish drama in education as a discrete form of dramatic art is that it is quite differently mediated from any form where the primary narrative viewpoint is that of the audience. Ken Byron elucidates this for English teachers, who naturally tend to privilege narrative in a literary way: 'what is happening is a first-order abstraction'. He goes on to categorise three key components:

- difference in viewpoint – in narrative fiction, the reader's viewpoint is selected for him by the writer, who mediates the fiction to him; in drama, because we are present at what is happening, and operate directly upon the fictional events, participants can select their viewpoint;
- difference in use of sign – while narrative fiction operates through a single sign system (written text), drama uses multiple sign systems in combination [i.e. the combinations of human interaction in the **real context**];
- different use of time – while narrative tends towards linear,

sequential development, drama dwells in the present moment.[13]

For these reasons, teachers who attempt to recreate a strong narrative experience by asking their students to 'act it out' are transforming it not into drama – which in a participant genre *is happening* – but into a representational schema of what *has happened*. Therefore the drama leader, during initial negotiation prior to establishing a scene from a story, must instead use focussing questions which mediate from the second order towards the first order of abstraction: 'What might happen if . . .?', 'I wonder why this happened?', 'Can we discover what would happen to these people now?' – moving from the third person/past tense towards the first person/present tense in which drama operates. Current Canadian work emerging out of negotiation between the genre of drama in education and the peculiarly Canadian one of story theatre is proving particularly valuable in mapping the structural distinctions between story and drama in education, and developing appropriate strategies for transformation between the two.[14]

This range of strategies is not unknown to theatre practitioners, often manifesting itself in Stanislavskian forms of 'first-order' improvisation used by actors in rehearsal, and in some participant genres of theatre in education and fringe theatre. The British director Bill Gaskill, in a detailed account of such rehearsal techniques, uses terminology familiar to drama in education, of a 'held-frame', to contain such first-order dramatic activities.[15] It should be noted, however, that the viewpoint of an actor is also quite different from a participant in a drama in education – the actor may be endeavouring to get to grips with the narrative *as if it were* a first-order happening, but it is not; it is received text, a major part of which, including the narrative viewpoint, has been given to that actor by a playwright.

To return to drama in education: the participants have their expectations set towards a resolution which is being made difficult by forms of retardation; these expectations can be partially altered to set up other tasks, either(a) synchronously – continuously if the intervention has been made without stopping the drama, or restarted; (b) in another synchronous time-scale, by moving into a different frame; (c) in diachronic time.

To take an example where all these time-scales operated at

different points, I was working with a group who had chosen to investigate the theme of 'misunderstandings which lead to war'. Preliminary negotiation had established the idea of a central emblem which could be developed within the drama to represent opposing symbolic meanings. The class was divided into two groups, both strongly enrolled. One group were a 'fortunate people who worshipped a great Eagle, the source of their good fortune'. They were involved in the task of making with reverence and care a giant papier-mâché statue for a ceremony of thanksgiving. The others were enrolled as a 'people who had suffered great misfortune and regarded the eagle as a bird of ill-omen'. They were trained to hunt it.

The action proceeded in synchronous experiential role-play as we had negotiated in advance, to the point where the 'unfortunates' hunting their eagle discovered the replica, and were just about to smash it, to the horror of the 'fortunates', who, unarmed, could only look on. At this point the tension was very high and, I felt, barely controllable, even though the 12-year-old students had some considerable experience of this kind of drama. In order to ensure that the emotional responses of the participants remained entirely within the **fictional context**, I changed the convention entirely. Just before the Eagle was destroyed, I froze the action, suspending the time-scale. I asked the group, nominally out of role but still affected by their strong identification with their roles, if there was any way in which this moment could have been avoided, given the totally opposing views of the tribes. Some suggestions were made, mainly involving the characters' negotiating with each other. I asked the group to pick up the action in the same synchronous way. They attempted to do so, but quickly found that the internal negotiations broke down in fixed positions that were not really negotiable.

Emerging at this point was an underlying strong feeling among the participants that they were being short-changed by the whole drama, and that the tension of conflict was clearly not going to be resolved in the proper way, with the expected destruction of the Eagle. To my surprise, this was voiced by one of the 'fortunates', who broke out of role to do so – thus suspending the synchronous time of the role-play. She was supported by a majority of the group in an *ad hoc* extrinsic discussion, rejecting my limply worthy intervention. (This may be seen to reinforce the example given earlier of young participants who, when offered the chance to negotiate the tension, choose a continuation which is imbued with the strongest potential for tension.)

Accordingly I proposed that the drama be restarted, from a point just before the 'unfortunates' discovered the Eagle, but this time incorporating the unsuccessful internal negotiations. In other words I asked them to go back in time and re-enact a modified synchronous action. This they willingly did; they quickly stepped back wholeheartedly into role, and the tension built very fast towards what I was still concerned might be too raw a moment of unrefined release through violence. This point had also been raised by a couple of class members, who were apprehensive about the possibilities of violence. To assuage our anxieties, I warned that I would intervene, not to stop the destruction, but to change the focus.

This I did, again at the moment before destruction, and I changed the convention entirely to a diachronic symbolic dance-drama sequence, to the finale of Stravinsky's *Firebird* Suite. I asked the 'unfortunates' (all but two volunteers) to enact in dance the destruction of the Eagle, and this time *actually* to accomplish the real destruction of the lovingly built representation, to show how this event started the war. However, the constraint I put on them was that the dance during which this was achieved should incorporate not only their own hatred of this malevolent object, but the love and grief of the other people, who were also to take part in the dance (all but two). In other words, their enrolment as characters was overlaid by an enrolment as dancer/actors representing their characters. In order to distance this further, I re-enrolled the two volunteers from each group as choreographers. They accomplished this with absorption and a fine climax.

Following this sequence, we took a time-jump into the future (into present time in fact), and I re-enrolled all the students within a quite different synchronous time-frame as members of a European archaeological expedition. They had discovered the smashed remains of what was obviously an important artefact, that might throw some light on the causes of the unknown conflict which had laid waste a prosperous area (shades of an earlier drama with adults!). Having developed theories of what might have happened by examining the evidence (a double suspension of disbelief which the children accomplished without difficulty), some of the children were re-enrolled as 'survivors of the war, scared to talk', and the remaining archaeologists travelled through time to interview them and check out their theories.

I had envisaged as a climax and resolution a final brief time-jump to the beginning of the war, to give the students the chance to use 'what they knew in hindsight' to stop the war. In fact, the source of tension had changed, and the students were finding the interviews with the survivors to be both tense and moving, and they managed them with considerable skill and consistency – nobody dropped role or appeared confused between what was known from within other frames. The drama was briefly stopped for one final extrinsic negotiation, where my proposal was overruled in favour of a climax, suggested by the children, where the archaeologists would help the survivors bury the remains of the Eagle, and with them the animosity that had cost them so much. This ritual was accomplished with control and sincerity.

TENSION AND AUDIENCE

As well as showing the negotiability of, if not tension itself, then at least its sources, the account above also clearly shows the second elemental dimension in which tension operates, that of *audience* – in this genre a particularly complex and problematic concept. A brief review of the psychological and social origins of the audience function in dramatic activity is revealing, and a necessary background to examining the way in which tension works through this element.

Psychological origins

I have already suggested that one of the origins of drama is the phenomenon of dramatic play. This has a complex relationship to the concept of audience. One relevant dimension is that of

absorption   ←   consciousness   →   alienation.

This relates indirectly to the continuum in art and play between exploring and fixing, discovery and rules, referred to in chapter 3.

In an embryonic piece of dramatic art at the exploratory end of the artistic continuum, a 3-year-old child plays on the kitchen floor at being a train. A number of 'audience' positions on the absorption dimension may be operating.

1 There may be no other person of whom the child is conscious, and the play is mainly operative in the fashion of the child exploring and internalising for herself the qualities of 'train'.

2 While this is happening, the child may be talking to herself, showing some consciousness of an aspect of herself *as* an audience, externalising the drama to herself.

3 If there is someone else in the room, the child may be oblivious to the fact that there is an audience; the signals that this audience receives will be very incomplete because externalised representation of the train may be little or fragmented, and what there is relates only to the internalising purposes of the child.

4 On the other hand, the child may be aware of the audience, and the *purposive* act will be accompanied by a *communicative* act – 'look at me, I'm a train'. The externalised representation will be more foregrounded, and the internalising purpose affected and weakened, the more the child is made conscious of the audience – for example, by the audience saying 'that's clever, darling' or 'it doesn't look much like a train to me'. In other words the audience is now affecting the representation, which as it becomes more self-conscious will strive more for artistic artifice and control over artistic form in order to have even more effect on the audience. The 'train' will be what the child is confident of producing, showing off what she already knows. There are very significant implications of this for drama in education, in terms of the practical distinctions which need to be made between exploratory and performative components in managing dramas – 'get into groups and make up a play to show us about an air crash' is unlikely to produce either valid exploration or good performance. The children are more concerned with safely showing knowledge (or, failing that, stereotypes) they already are confident of than with discovering anything new. Moreover, their performance skills are tested and threatened by a too-familiar audience reluctant to suspend the **real context** very far.

5 Back to the 3-year-old. This vestigial dramatic action demonstrates the simplicity of the step between audience and participant, responder and initiator. The audience will often seek to enter the drama, either formally ('Can I be on your train?') or

informally ('Make your train go under this tunnel'). Immediately, negotiation has to be called into play (into *the play*), and agreements have to be made on **fictional context** and narrative, if in fact this play is to continue, and not be called off by the initiating artist.

6 Also at this point, a second level of communication is invoked. Once the agreement to incorporate the other role-player into the dramatic situation has been made, the players need simultaneously to be the characters and signal to each other what they are doing, so that the other character may respond appropriately. This is an audience function subsumed into the purposes of the drama – without which the drama cannot continue. An experienced role-player may be able to respond with the awareness of these signals also subsumed almost entirely within the role, that is, intuitively. An added factor is the level of the child artist's symbolic understanding and consequent mastery over the level of symbolism employed, so that the objects within the room which may be incorporated into the train drama can be agreed and the dramatic negotiation does not break down. For example:

Adult: This can be your carriage.
Child: No, it's a chair.

It is of course not unheard of for the child to be more symbolically attuned than the literal-minded adult, with that interchange happening the other way round.

7 One further position on the audience dimension is worth noting. When the original artist representing a train is joined by another player, they now have the capability to enter into the kind of dramatic relationship which is necessary for any complete dramatic action. If there is a third person in the room *watching* the action, say if the participants decide to turn their intra-communicative act, which is initially in the **fictional context** alone, into an inter-communicative act within the **real context** (e.g. 'Let's show our train to Mummy'), they are entering into a simple form of a conventional performance. However, the notion of the 'detached audience' is still quite unreal. The audience is anchored in the **real context**, and the children's performance will resonate with that. The child's mother will take pleasure from the enjoyment of the children. If the audience is a psychologist instead of the child's mother, the audience purpose

and the meanings derived will be quite different – an observation of developmental stages. If the audience is the child's mother who *is* a psychologist, both sets of audience meanings will be present. If the play is occurring on the morning after the mother and father had a family quarrel, or the day before they are taking a train trip, if it is taking place in a palace drawing room rather than a suburban lounge, if the date is 1915, if it is interrupted by the child falling over and hurting herself or by the arrival of the plumber, each time the audience will have a quite different experience. In other words the meaning of the performance will be quite different according to what the audience brings to it, and that audience's real relationships to the performers. The performance itself will be organically affected too. The child may seek approval from the mother by confident risk-taking display, but be tentative and conservative in play with a watching psychologist, and show off to a family friend. If the audience walks out of the room, the dramatic game may change. Players and audience alike, you can't get away from the **real context**, and this embryonic drama shows how part of the meaning is made up of the metaxis between the contexts. More on this is to follow.

Given these variables and this complexity of relationship possibilities, it is hardly surprising that with 3-year-olds this kind of drama usually breaks down quite quickly. Nor, with a group of twenty or thirty participants at any age with varying levels of commitment to the negotiation of a drama, is it any more surprising that breakdowns occur.

Social origins

The dramatic and performative acts in which the people engage by taking upon themselves the functions of audience, playwright, actor, etc., take place within societies, and as well as having individual functions such as those described above, they have social purposes and collective implications. A brief look at the origins of formal drama within societies may prove helpful in dismantling the apparent separateness of audience from performer (as separate person, rather than as partially separable function).

In some social contexts, such as an Aboriginal corroboree, drama, dramatised narrative and narrative dance, etc., are very much shared activities. When a group of Pitjatjantjara elders and a group of Sydney tertiary drama students exchanged their theatrical conventions, at the suggestion of the Aborigines, they discovered that almost the only basic convention of western theatre form which the Aborigines did not share, and had difficulty in grasping, was that of a passive audience distinct from the actors.[16]

Origins of European drama do not show the fourth wall which later practice put between the performers and the audience. The emergence of drama in medieval European liturgy shows a similar functional collectivity. A central tenet of Christian worship is that even though the roles of the priests are clearly marked, the activity is a *communion*, in which all are engaged, and there is a commonality of role engagement (necessarily under the watchful audience gaze of God). This concept of commonality of role engagement would have been taken for granted by the Pitjatjantjara elders, too. In the Quem Quaeritis and similar early medieval tropes (or proto-dramas), it is almost certain that the audience had an actively responding role, as they do in most liturgies. As these proto-dramas developed into processional interludes, the congregation would be part of the procession, and gradually more and more lay members of that audience would be incorporated into the performance (without, so far as we know, any 'difficulty' theologically or aesthetically). The **dramatic context** of the dramas was well known to all, shared and periodically reinterpreted by all. This communal and processional nature lasted until well into the Reformation, long after the plays had left the church and taken to the streets (now formally written with the help of priests and monks).

Audience and tension in modern theatre

The web of psychological interdependence between the originator, the actor and the responder as it exists in the young child, and also the sociological network of relationship which exists in any act of theatre, have been charted above. Even in formal literature, where there are physical and temporal gaps between the originator, the medium and the responder, this network exists in implicit form, as Roland Barthes and the later post-structuralist critics have shown.[17] Theatrical conventions may be conceived of as a continuum akin to the absorption/alienation dimension referred to above, but not identical.

entirely separate functions   **←**   **→**   functions fused

At one end, with the gaps between functions at their greatest, would be the theatre of 'illusion', where the audience are made, by curtains, lights, the pretended completeness in itself of the action and the shape of the theatre, to feel that the action exists entirely outside themselves. In this kind of theatre paradoxically the greatest demands for empathetic identification are made. The audience act upon the offered and apparently self-contained material, transforming it through their associations, emotional dispositions, values and attitudes into their own modified meanings – which in a full theatre incorporates some shared meaning, as well as a further shared feeling that this shared meaning is significant. This may be so, but the *major* source of the tension in for example *Ghosts* exists entirely within the fiction as each member of the audience identifies, alone, with the dilemmas of the characters. In this, as in most feature films, which rely on an essentially naturalistic setting and style, the theatricality is obscured and focussed on the interior of the drama, so that there is an easy congruence between audience and actors in joint identification with the characters.

Moving along the continuum would be Brechtian forms of theatre which, in seeking to alienate the audience from the thrall of empathy with the fiction, create another paradox. In revealing the artifice underlying the presentation of the fiction in order to detach the audience from that empathy, this theatre acknowledges the audience's role as an integral part of the whole event, whose meanings are only partially contained within the fiction. A major part of the tension exists between what is being depicted within the **fictional context**, and the **context of the medium** to which the form of the drama is also drawing attention. This is worth examining briefly in terms of congruence and incongruity. The technique of creating tension directly within the audience members rather than within the characters may be seen in the musical *Cabaret,* whose central narrative love story embodies little tension, but the interpolations of the grotesqueness of songs like 'If You Could See Her Through My Eyes' juxtapose ironically a congruence of setting and ethos with an incongruity of form and message to set up a discomforting 'eddy', a tension within the audience as distinct from within the characters. The effect of this upon the narrative is to thrust the background into the foreground, to turn the lead-up to war in Germany into the primary narrative, and the apparently central individual figures into merely commentators, a secondary audience eye. This is particularly noticeable during the song 'Tomorrow Belongs to Me', which is beguiling alike to the main characters – who are also at this point sidelined as an audience, for the event of the song and its singer has little integral significance in *their* narrative, but who suspect what its significance may be – and to most members of the real audience, who, with the added tension of hindsight, would be expected to know the sinister significance of similar Hitler Youth songs – such as the 'Horst Wessel Song' – in the historical situation. The continuous process of awareness oscillating between the **fictional context**, the **context of the medium** and the **real context** provides resonances within each of them from the other.

Further still along the continuum would be pieces of community theatre which in some degree invoke a shared recognition among the audience as a major part of the tension they create. In other words, such pieces invoke a dominant **context of setting** and bring it into the **fictional context**.

Though falling short of integral participation, a local community theatre show like *Yarranlea Years* engaged the audience in a piece of 'location theatre' – see chapter 5 for more detail of what this term entails.[18] The setting was a one-teacher school which the elderly audience members had all attended; that particular location itself contained strongly specific associations for the audience, who during the play saw 'themselves' being replicated, at least in generalised terms, in the action which they were watching. Part of the tension for them consisted of the incongruity of the very congruence between the real and the fictional – thirty years on, being asked to sit at their own desks and watch strange actors, adults and children, enacting generalised aspects of their own childhood, and anticipating which specific memories would be tapped into. One particular set of memories involved the suicide of a Vietnam veteran, the son of two members of the audience, also the two most respected members of the community. This suicide had caused long-running friction within the community through the parents' inability to come to terms with the event. In discussion after the performance, some members confessed to feeling genuinely apprehensive about whether and how this event would be handled within the play – a metaxis which the team had anticipated, and so they had prepared this section with particular care. Another, quite different source of retardation, and therefore tension, was the shared sense of *ceremony*. From the initial contacts made between performing group and audience, through the nature of the invitations to the audience and the souvenir programmes, the semiotic of a celebratory, ceremonial event was built into the play, and pervaded each scene. The finale was a 'Pride of Erin' dance, used as the holding form for dramatised recollections, in which the whole audience joined the actors.

Though essentially a performance, the elements of participation, the concentration on using subject matter familiar to the audience, and in particular the major sources of tension – shared recognition, ritual and metaxis – bring this genre close to that of drama in education. Implicitly or explicitly, all these sources of tension had been negotiated in advance by the team and some audience members, operating as spokespersons for the community audience as a whole, who had assisted the team by providing the raw subject material. There were, no doubt, many matters and issues of conflict and disagreement among the community, or between family members, which they did not reveal to the performers, or suggested that they should not be dwelt on. In other words, the piece could not rely on the more usual sources of conflict and dilemma for the tension, and the event clearly had to fulfil primarily a celebratory purpose, rather than a dramatic, narrative or polemical one.

AUDIENCE AND TIME

The formal relationships between performers and audiences are being renegotiated in other contemporary processual forms of theatre. Audience participation in theatre is a contentious issue, in terms of the *expectations* of audience, and what effects the incorporation of audience can have on the nature of performance and on the audience's construction of meaning.[19]

In the genres of drama in education and theatre in education with integral participation, the gaps between artist (playwright), medium (actor) and responder (audience) are at their most vestigial, and the sources of tension become most negotiable, as at least three personas are operating simultaneously, each involving a separate management of tension and its sources at all levels.

1 The percipients *are* the characters in the drama (i.e. the characters exist entirely as shared constructs of the participants' intentions in creating, defining and accepting their characteristics). In this persona each percipient experiences the tensions of that character's attempts to realise his or her goals, the primary 'first-order' tensions of the task, of conflict, mystery and secrecy.

2 The percipients are also *participants playing* the characters in the drama – with a degree of identification which involves a measure of commitment of themselves, variable according to the kind and level of role-play being used (see Figure 3, p. 87). In this persona, sources of tension include the metaxis of the real conflicts and relationships with those in the dramatic situation, and the embodiment of tasks which is the dramatic management of the character.

3 The participants are also *audience* watching the action, and that includes watching their own involvement in the action as participants and as characters. In this persona, a further set of tensions of mystery and secrecy are created, to which the distinguished drama educator Cecily O'Neill has recently drawn attention, implying that these are in fact perhaps the primary ones for any audience:

> Theatre is about watching . . . and watching for something which is being gradually uncovered to our view, gradually defined . . . and this is true for roleplay, too. We know the tension between the inside and the outside of the situation and our task is to find out the truth.[20]

In terms of role-play, O'Neill puts it simply: 'whenever I stumble upon a double role for my students, the drama seems to come to life.' As another worker puts it: 'working in role, or taking on a role oneself is always accompanied by a highly productive ambivalence – we are transformed into something we are not, and by multiplying the forms we take we are transformed again.'[21]

In the practical terms of structuring drama and participatory theatre in education, it is crucial to understand the essential distinction between these three levels of perception in terms of management of the tensions of mystery and secrecy. It is the difference between a successful drama and a failure, or a successful drama and a confidence trick. It is embodied in the difference between the willing suspension of disbelief and the manipulation of belief and truth.

O'Neill goes further and suggests that 'what is most frequently being uncovered is the truth about *an identity*', and further still – 'Identity is the major theme of drama.' In this she lines herself up with the arts education theorist Peter Abbs, who claims that 'the great unspoken questions of our time which all art must engage with relate to identity and community – the need to be and the need to belong'.[22] She then uses this as an overall frame to interpret the primary operation of tension as 'the tension between the characters' ignorance and the audience's knowledge of the truth'. In broader terms, her restatement of this as 'the tension between a given situation, and what it might be at its completion' not only restates the interconnectedness of tension and *time*, but also harks back explicitly to Suzanne Langer's influential notion of 'the tension of the future in the present' – Langer was one of the first arts theorists to use the term 'tension' in approximately its current use:

> Drama creates a virtual future . . . Even before one has any idea what the conflict is to be, one feels the tension develop-ing. This tension between past and future, the theatrical 'present moment' . . . (the perpetual present filled with its own future) . . . gives to . . . situations the peculiar intensity known as 'dramatic quality'.[23]

TENSION, POWER AND CONTROL

Without in any way refuting this perception of O'Neill and others that the major sources of tension in drama are within the audience dimension and are concerned with attempting to recon-cile conflicting patterns of identity, I want to propose another perspective, which in fact subsumes this, and subsumes all the various dramatic tensions (of the task; of relationships; of mystery, secrecy and surprise; and, most potently, the tensions of metaxis). If indeed art is primarily concerned with 'identity and community – the need to be and the need to belong', then it must be concerned with *power and control* – the personal *power* to create and assert identity, and the *control* over the communal situation that enables people to belong. This proposition relates to social constructive/interactionist theory in psychology, that it is from interaction in context that humans derive the touchstones which define not only social but personal identity.

Since the notion of 'empowerment through learning' is also a commonplace phrase in the cant rhetoric of education, it is unsurprising that drama teachers often use this to justify the work they are doing, though usually in terms of the specific learnings to which the drama is giving the students access, rather than in terms of any sense of empowerment through the art form itself.

The urge for power and control is the primary source of dramatic tension. The tension exists in the space between the urge and its fulfilment. In Aristotelian dramatic terms, the resolution of tension is the essence of classical comedy. Tension is created by the *questions* which the drama raises in the audience; the resolution comes in the form of *answers* which satisfy that infantile need for the comfort of 'sequence, causality and selectivity',[24] the affirmation of an ordered world. This phenomenon is not confined to drama and literature, but operates in society at all age levels. An interesting study in social psychology, *Questions and Politeness*, has explored the networks of everyday social interactions using an entirely compatible notion of tension.[25] This study demonstrates the close connection between questions and command, and explores how socially significant is the reassurance and redress which answers, the resolutions of questions, provide.

Classical *comedy* operates at the 'rule-fixing' end of the continuum of art and play; the kind of comedy which emanates from the other, 'exploratory' end operates by calling those very rules into question, and gives a *dis*comforting experience where anarchy, immorality and misrule are temporarily validated, and may be left so – in a black comedy such as *Measure For Measure* it is only the questions of plot which are answered.

In a classical *tragedy* as defined by Aristotle, tension can exist equally in the gap between the urge for power and control, and its denial. Here the hero's destruction just as certainly resolves the dramatic tension caused by the questions which the action raises, with answers that serve to confirm our known powerlessness – in the face of death, of fate or the gods, of the rules of social order. This fulfils equally the affirmative function of sequence, causality and selectivity, of an ordered world where we can see not only *that b* follows *a*, but *why* it does.

Both these classical forms of drama are concerned with *answering* a number of what may be quite simple kinds of question which are the immediate sources of tension:

(a) Passive questions of 'identity and belonging' posed to the audience by the playwright's narrative:

- Who are these people . . . with whom *I* identify sufficiently to be interested in their story?
- What is happening to them?
- What will happen to them?
- Will what I hope/fear happen to them?
- Why is this happening to them?

The passive nature of these questions reminds us of Cecily O'Neill's words: 'The most tyrannical form of suspense is to let us know what's going to happen and then keep us waiting to see it happen.'

(b) Active questions posed to the audience by their own urge for power and control:

- Will these people – with whom I identify – succeed in attaining their goals?
- What can they do about their predicament?
- Why doesn't he or she do this, which I can see would resolve his or her predicament?

(c) The further questions posed in the **context of the medium** to the audience-as-participants:

- Will this narrative satisfy my need for reassurance of an ordered world? (urge for control)
- What can I do about this, which I see as analogous to the real world? (urge for power)

The Third-World theatre activist Augusto Boal has pointed out that 'the poetics of Aristotle is the poetics of oppression: the world is known, perfect . . ., and all its values are imposed on the spectators'.[26] What imposes those values upon the spectators is the way in which, having created tension by causing certain questions to be asked, the playwright's narrative answers those questions. The world is, if not perfect, complete. 'In its purest form, the closed dramatic ending is clearly marked by the resolution of all open questions and conflicts and the abolition of informational discrepancy.'[27]

The response of Brecht and his successors in didactic theatre, seeking to use theatre to change rather than to confirm the values of the *status quo*, must therefore include an implied negotiability of tension, the notion of *not* resolving the tension, but rather leaving the audience with questions unanswered for them to answer as they will:

> Closely observe the behaviour of these people:
> Consider it strange, although familiar.
> Even the simplest action,
> Observe with mistrust.[28]

Or in Boal's terminology: 'the spectator no longer delegates power to the characters either to think or to act in his place.'[29] This may be tracked further back to the audience who more normally delegate power to the *playwright* to create characters that think and act in their place. Brecht's practice at least warned the spectators that the playwright and players were usurping their power to think and act. Boal's practice took the notion one step further and invited the audience to become actors both literally and figuratively.

Participatory TIE and drama in education can clearly demonstrate the purposes for which tensions are created, and how the underlying questions are posed, because the audience are simultaneously also the participants and the characters, and may be given certain powers of the playwright. In fact, from Heathcote onwards, the crucial importance of *explicit* questioning in establishing both dramatic tension in the art form and the potential for learning have been stressed:

> One striking feature of Heathcote's work with classes is the speed with which she gets the group drive going . . . Questioning is her most important tool.

> Questions are both the material and the negotiating medium of drama. Drama is an investigative form; it is concerned with probing questions raised (by the content) about some aspect of human experience: what would happen if? what would it be like if? what would we do if? what does it mean to be in this situation?[30]

TENSIONS OF THE TASK

Because the participants are also the characters, the first set of tensions to be examined *within the drama* are the characters' tasks. The characters have questions to be answered in terms of goals to fulfil which are concerned with their own power and control over the situation. Those goals are to be fulfilled by tasks which impose challenge and take time – only the infant is satisfied by an immediate gratification of the need for an answer. How these goals are frustrated by other constraints imposed by the situation or other characters will be dealt with later. The tasks themselves form the first level of retardation.

The teacher/playwright has to make the question interesting and urgent enough of itself to generate the tension required. Two dramas referred to earlier, *The Industrial Revolution* and *The Nativity*, both depend primarily on the tension of the task – in fact, in the former there is no conflict, no dilemma and almost no secrecy.

The TIE programme *Spacemen Have Landed in Leeds*[31] is similarly unusual for the complete lack of both conflict and dilemma; there was no ritual and no secrecy, and even the tension of mystery was withdrawn during the second visit of this two-part programme.

1 In visit 1 the children, in that flimsiest of roles as 'themselves in the fictional situation which is set in the real classroom', had to help scientists solve a series of practical problems so that a friendly alien could make communication and then land on earth. The alien, spoken to through a device resembling a Dalek, which the children helped to piece together, gave the 'children' two tasks for the following week when 'my co-pilot and I will return', to identify from photographs and a sound tape 'how my planet began to die', and to 'show us how people on your planet can be happy and enjoy themselves'.

2 The following week, two unthreatening humanoids emerged from the 'Dalek', and engaged in a gentle greeting ceremony, then delivered themselves and the whole drama over to the 'children', who had prepared explanations of how the planet died, and some demonstration of how humans enjoy themselves. This section of the programme varied radically each performance, according to what the children had prepared – in the filmed version, a demonstration and training session for children's games including marbles, skipping and soccer, and a walk through the (real) snow; on other occasions parties and even a banquet cooked for the spacemen.

In fact, the children had met the whole team before the

beginning of the first session of the programme, and had assisted in unpacking and repacking the company's van. The mystery was only within the drama for the 'children', not outside it for the children themselves. O'Neill's terms of the central tension being mystery connected with identity or belonging would explain the children's absorption during the first session. However, in part 2, it would seem surprising for the children to engage in the tasks when all other motivational tension had disappeared, with the obvious relish and absorption displayed on the film (and having witnessed another performance, I can vouch for it). These children were mildly subnormal, officially with poor attention spans, yet they remained on task for virtually a whole morning during this second part.

In this programme, there was another very strong motivator, closely connected with tension itself and to do with harnessing the urge for power and control. The children were put into positions of power and control within the drama. Their power was having more knowledge than the aliens; the control they had was in being able together to save the aliens by sharing that knowledge. These were children whose normal experience at school – and in many cases in their home environment – was of being dependent, of being the ones who did not know, and who could not cope. This was why they were in a Special School. In the drama, enrolled as 'themselves' (so that it did not matter in real life if they were not very capable of helping) they were given a number of manageable tasks – 'just ordinary tasks, like screwing nuts and fitting a jigsaw together, but here they are doing it for a purpose',[31] the dramatic purpose of helping the aliens land.

The team's central questions were deftly phrased and timed. At the start they used the *mystery* of the aliens and a ticking box to create an initial tension and make the children want to know the answers to the mystery. This also established that the task – finding the pieces of the space vessel, 'blown up just overhead' and so hidden round the school – would be within the children's natural capabilities. They then asked their own key question, 'Will you help?' to which the response was invariably enthusiastic. For session 2 the questions had to tap into the children's expertise in such a way that these children, many of whom were used to believing that they could accomplish little for themselves, could take over and run the drama for most of a morning. The tasks therefore related to knowledge which the children did have as a matter of course – knowledge of the locality, and how houses were made, would answer the aliens' first question, and knowledge of how human beings had fun would answer the second. There was a serious dramatic logic to the task: if we do not help, these aliens will die.

Within the action of week 2 the main strategy which kept the tasks fresh and the tension level high was the way in which the aliens reacted to what the children took for granted, as fresh, unknown and even to be feared. Each time an alien took a piece of chewing gum and looked at it as if it might be poisonous, each faltering stumble over the skipping rope, each look of wonderment at the children's paintings and descriptions of bulldozers or birds, all reinforced the children's sense of being in control of the source of power. The alien uncertainly chewing through a fairy cake complete with waxed paper base brought an exceptional frisson of tension and release into mirth – partly in this case accompanied by an extra frisson as the audience-as-participants knew they were tricking the actor-as-alien into a gently unpleasant experience, which he could not get out of without breaking out of the drama – another momentary level of empowerment in the **contexts of the medium** and **setting**.

This programme has been described in detail, as it is a signally vivid example of what is in drama in education practice not only a very important teaching strategy towards empowerment in education, but also a particular management of the element of tension within the art form which is unique to participatory drama. This example is doubly significant because it is particularly rare in theatre in education, where it is more common for the participants to be placed in positions and roles structured for them to respond rather than initiate, so building-in dependency.

The playwright goes some way towards giving a conventional audience the same sensation when they are placed in the position of knowing something of which the characters are unaware. The audience can know it, but, separated from the character and the situation, they are powerless to act on it – that is the source of tension. The participant/characters in a piece of drama in education can leave the audience and take upon themselves the power to act, and their action will resolve the tension. Therefore, their actions themselves are redolent of tension, that of the to-be-completed-task which, being urgent and important to the

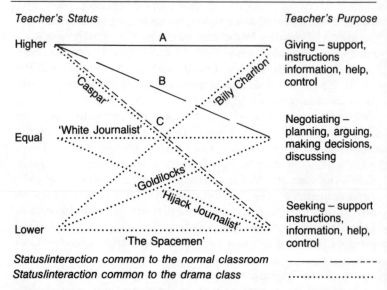

Figure 5 Teacher-in-role: managing status in the classroom

characters, assumes significance to the participants/audience. In Boal's terms it 'changes the people – "spectators", passive beings in the theatrical phenomenon – into subjects, actors, transformers of the dramatic action'.[33]

The actor/teachers in *Spacemen Have Landed in Leeds* were providing an extension of the convention of teacher-in-role, which has already been mentioned in several contexts. The three-way connection between tension, empowerment and negotiation operates very forcefully through this convention. It can be a mode of empowerment in the real learning situation. The drama provides a frame whereby the children and teacher can *partially* suspend the real relationships of the classroom and explore other relationships. In terms of status and negotiation, this has important ramifications for schooling. Figure 5 shows the possibilities for renegotiating through drama the interactive purposes of the classroom.

There may be seen to be a rough correspondence between the status and the purposes. In classrooms this is normally ratified into a limitation upon the possible pathways, so that line A is the norm, with line B used less frequently – denoted by the broken line. Line C is rarely invoked. Though the word 'seeking' does imply questioning behaviour, the great majority of questions asked in class are ones to which the teacher already knows the answers, and they are being used as a checking device, to maintain control, and so belong among the interactions on line A. There are many factors which together ensure the teacher's status remains permanently higher than the children's on almost all classroom fronts – school authority and convention, age, amount of valued knowledge, level of valued skills, *statu parentis*, and in the junior school physical size and strength. Therefore, other lines of interaction can rarely be used at all.[34]

There is an obvious correlation between status and both power and control. A classroom is a **context of setting** which naturally disempowers its clients, rendering them under the control of others. It is common practice in drama in education to use the convention of teacher-in-role specifically to reverse the norms. Accordingly, roles along line A or line B are discouraged, as being merely extensions of the real interactive network. Roles which give the opportunity for the students to exercise power, or at least joint power, give more scope not only for the students to experience temporary empowerment but for the drama itself to contain the tensions of the empowering task. The double tension referred to is that between the teacher-in-role and the audience/ participant function of the percipients. The frisson of making the adult eat the fairy cake, wax paper and all, and watching it happen, made invulnerable within the **fictional context**, is that experienced by children in a drama lesson who can flout or exercise unwonted authority, contradicting the teacher, ordering him/her about or castigating his/her ignorance.

There is considerable controversy among workers in drama in education as to how much this technique, or any of the empowerment elements of a drama in education, actually empower the clients beyond the drama, in other words within the sphere of useful learning. Central to this must be the question of the effect of congruence between the **real context** and the **fictional context**. This has been dealt with at other points within the book. However, this chapter is about tension within the art form, and its negotiability.

The TIE programme *Labour for the Lord*[35] throws this into relief, for within the drama itself the children were put into a position of powerlessness throughout, a powerlessness that was twice brutally reinforced by an imposed tension of surprise and deception. They were enrolled as workers in a chemical factory during the Industrial Revolution. The boss was not a villain, but a benevolent tyrant whom from the start the children were made to respect. Two actor/teachers played entirely sympathetic fellow workers, Jack and Bella. The tasks which the children performed, though they were intended to represent drudgery, had both novelty and a ritual quality within the glamour of the powerfully realised scene-setting (a smoke-laden chemical works) for the children to enjoy doing what they were told for the duration – the tension of the *task*, and of *ritual*. A philanthropic gentlewoman seeking to ameliorate conditions in the factory unwittingly led to the first betrayal – and the 10-year-old children were sacked for not being old enough to satisfy the conditions of the new act she had promoted in Parliament.

This hiatus, which corresponded with morning break, and seemed to spell out the end of their participation in the whole dramatic game, caused the children/participants a frustrated anger appropriate to their characters, the child labourers losing their jobs. In the playground their friend honest Jack offered them the inducement of getting their jobs back by just lying to the boss about their age – he still needed the workers, had no love for Lady Bountiful and would probably turn a blind eye. Apparently empowered again – at least permitted to take part in the 'drudgery' – the children joined in with a renewed tension of the task, which now included assisting Jack to invent a new chemical packing machine to ease the toil, and persuading the boss to try it. Their reward was another ambush, another betrayal: they were found surplus to requirements, and sacked again, finally this time – the pretext being their lies about their age, betrayed this time by their friend Jack. There was no recall, no appeal, and they had to suffer the further indignity of a lecture on honesty from the philanthropist. Their only satisfaction was the sight of Jack himself being double-crossed by the boss, as a quite natural part of the order of things. As they filed out, some of them left in tears, all of them left very angry. The tears and anger of the participants were real. One of the team then spent twenty minutes talking to the children, de-roling them, defusing their anger, and encouraging them to discuss the implications of the drama.

The purpose of the team was paradoxical: by making the children personally experience the causes of powerlessness, and in particular unemployment, in a situation analogous to that in their area today (industrial Tyneside, UK), the team hoped that the children as audience would be stirred to question the necessity for it. Whether the programme did so, or merely confirmed the children's perceptions of their natural impotence, depends greatly on how the ending may be interpreted in terms of tension. If the ending was a resolution, an Aristotelian-tragic affirmative answer to the question 'Did this have to happen to me?' then we must infer that the programme was subverting its own aims. If on the other hand it is interpreted as a non-resolution of the tension, where their tasks and goals were hijacked by the boss and his duplicitous lieutenant, the question left unanswered and the children stirred to question their **real context**, then the programme's Brechtian aims were achieved. Certainly, the team, by inserting the postlude discussion, intended to ensure that this happened. Unfortunately, this discussion was not well handled by the actor concerned, and both tension and focus were diffused, rather than defused. The children were aware that they had had a strong experience, most of them in retrospect had enjoyed it – even the ending – but few could verbalise the point of it.

TENSIONS OF RELATIONSHIP

Voluntary

For obvious reasons related to the control patterns of schooling, the tension of *intimacy* is rarely used in classroom drama in education. When it happens, it is usually an unplanned product of the strength and cohesiveness of the dramatic action. It is likely to be the retardation of a moment which has a particular symbolic significance within or beyond the drama. One such moment – within and beyond – occurred during a drama to be dealt with later in this chapter, where a black South African teenager in role as a social worker spent well over ten minutes gently cradling, stroking and crooning to a white Afrikaaner adult, in role as a collapsed drug-dependent.[36] As this example bespeaks, such action and the tension it embodies are entirely in the hands of the participants to permit or deny – to this extent it might be said to be the most negotiable component of tension as well as the rarest.

Ritual is an extremely important form of retardation, and is, in a sense, not negotiable. It is a form of voluntary compulsion – it demands that the participants voluntarily commit themselves to action which cannot otherwise take place, and which has no necessary extrinsic meaning. Ritual is usually seen in terms of its value as a management strategy, but in fact this is indivisible from its function within the art form. Ritual tends to be used towards the beginning, or towards the end of a drama. If near the beginning, it is usually employed as part of the enrolment, as a way of committing the participants to each other and to the drama. To help a disparate group of children, with varying depths of commitment, establish a group identity as a gang of bushrangers, the teacher demands that all swear an oath of loyalty to each other and ratify that in writing; each must walk to the centre and place his promise on a pile.[37] Though primarily an enrolling device, it has the same effect upon the participants as it does on the characters within the drama, creating a necessary congruence of interest, and a confirmation of this.

Ritual at the end of a drama is normally a rounding-off, used not to stave off the resolution of the tension, but to affirm that it has been resolved. It may also highlight the symbolic signifi-cance of the action which has preceded it – where the new leader is crowned, or the railway which has taken so many lives is opened.

One TIE programme which used ritual throughout both for retardation and for operative purposes, *Be Aware*,[38] was based upon the real-life rituals of the State Emergency Service. The tension of operative necessity, where life-and-death urgency had to be set against the slowness of life-and-death caution, was harnessed to fuel the dramatic tension. Its effect was to build tension throughout a whole day, and simultaneously provide the control to manage that tension.

1 The groups of mildly intellectually handicapped adolescents were first ritually enrolled, literally and metaphorically, as 'SES trainees' in a ceremony where they received suits, badges and official numbers replacing their names, and took an oath.

2 Their training had barely started when they were called upon to help decode a 'Mayday' call concerning a bushfire and then discover the story of further victims in deadly peril, from a survivor (by watching a segment of performance drama). This introduced a quite different set of tensions of suspense and

mystery. Their training programme then had a new urgency, for they needed to be properly trained in order to perform a fire rescue safely. The training, which is highly ritualised, followed the real SES procedures closely.

3 The rescue itself was carried out by the students, entirely on their own, but operating under the ritualised forms of words and actions they had learnt.

4 The final segment of the programme, again based on SES procedure, was a formalised debriefing. This programme was very close to a simulation exercise; it contained, however, a strong dramatic identification with the prospective victims, and the theatricality of the rituals bound together the fictional and the real components of the programme.

Involuntary

The belief that *conflict* is the principal source of tension within this genre – or any genre – is initially beguiling, as most formal dramatic situations contain some conflict, and moreover, anger and frustration are among the easiest emotions to engender in role-play – much simpler than grief, safer than intimacy, more authentic than shock (where the truth is known to the participants though not the characters). It has not proved a particularly productive central source of tension, for a number of reasons:

1 These emotions are readily aroused, but raw; they tend to overpower thought and do not lead easily to the subtler refractions of distancing devices; this is particularly noticeable within group conflicts, where anger binds together with group feeling to create what is sometimes known as the 'yahoo effect' – a participant crescendo of group indiscipline and loutishness under the guise and protection of the dramatic conflict which invariably wrecks the drama.

2 Once roused, they are hard to control, and can easily overspill unclear boundaries between the behaviour appropriate to a character and that appropriate to a participant.

3 Most importantly, school classrooms and schools themselves on the whole actively discourage conflict as unproductive of learning or achievement; social development of children is usually framed in terms of how well they learn to diffuse or repress anger and frustration, and avoid conflict. Small wonder,

then, if the loud confrontations frequently bellowing forth from drama classrooms have played their part in maintaining the school managements' perceptions that drama is eccentric and marginalised from the real business of schooling.

This bleak view of the usefulness of conflict as a source of tension is by no means the whole story. Firstly, however, to see how it was so facilely seized upon as a convention, it is necessary to trace the idea to its origins. As with so many of our current perceptions of drama, this was in the theory and practice of ancient Greece, in this case refracted through the discourse of post-Renaissance Europe, Hegel to be precise.[39] Hegel refined the Greek practice of balancing protagonist with antagonist and strophe with antistrophe, into a dialectical system of thesis and antithesis. This contributed to his 'discovery' that the dialogic mode is the essential element that characterises drama. This in turn inevitably drew attention to conflict, an inevitable feature of the interaction of characters and their situation in most plays, as *the* central element.

One problem of drama and theatre in education and other processual genres, if we may interpret them as *new* genres based on the joint participant rather than the separable playwright/ medium/audience of western theatre, is that the available discourses inevitably limit thinking and the ability fully to manage the possibilities of the medium. The most readily available discourses are those of theatre and theatre study. Even Suzanne Langer, in the very act of proposing a radical new definition of tension which has become influential and valuable in developing the genre, is looking over her shoulder at Hegel: 'even before one has any idea what *the conflict* is to be . . .'[40]

Though a few of the examples of dramas within this book and this chapter contained no conflict at all, yet sustained tension throughout – for example, *Spacemen Have Landed in Leeds* – most drama clearly does incorporate those elements of anger and conflict quite proper to the interactions of characters in a situation. One teacher's definition of his practice as 'I just put the children in a hole and then let them argue and fight their way out of it' is still regarded as a classic compression of acceptable practice.[41] Another, more recent: 'If emotions are to be engaged, then the most useful is a sense of righteous indignation.'[42]

Since the territory of drama in education is rarely concerned with just *personal* characteristics, conflicts usually arise within the situation as clashes of values and attitudes, or the conflicts which the predicaments of the situation evoke, more usefully classified as *dilemmas*. The conflict invariably arises as a product of the situation, and has to be managed (rather than avoided, as classroom practice in other disciplines would usually assert), and the implications of the values and attitudes dealt with. These implications, together with the emotions which have been aroused, and the central dilemmas themselves, all become problems to be solved within the drama, in other words, part of the corpus of tasks to be faced, thus part of the constraints of retardation and impedance lying between the characters and their goals of empowerment or control. The aims of the drama thus actually converge with the aims of the schoolroom, where practice in problem-solving is a highly acceptable activity:

> enrolled in situations where they were made angry by injustice or convinced that something needed to be done about a situation . . . because it was their duty to handle it. Their determination to take the problem and solve it was so over-whelming that they could be motivated to change the system . . . with all the power of their temporary authority.[43]

TENSIONS OF MYSTERY, SECRECY AND SURPRISE

In her speculations on the centrality of mystery and secrecy – and therefore also surprise, which may be defined as the eddy caused by a secret revealed – O'Neill notes that these depend on deception. She also notes speculatively that 'it is difficult to think of a great play which does not at some point use disguise and pretence as a real structural device'.[44] At this point she is drawing attention to the relationship between audience and characters which omits participants. The pretence may be hidden from audience and characters, perhaps to be revealed as dénouement; it may be hidden from the audience but not all the characters, where it is clear that Miss Marple or Sherlock Holmes has the answers well in advance of the audience; it may be revealed to the audience in a complicity of audience and playwright, but not to the characters.

Mystery, secrecy and surprise are forms of *suspense*. In the terminology of Manfred Pfister, one of the few literary critics to

have attempted to define the elements of drama, they all
incorporate 'informational discrepancy'.[45] In a useful but limited
definition of suspense which appears to incorporate all aspects of
his concept of tension, he mentions the word 'tension', but
allows it to remain undefined, reducing the value of the definition, wherein suspense is privileged as the only explicit form of
tension (he too rejects conflict as a major drive), and to be
indissolubly linked to the transmission of information.
'Suspense always depends on the existence of an element of
tension between complete unawareness on the one hand and a
certain level of anticipatory expectation based on certain given
information on the other.' His definition depends on an interpretation of dramatic meaning as flowing one way from playwright
to spectator. Suspense is one certain assertion of the power of the
playwright over the spectator, to create particular demand and
retard the satisfaction. Although Pfister acknowledges the limitations of reception theory in defining suspense, which he also
defines as a 'relation within the text', he gives up the whole task
for lack of an 'as yet non-existent system of pragmatics . . . [to]
. . . comprehend the individual and supra-individual factors'.

Unsurprisingly, Pfister, dealing with received theatre texts,
does not recognise a processual component of even the tension of
suspense, which is what O'Neill follows Dorothy Heathcote in
acknowledging as a key factor. The informational discrepancy
may be real or it may be *virtual*, an accepted convention which is
part of the suspension of disbelief that is the basic contract
essential for drama. That in itself is a *voluntary* deception;
Heathcote calls it 'the one big lie'.[46] Where the percipients are
sharing the functions of playwright and characters as well as
audience, even if the leader appropriates the bulk of the
structural playwriting, the informational discrepancy only needs
to exist at one level. The participants as playwrights may know
because they have decided it all in advance, and even acted out the
epilogue after their rescue, that they as hostages will eventually
trick and overpower the hijacker, but the climactic scene is still
full of tension. In the event, the children's impatience to resolve
the tension causes them to go outside the parameters of belief
with importunate bravado, and undermine the tension of
suspense. They then willingly renegotiate the re-enactment of
that scene, with a high level of breathless tension evident in the
way they permit the leader/hijacker to retard the scene excruciat-

ingly long; evident, too, in the controlled excitement of the
release as their trick finally works, and they overpower him.

The dexterity of very young children, and the great pleasure
they take, in managing more than one level of suspension of
disbelief simultaneously has also been noted, in for instance the
Goldilocks drama. Part of the pleasure may be said to be the sense
of both power and control which the convention affords them;
they are able to be simultaneously powerful and striving for
power at different levels – the pleasurable tension of the urge for
power at the level of character juxtaposed with the pleasurable
exercising of power at the level of participant.

The surprise ambush of the character/participants by the
leader/playwright – in order to throw in a new piece of information, a new constraint or a new level of deception – is valuable
to deepen sagging tension. It may even be appropriated by the
character/participant/playwrights – even from within the drama
itself, without breaking role: as Lewis and Clark's 'scouts'
discover Eldorado. Real ambush is not necessary for participants
to experience the tensions of deception and mystery. This is
clearly implied in the journals of a class of 14-year-olds, about a
drama on *Nuclear War*.

> Christy had the very good suggestion of somehow handi-
> capping ourselves, and we decided on making a blindfold with
> holes cut to give limited vision. We'll be trying this idea next
> lesson. (Fiona).

The effect of this renegotiation on three participants was:

> All through the drama I was scared witless. The sudden
> realisation that this [a real nuclear war] might happen, that
> this supposedly over-exaggerated drama could actually come
> alive one day. What we did was actually under-exaggerated.
> It's all very frightening. (Kathy)

> I think the improvisation was a valuable one and the strongest
> and bleakest I'd been involved in. (Katherine)

> I loved every minute of the drama today . . . it really got your
> emotions involved thinking . . . (Fiona herself)[47]

These four quotations taken together indicate, in spite of the
superficial differences of response, the clear grasp which these
participants had of the purpose of the renegotiation, to provide a

stronger constraint to make the drama more difficult – *zatrudnyennaya forma.*

The instinct of some teachers and TIE teams to make a mystery of the whole **context of the medium**, and withhold from the participants even the knowledge that the event is a drama – the 'adventure programme' – may be seen from these examples to be based on a misunderstanding of the nature of dramatic identification. As a rule it relates more to the teacher's own needs for power and control beyond the dramatic context than to any operative forces within the drama itself. This has been dealt with elsewhere in this study.[48]

THE TENSION OF METAXIS

The *dual affect* of Vygotsky, where the child 'weeps as a patient, yet revels as a player', incorporates a tension caused by the gap between the real and the fiction, and a recognition of that gap. This is the tension of metaxis. In both the *Goldilocks* and *Hijack* dramas referred to above, knowledge was being consciously withheld. The levels were reversed, however. In *Hijack* the real knowledge of the participants was used by them as playwrights to control the narrative, and ensure that it reached the prearranged conclusion, with as much difficulty as possible – the constraint pushed to its uttermost – while the characters themselves remained in ignorance, and therefore in suspense right to the end as to whether the trick would work. In *Goldilocks,* the knowledge which all the participants had *as characters*, they withheld in the real classroom to create, as has been noted, a further dramatic frame outside the drama itself, a *virtual* 'classroom'. This example, incidentally, illustrates the close relationship between drama and jokes, whose framing of aspects of the real have led to their being dubbed 'a kind of dramatic text'.[49]

A not insignificant part of the tension of both dramas also related to the fact that the *character* on whom the deception was being played was in fact the teacher (in *Hijack* the teacher as hijacker, in *Goldilocks* the teacher as 'teacher'). The children were exercising both power and control over the person who in real life exercised both over them by virtue of position and status.

The suspension of the rules of the **real context** in order to enter the dramatic fiction is never total. The **real context** is still manifest – in the nature of the event taking place usually in school time, in a school classroom, as part of a school subject. The drama gives a permission, as Linnell calls it, for a 'temporary authority', wherein status may be reversed, as has been shown, and where behaviour normally interdicted may take place. The temporary authority of Goldilocks's helpers, and the bravery of the hostages, are entirely appropriate to the **fictional context**, but patently not to the **real context** (one group lying to the teacher, the other assaulting him). A strong subsidiary tension is created in the metaxis between these dissonant actions.

Occasionally, the tension of metaxis is so strongly created that it subsumes any others. This may happen briefly, as it did in the *Madness* drama referred to in chapter 2, where the drama provided a platform for Mary to reveal, and the group to share, some of her real feelings about her restricted growth. It may happen by accident – and usually has a fortuitousness about it – as in the *Utopia* drama described at length in that and the following chapter. There may be an element of management about it, however. Instances of metaxis were a consciously planned component of Paul Davies's *Storming St Kilda by Tram*, a piece of performance theatre to be discussed in detail in chapter 5, though the particular incidents which provided the metaxis varied from performance to performance.

Part of my aim and planning, working with black students in Johannesburg in a drama on their choice of topic *Dealing with Drugs*, was, I hoped, for some moment of significance to the **real context** to emerge from the drama.[50] In South Africa the **real context** makes the issues for drama palpable.[51] Not knowing the students or their environment well, I had to negotiate connections with the **real context** carefully with the group and, equally, permit the group to avoid them. The **real context** was a volunteer group of twenty black adolescents, working with me in a demonstration of drama in education in front of eighty observers, mostly white teachers and drama workers.

Predictably, the first session contained a great deal of tension, but entirely *outside* the drama, within the **contexts of the setting** and **the medium** – the number, the status and the dominant colour of the spectators posed no small threat to the participants. I worked slowly towards establishing a believable dramatic context on the topic of the students' choice, *Dealing with Drugs*, and hoped that this extraneous tension might be redirected into some form of metaxis. During the first break, I asked the students, away from the audience, if they would be prepared to 'use' the audience in the drama. After discussion, the group agreed, very tentatively.

I used the *mantle of the expert,* enrolling the students by their choice as police, social workers or doctors, all with experience of drug offenders but with three different orientations towards them, whose overall task was to design and then operate a high-security drug offence institution. Within the drama the students made initial contact with the audience, whom I asked to take role as 'relatives of drug offenders', in the task of seeking advice about appropriate design. This did break the ice. Prior to the students returning for the third session, I strongly enrolled the audience as convicted criminal drug offenders, and forced them to sit on the floor, awaiting their fate. They all consented to the enrolment, many adopting a range of pathological symptoms such as withdrawal or aggression.

The students on their return had power and control within the dramatic context, evidenced by the adults' physical abasement – a feature which appeared to cause the students considerable startled excitement.

The next task was physically removing the offenders to 'a waiting room' – adjoining – while preparing the institution to receive them. This demanded actions totally prohibited in the **real context**: complete physical control over white adults by black children, typified in advance by their role as 'caring' (the social workers), 'uncaring' (the police) or 'dispassionate' (the doctors). Even in Australian schools, touch is rare enough between adults and children. The students used the licence of the drama to reverse the normal order of their lives for the next hour. 'Social workers' carried, stroked, caressed and cradled, sang to and cajoled their 'charges'; 'doctors' carried theirs about with disinterested care and gently humiliated them with examinations; 'police' lifted bodily, threw around, insulted and humiliated theirs. All this was done by the students with *control,* allowing the drama to remain unbroken. Nobody, students or adults, came out of role, and some of the adults deliberately used their role to permit or push the police and social workers into more extreme manifestations of their 'temporary authority'. (Afterwards, some of the adults admitted that they had felt nervous and even threatened personally by the experience.) Throughout, there was enormous tension. One very experienced participant recognised that this tension was caused by the dissonance of the **fictional event** with the **real context**. Further, she recognised that though the same tension of metaxis was shared by all, there were differing, even opposing, personal reactions to that dissonance, and the possible implications in the real world of the power relationships which the drama was exploring:

> When those seventy black kids took complete charge of not only eighty teachers, but seventy white teachers, I was really moved . . . I watched them [the teachers] very carefully. I think some of them felt the same way that I did – moved, and in a strange kind of way saying to myself 'this is a moment of sanity' – but I also watched other people, and I think some of them felt threatened, because in their heads they say 'yes, this is OK, this is fine' but when it comes to the experience they withdraw.[52]

The tension of metaxis is as susceptible to resolution as the other tensions outlined, and responses to the above drama highlighted this. The dynamic of the question/answer network and its application to the real context is extremely problematic. The above observer's warm reaction suggested a sense of resolution, which Brecht or Boal might consider dangerously reassuring, as did another of the adults:

> Whether the audience could make effective use of . . . [this lesson] would depend on the attitude of members . . . and the extent to which they are trapped within the elitist structure. I have seen little evidence that [they are] reaching out.[53]

The playwright Athol Fugard, commenting on this drama after hearing my description of it, took a more optimistic perspective which, without contradicting the above, suggests that he perceives the learning potential of such events in the real world as being their capacity for asking questions to which the dominant ideology has no answers:

> Theatre is about communication – this kind of drama for youth and teaching is trying to break down the barriers which are imposed by way of government policy.[54]

This may be phrased in terms of *questions*, that the potential for residual affect in the **real context** from this form of tension, and from all the other forms of tension outlined here, is in direct proportion to the extent to which the drama is 'an open question, an incomplete proposition'. If the drama 'provides the missing clause', it presumably just takes its place in the network of ritual reassurance and redress which maintains the *status quo*. If it leaves some aspect of the tension unresolved, breaking the 'code of politeness',[55] it might have the potential to command further action or interaction.

Chapter 5

Location: renegotiating expectations

A PLACE OF SPECIAL SIGNIFICANCE

One of the features that distinguish drama from other literary forms is the fact that it is experienced in space, directly, at *all* the following levels:

1 The **internal context**, the subject matter, is made physically manifest, in a way that the Brothers Karamazov and their story, or Wordsworth's Daffodils, are not.

2 The **medium** for that internal context, the machinery of presenting the art work to the percipients, is a major element. In a literary event it is usually vestigial – most abstracted in the shape and typography of a book, more visceral in the person of the storyteller or voice of the poet – whose explicit purpose is usually to obscure itself in focussing attention on the internal context. In drama, 'A very large number of signifiers are simultaneously unleashed upon the audience [including] the elements of the setting.'[1]

3 In the whole event, the **fictional context** rarely fits in unobtrusively with the **real context**. Drama demands a special attention. A book can be read at home in bed or waiting for a bus. Drama, to begin with, is a group art, and demands the coming together of all the percipients. This automatically registers drama as a 'special' event, which is augmented by its performative nature. This is why, as many commentators have similarly commented, 'the performance space . . . has a vital and truly fundamental aspect: by its very existence it generates meaning',[2] or strictly in the terms of audience perception: 'as multimedial texts, dramatic texts are conditioned structurally by the spatial dimensions and technical sophistication of the stage

they are performed on.'[3] Even for a conventional audience in a conventional theatre, this multiple layering of significance is often seen as a paradox, as Jan Kott puts it elegantly:

> We watch a performance and therefore everything that happens onstage is not 'for real'; we are in a theatre, we sit in a seat and look at the stage and so everything that happens there, happens 'for real' . . . The theatre is both the reality of illusion and the illusion of reality.[4]

In order to examine this paradox, Kott takes Suzanne Langer's notion of the tripartite distinction between signs, icons and symbols, and retranslates it into 'literal, mimetic, and symbolic signs':

> The action takes place in a specific part of a theatre building: on the stage, in an arena . . . Before the beginning of the play . . . the stage and decorations are literal signs, which the dimming of lights can change into mimetic or symbolic signs.[5]

The implication of his word 'change' seems to be that any space can be equally removed from its literal semiotic – that by this change, the literal disappears or is suppressed. This rather simplistic idea seems entirely to have overlooked the Russian Formalists, whose concept of *ostranenie* means making *strange*, quite the reverse of making *disappear*.[6] This concept had a crucial influence on Brecht and all his followers, who strove to reassert the literal setting and location as necessarily coexisting with any mimetic or iconic signification. Further, for Brechtians a usable dramatic symbol is not one which has been totally divorced from its referent, but one which will automatically be referred back directly to resonate with the literal and with the associations from beyond the drama accompanying that literal sign, and suggest action. This may be seen, for instance, in that classic example from theatre in education of a dramatic symbol, an axe being transformed within the dramatic action from a tool to a weapon.[7] This is discussed further in chapter 8.

Participational drama reveals the oversimplification of Kott's position far more immediately. Drama teachers have found that the improvised theatre in which they usually work retains its full sets of expectations and of messages of the space, partially submerged but never totally suspended, even while the mimetic and symbolic semiotic networks are being evoked. We may be Vikings looting a monastery, but we are simultaneously still children with our teacher; we cannot actually destroy the 'priceless illuminated manuscript', because it is in fact an expensive library facsimile; nor can we even in simulation rape the nun guarding it, because she's our teacher. Both the iconic sign (burning the book) and the mimetic sign (pretending to rape the nun) are quite appropriate to the dramatic context, but they are precluded, both by the real network of taboos and by the purpose of the drama – at least the teacher's, which is certainly not for the children just to experience 'being a Viking'.

Drama normally takes its 'special' place in a specialised space designed for the purpose, a theatre. Renegotiating this specialised space can considerably affect the dramatic product and the meanings available to the audience, as well as the expectations of the audience – the whole contract for the event, in fact. Many modern theatre workers have chosen to address this, by working outside the 'specialness' and normative confines of a theatre. TIE and drama in education workers, for whom theatres are rarely available or appropriate, have had to address it. This process entails a renegotiation of virtually all the other elements of dramatic form, as well.

RENEGOTIATING EXPECTATIONS IN ADULT THEATRE

In order to gain insights into the significance of location for drama in education practice, it may help to consider closely a different form of adult theatre, which has specifically concentrated upon the question of location – and for which the very term 'location theatre' has been coined. Paul Davies regards himself explicitly as in some degree a processual playwright, who welcomes the input of actors at various stages of a draft script, and perceives himself as 'the author as repairman, or rather, damage control officer'.[8] In the case of *Storming St Kilda by Tram*, performed by his company, Theatreworks, the major focus of renegotiation was the space, which had immediate implications on the expectations of the audience. All performances took place in a tramcar actually travelling from St Kilda (a seaside suburb) to the centre of Melbourne and back. Davies is particularly concerned with the relationship between performance and audience. Noting the specialness of the event of theatre – 'people actually have to leave their homes, buy a ticket and gather together' – he classifies a conventional play as a 'coming together of strangers and friends . . . a "community of one audience" . . . a Community Encounter of the First Kind'.

A 'Second Kind' involves a renegotiation of the audience relationship 'where the actors and audience share the same status, interact on the same level' – in other words audience participation, whose difficulties Davies rather underplays. The three dimensions of this convention – *integral, peripheral* and *extrinsic* participation – as it operates in TIE, the predominant theatre form to use it in recent years, have been dealt with at length elsewhere.[9] In adult theatre it is even more problematic, because the normal expectations of the audience preclude it. I experienced a notable contrast in two events occurring within days of each other in neighbouring theatres.[10] The first, *The War Game*, was a simulation *workshop*, held by actors for teachers, which lasted for over three hours of continuous physical participation using the whole auditorium not as a theatre, but transformed into an adventure space, The participants were mostly strangers to each other, but we participated with enthusiasm and without reservation. A few days later, at the end of a conventional stage play, I was pressed to come on stage and participate, with some of the very same actors, in a final celebration dance. I felt acutely awkward, and refused. This reaction is entirely common. The audience's expectations of an event, and the messages of that particular event, rule what they are prepared to do. In most cases, a play is an event to watch, and a theatre is a place to watch it.

Storming St Kilda by Tram is of yet another order. In Davies's words, a 'Community Encounter of the Third Kind'.

> Third Kind Encounters occur when the audience and actors can be identified together as a group which is quite separate from, but nevertheless interacting with, an omnipresent reality outside the perimeters of the particular play. In this instance audience and actors share a complicity for the play's events in relation to the outside world. This bond is largely unstated.

Here Davies puts his finger on four key, interrelated elements in the nature of process. (a) As he makes clear, the **real context** is neither obscured nor suspended, but coexists with the **fictional** context. (b) The **fictional context** of these participants interacts with the **real context** in some significant way – metaxis is a vital ingredient of the impact of the play under analysis. (c) Although he is still talking of actors and audience as distinct functions, there is an implicit recognition of what both share as participants. (d) His use of the words 'share', 'bond' and 'complicity' also implies that there must be a renegotiation of the expectations of the audience, to include a participant role which may be as character in the dramatic context, or as part of the dramatic **medium** and **setting**, sharing the roles of author and actor.

To see how this process is expressed in relocating a play, it is worth considering the particular performance qualities of a tram by comparison with a theatre. There are a number of similarities, of which those denoted with asterisks have been consciously recognised by this playwright:

- It is an enclosed environment, insulated for the duration of the event from the outside world.*
- It can normally only be entered on payment.
- This is a purposeful act – one does not enter either a tram or a theatre by accident.
- Participants sit down, and remain seated throughout the event.
- The participants usually have freedom and time while taking the tram to watch and observe events which do not impinge on their actual lives.*
- For many people it is a pleasurable and relaxing experience.*
- Other people enter and leave frequently, as do characters in plays.
- In a theatre, watching a play unfold, audience members often feel that they have been on a journey.

There are also a number of significant differences, which provide the playwright and audience with constraints to exploit or overcome:

- A tram with its broad glass windows has a possibility of 360° vision, whereby participants (audience and actors) can watch the outside world from which they are insulated – and can themselves be watched.*
- Virtually only one internal fictional setting is possible: a 'tramcar'. It is an extreme example of a dominant **context of**

setting. The literal messages of a tram are too loudly distract-ing for the audience easily to suspend their disbelief into an incongruent fictional location.

- One implication of the venue actually moving is that char-acters' entrances and exits have a finality about them quite unlike a normal theatre; they can only re-enter where they exited.*
- A second implication is the extreme difficulty for an audience member to leave the venue during the performance – though voluntary, they are effectively a captive audience.
- A third implication is that, by moving, the venue is itself passing through a number of 'outside worlds' which may literally or by implication be included in the action.*
- A tram makes a clearly recognisable and not inconsiderable noise.*
- A tram holds only fifty seated passengers, and has problems of sightlines.
- A tram, unlike *most* theatres, throws people together from all class backgrounds – it traps them there together.*

PROCESSUAL IMPLICATIONS

From this base, the playwright set out to provide an acceptable theatrical experience for an audience, one which would allow them to feel comfortable even as it renegotiated their expectations of a theatrical performance by incorporating the possibilities and the constraints inherent in the location. In other words, the playwright had to turn a very dominant **context of setting** into an acceptable **context of the medium**, with the complicity of the audience – a factor not always automatically available in pro-cessual genres such as street theatre or drama in education.

In such an example, not only the audience expectations have to be renegotiated: these sets of similarities and differences contain implications that demand the renegotiation of virtually all the elements of dramatic form, as well as the subsidiary theatrical or performance elements – which in this play were among the first to have to be negotiated.

Scale and logistics of production

Every theatre building dictates the scale of production possible, and the budget which can be managed, as well as implications for the *kind* of audience. In this case the location actually mediated against this writer's expressed policy of 'writing to the widest possible local audiences . . . crossing class boundaries'. Davies certainly expressed the social class eclecticism of a tram in his *characters*. However, at least in the performance I witnessed, the *audience* clearly consisted of experienced middle-class theatregoers. The limited size of the tram, the necessity to go through fairly complex booking procedures, and the out-of-the-way starting point all reinforced this.

The location demanded a modification of the functions of both actors and director, as Davies indicates:

> In the case of the mobile plays, these events have to be timed and orchestrated with a precision that matches a film script. The execution of the plot depended on the actors getting on and off at certain exact moments in the action . . . a car accident across the tracks could throw everything out. In these cases the ability of the actors to improvise within their characters and within the broad direction of the script became crucial.

Plot – narrative and purpose

The real location was allowed to dictate naturally the outline of the fictional plot: the play would be about people taking a tram journey, characters whose lives and purposes would cross only for the time they were in the tram. Within this outline there was room for flexibility – events beyond the normal (though not beyond the recognisable) might happen; old friends might unexpectedly meet on this tram; the characters' lives might be temporarily or permanently changed by these events, though only the circumstances on and around the tram could be part of the dramatic action itself. The actual route taken was significant: because the second half of the journey reversed the first, characters could leave and rejoin the action once only.

Mood

In this book mood is dealt with late, in chapter 8, perceived as part of the meaning, an end-product of the structuring of other elements. In the case of this play, as in much drama in education, an appropriate mood was also a *precondition*. Since the audience were effectively captive, and could only escape by putting themselves to great inconvenience, it was obviously important to ensure that they had a good time. This meant that without being able to prenegotiate with the audience members their personal boundaries, the play must not be offensive, nor in any way sufficiently discomforting or threatening to risk anyone deciding to leave. The action also needed to be robust enough, engaging enough and painted in broad enough brush strokes for the audience to follow in spite of the distractions of the passing landscape and the noise of the moving tram. In other words, *good humour* must be engendered and maintained. Davies chose a humorous approach, based on mildly satirical situations and likable but laughable characters. Violent action, such as a hijack, a fight and arrests were kept firmly in comedic, slapstick vein. When potentially controversial subject matter was introduced – such as one character's revelation that she resorted to prostitution to bring up her children and keep them at good schools – it was kept tongue-in-cheek. The audience's attention was focussed not on the nature of the subject, nor the character herself, but on the problems which the information created for her amusingly contemptible ex-lover.

Context and roles

The above preconditions forced the playwright to renegotiate his normal approach, which is to work with an explicit political concern that dictates the whole **fictional context**, both situation and characters. In this case the location *was* the situation, it dictated the characters, from which the narrative could then emerge. 'A tram throws people together from all class backgrounds, it traps them in there, together.' Davies and the actors travelled on trams, observing behaviour, then sharing and workshopping their observations. This was an unusually processual approach for Davies, who usually incorporates his actors only after a draft script has been devised. After this process, they decided that all the characters should be recognisable as common types, and from a contrasting variety of recognisable class backgrounds, chosen to cause a strong reaction to each other. They must have a stereotypic quality, but be individual and surprising enough for the audience to be interested in relating to them personally, if the peripheral participation demanded it; this also meant they must have *charm*.

Focus and tension

The team decided that a number of pieces of action should occur among these characters, which should be recognisably within the aegis of a tram journey, *but only just*. In that gap between the expected and the unexpected would lie both the dramatic tension and the humour. All the main connecting incidents of the plot are of this ilk: a coincidental meeting between embittered ex-lovers is both unlikely and believable, until they reveal their true natures, and the audience is immediately involved in the comic soap-opera tension of their bizarre lives and quarrel. A modern audience is familiar with the grandiose concept of a political hijack of a public conveyance, but a tram being hijacked by a derelict with a trick knife deflates it into gentle burlesque. Policemen intervening in a brawl and causing more confusion is standard material for comedy, and it is also recognisable as commonplace – further, many members of a Melbourne theatre audience would recognise the parodic echoes of David Williamson's *The Removalists*.

Time and timing

The location of a tram, and the fiction of the tram journey, have implications for both time and timing. For one thing, the play had to be *entirely synchronous* since the fictional action took place during the real journey, and entrances and exits were tied to tram-stops. This in turn predicated complex logistics of production, and split-second timing of action and dialogue within the tram. This was the source of the metaxis that was a major element of this play, and not always predictable. Among the times when the actors had to improvise were breakdowns in the tramways schedule, and the entirely unprepared-for interruption when the cast was interrogated for twenty minutes by real police.

Language and movement

A tram is in two ways an unusual auditorium – it is very long and thin, and it is noisy. This imposed certain constraints upon the action. First, important plot and character revelations had to be heard right down the car; this predicated very clear, simple and brief dialogue, with a lot of it spaced out so that the characters needed within the dramatic logic to shout at each other. In movement terms, it necessitated a lot of linear movement, with characters needing motivation to move regularly from one end of the car to the other – walking off in pique, moving over threateningly, etc.

> Particular stress was placed . . . on voice projection and . . . an ability to convey as much through gesture as dialogue. The upshot was the evolution of a kind of *commedia dell'arte* style of performance which counterpointed the apparent ordinariness.

Such simplistic stridency could not be sustained for long periods, so the playwright on a number of occasions used the device of split focus, where two or at one point three pieces of action were going on simultaneously in different parts of the car. All of these were actions which reinforced what the audience already knew of the characters and situation, so that none were crucial for those out of earshot. In fact, this device added considerably to the appropriately fragmented texture of the audience's experience, along with the various distractions outside the window.

Expectations – the metaxis of fiction and reality

As has been indicated, part of the attraction for the playwright in the choice of the location was the opportunity it afforded him of renegotiating the audience's expectations. This was possible because the audience had not one set of expectations, but two: those of a theatre, and those of a tram journey. The similarities permitted him to juxtapose the two and then play on the dissonances between them, using 'tram' as the primary expectations. The play started with a conductress giving each member an authentic-looking travel card and a sickness bag (a humorous juxtaposition from a third genre of passive journey), and assisting them to board the tram. From then on, a number of different forms of metaxis occurred, variously between the wider **real context** and the **setting**, and between the **real** and **fictional contexts**.

1 When passing pedestrians or motorists saw and reacted in

good faith to one of the events of the dramatic fiction, such as the arrest, their reactions were visible to the audience, and provided a pleasure of the same order as *Candid Camera*, the order of the practical joke, that of shared security and superiority over others in a position of minor risk. The passers-by being outside, there was no risk of real contact for the audience, in on the joke and safe behind their glass windows.

2 Of a slightly more uncomfortable order of humorous juxtaposition were the occasions when passers-by tried to board the tram as a tram. The audience were watching the discomfiture of a real person in the doorway, not just of a deconstructed figure beyond the glass, and were powerless to intervene. Clearly aware of the ambivalence of this event for the audience, the actors dealt sensitively with these unsuspecting intruders, and the frisson was not permitted to destroy that necessary mood of good humour.

3 On a number of occasions, reality intruded on the fiction in ways which the team had not foreseen, such as by a delay in the tramways schedule. On several occasions, although the Melbourne Police had been advised of the nature of the event, individual officers had not been apprised, and intervened in what they saw as a brawl on a public tramcar.

4 Examples of metaxis were actually scripted into the play. One character's purpose in boarding the tram was to go to the Melbourne Theatre Company's current show, and she duly got off the tram outside that very theatre, as other late patrons were arriving. At this point, in a further layering of metaxis, the 'tram inspector' revealed that he was a fringe theatre worker (true), and only working on a tram because he was 'resting' (fiction, but likely). He then hung out of the tram shouting humorous insults at the Melbourne Theatre Company and its real patrons until the tram had passed the building.

5 This gentle metaxis of real and dramatic contexts was layered further by a Brechtian ambush of the whole convention, bringing the **medium** into the metaxis. Maintaining his 'officious tram inspector' persona, this actor simultaneously overlaid it with the real role of the Theatreworks stage manager explaining the interval procedure for the audience, including prearranged drinks at a city hotel bar.

The impotence of the audience to affect the events of the **setting**, the **medium** or the **fiction** renders this metaxis of a very different order from that envisaged by Boal, who perceives it as a liberating device for the audience, to activate them. It is therefore in the same way different from the metaxis of a drama in education experience.

LOCATION IN DRAMA IN EDUCATION

In comparing how audience expectations are renegotiated in location theatre with drama in education, it is useful to refer to the list of similarities and differences shared by tramcar and theatre. Drama in education and the substantial touring percentage of theatre in education usually take place in a limited range of spaces in schools and colleges. The most common location is the classroom, particularly in primary schools. Alternatively, some form of activities space or assembly hall may be used. In secondary schools and colleges, a designated drama studio may be used.

Some immediately obvious differences among these other spaces affect the specific nature of the activities possible within the drama, and thus the choice of framing devices used for focussing.

- A classroom is usually cluttered with furniture, hangings and objects which impose severe restraints on the use of the space, but also offer possibilities.
- It may impose an equally severe constraint upon the amount of noise allowed.
- It may be partially public and overlooked.
- Activities spaces tend to be cleared of furniture and carpeted; they are often shared with other users.
- Assembly halls are usually, by comparison, very large, and either entirely empty of furniture or full of chairs. They normally have a stage. They may have lighting.
- Drama studios are usually fairly clear, with some of the recognisable accoutrements of a theatre, such as movable rostra, stage lighting and sound systems.

Teachers may on occasion be able to choose to work in more than one of these locations within a single drama.

Although the contract for willing suspension of disbelief permits the space to be used with flexibility and imagination, teachers generally find that a degree of congruence is at least helpful and even necessary between the fiction and the reality. I have already alluded to the impossibility of enacting an Olympic distance race final with any kind of physical authenticity in a classroom, or even on a school oval.

These fairly substantial differences among drama in education spaces are also pre-empted and modified by a set of similarities. All the spaces are within the confines of a school or college, and subject to the strong expectations of that setting, in terms both of formal rules and of ethos, the shared understanding of what behaviours are appropriate to that setting – for example, obscene language may be both appropriate to a character and normal to the participant playing the role, but precluded from the drama by the fact that the Principal might overhear.

School spaces impose particular problems of management on teachers, not just for drama. Special spaces have special sets of behaviour. A secondary school assembly hall is often associated with rituals devised to accentuate some of the most significant messages of schooling – group loyalty, patriotism, respect for authority, reverence for God, acclamation of the successful, joint celebration of the very identity of the school.[11] It is not coincidental, nor just a concomitant of its size, that an assembly hall is seen as the most common and suitable location for a visiting theatre or theatre in education company to perform a play.

A classroom is to some extent an enclosed environment, somewhat like a theatre insulated from the outside world. Entrances and exits may belong to that **external context**, such as the Principal, a parent or a student from another class with a message. They may belong to the **context of the setting** itself, such as a participant going to the toilet, or the teacher aide passing through. Students do not pay to enter the classroom, but events within are treated as if they impinge upon the students' lives outside, in some *indirect* way. Sitting and remaining sitting while watching other people doing may be *one* of the expectations of the classroom, as it is of theatre, but much less exclusively so.

The differences are equally revealing. Like the stage set within a theatre, but unlike a tramcar, a classroom is at least minimally decorated with items that reinforce the **context of the setting** – books, charts, pictures, a blackboard – and which the protagonists use within that context. Effectively the participants are as much of a captive audience as that in the tramcar – strong psychological and sometimes physical deterrents exist against leaving the event. Noise is usually a major factor, but quite unlike the tramcar: there are usually constraints against the drama making much noise at all. On the other hand, very different activities in neighbouring locations may cause unpredictable distractions and sound levels – the loud voice of a teacher through the partition, a lawn mower, the clatter of a passing class.

Perhaps the most significant difference of all is that the classroom *may*, like the tramcar, 'throw people together from all class backgrounds, trap them together', but unlike either theatre or tramcar audience, a class is a homogeneous unit in terms of age and familiarity.

Almost equally significantly, a classroom is not generally perceived by its participants to be an auditorium. The architectural nature of a theatre reinforces its messages of passivity for the audience, as do the conventions imposed upon the patrons. Once this might have been substantially true of a classroom, but not today. The patrons, as actor/participants, are familiar with the setting, and used to its possibilities and limitations. The implications of this are dealt with in the next chapter.

Chapter 6

The participant group

NEGOTIATING CONTRACTS IN THEATRE

Throughout this book, the words 'participant' and 'percipient' have been used with closely synonymous meanings. The word 'actor' has also sometimes been invoked, particularly when other writers have been quoted who come from a background of conventional theatre practice or theory. To recapitulate the distinctions: the word 'percipients' refers to the totality of real people directly involved in a dramatic or theatrical event – all those who perceive it at first hand, the people within the **context of the medium:**

- playwright
- actor
- participant
- director
- audience

It is more appropriate to regard them not as distinct individuals but merely as distinct functions which, depending on the processuality of the genre, may be simultaneously shared by some, most or all of the percipients. For example, in a drama in education such as *Nuclear War*, referred to in chapter 4, the students took control of the subject matter as *playwrights*, negotiating the narrative and the focus both outside the dramatic action and by intervention within. They took *participant* roles as the *characters* for considerable periods, though not specifically as *actors*, for there was no *audience* for them to communicate with beyond the other participants. They were *audience* of their own action, as their journal entries testify.

Just as the nature of the location and space produces certain expectations, so does the nature of the percipients. For any group of people jointly and willingly to suspend their disbelief, *contracts* are necessary. This is particularly true of drama in education, whose very existence depends on that willing suspension on the part of the whole group. A performance of a Shakespeare play has been known to happen without an audience, and the text has an objective existence for future re-creation. A drama in education only exists in the moment of its enactment, and only for the participant group.

The notion of contract is very important to the whole concept of process. As the elements of the dramatic event are renegotiated, contracts explicit and implicit have also to be renegotiated. *Storming St Kilda by Tram* displays a conscious, sophisticated and deft management of the implicit, tacit contracts of expectation between performers and audience, who were in fact quite separate groups.

The expectations of an audience are not only concerned with their location. If the event differs from their expectations too radically they will probably reject it, not necessarily because they would in all situations reject it, but because they feel that a contract has been broken. Explicit contracts include the paid ticket which entitles the audience member to see the show, and so the first reaction of an audience cheated of their expectation is invariably angrily to demand their money back, in other words to annul the contract in a substantive way. At a 1988 Brisbane Festival, a show labelled in aggressive promotion as a 'Cosmic Laser Spectacular' created considerable antagonism, and customers who not only demanded their money back, but threatened to sue the Festival for misleading advertising.[1] In comparison with other locally available laser shows this was not a laser spectacular at all. Essentially the show was a solo Japanese dance, in a setting of hi-tech sculpture. The theme was explicitly *cosmic*; in its own terms, of a display by a celebrated dance virtuoso, it was *spectacular*; it *did* include some simple *laser* effects. The three words put together had created a different expectation, however, and this was what was translated into the formal contract of the ticket.

In drama in education contracts the 'agreement to the big lie' may be implicit or explicit. A British Drama Adviser, Jon Neelands, asserts: 'The contract itself may be implicit – it's already there and understood in the way you and your class relate to each other; or explicit – it's been discussed and negotiated openly with your class. *But it must be there.*[2] In my experience it invariably needs to be made explicitly at some point, along with some other contracts concerning the rules of games, the game of drama and the way the group itself needs to operate – this is dealt with more fully below. However, Neelands goes on to define the exact purposes of the contract in drama in education:

The contract can serve several purposes:
1. It establishes a partnership between teacher and group.
2. It defines the investment being made by all those involved: 'this is what I'm putting in and what I expect to take out.'
3. It reinforces the idea that drama makes its own kinds of demands on both teachers and pupils and that if any of those demands are avoided the drama will lose its effect.
4. It demystifies drama both as a learning process and as an art-form: 'the teacher is not playing tricks with us'.
5. It provides a reference point for dealing with problems which may arise later: 'Which of the terms of the contract did we fall down over?'
6. It initiates a dialogue which enables both partners in the contract to comment and reflect, in a positive and productive way, upon what's actually happening in the classroom.[3]

CONTRACTS IN YOUTH THEATRE

Detailed analysis of an example from a somewhat more conventional genre, youth theatre (i.e. theatre performance by young people), throws light on the similarity of the contracts which must be negotiated in any dramatic event. This project was entitled *The Great Circle*, and was devised by Michael Doneman, the group's (adult) co-leader.[4] This has been selected partly because Doneman regards himself as a processual playwright and partly because the concept of 'contract' was explicitly acknowledged, though in the event the project was contractually ambitious and very problematic. Neelands's purposes will be seen to be relevant, in particular 4 and 5, which may appear to relate more specifically to the discipline functions in a drama classroom than to the all-voluntary atmosphere of a youth theatre.

From the start of *The Great Circle* the leaders were aware of the importance of contracts. The explicit contracts in theatre include the literal paper contract which binds an actor, director or playwright to the event, and any current statement of policy which may be binding on those who work in the theatre. The theatre, La Boîte in Brisbane, has been for many years concerned with young people and their relationship to the main body of work of the theatre, and with a processual approach to that work: 'a policy of balanced diversity, where public perception of La Boîte is a house style of *youthful orientation*'. This ethos first implicitly drew the leaders and some of the participants, then also explicitly bound them.

Doneman and the two other adult leaders were contracted to fulfil the policy outlined above. They were also bound by recent history. The previous year La Boîte, under Doneman, had produced a festival of three plays with some commonality of theme: 'Each indicated in different ways the need for a radical change in human consciousness . . . if the mistakes of the past are to be avoided.' The next project was to be related to that theme: 'Essentially they wanted to give youth theatre the chance to tackle classic and epic themes.'

Inevitably, one of the constraints of youth theatre is the lack of conventional acting skills. The principals accordingly pursued a second purpose, of creating an ensemble 'to work over a lengthy period developing a range of theatre skills . . . as the advertising handbill states: *to develop a new performance language which integrates dance, cabaret, circus skills and music*'. Thus part of 'the investment to be made' had been defined in advance and committed to another form of loose contract, that advertising handbill. 'Classic and epic themes' and 'circus skills in a new performance language' are two ambitious and disparate purposes for a youth theatre project. At the beginning, the leaders made only the second explicit to the participants, and difficulties resulted.

The initial contact with the group, two weeks' preliminary improvisation including exercises related to the intended theme, proceeded in Neelands's terms exemplarily. In fact some of the ideas and images which emerged during this period were incorporated in the final production. Some ideas also emerged which were dropped, not always with the entire consent of the group. The two weeks culminated in the development of an explicit, written contract, presented by the leaders, but incorporating suggestions from the participants. This contract was to be signed by all intended participants in the project itself. It specified a number of contractual responsibilities – time commitment, etiquette, facilities, work-sharing, authority and finances. The contract was phrased in a way which made it clear that there was not an equal relationship between performers and leaders, using the words 'we' and 'you' judiciously. It also specified a limited degree of democratisation:

AUTHORITY: While process and production will be democratised as far as possible, final authority rests with the director and others responsible.

(The use of the word 'process' at this point is consonant with the definition in this book.)

Although this explicit written contract represents an unusual sophistication of conventional youth theatre practice, which tends to be very informal and tacit, it was not entirely successful in defining the terms of agreement. Ambiguities in the way the contract was expressed left gaps in the *implicit* contracts: 'In the beginning . . . lack of communication and uncertainty over how the script would be developed led to dissatisfaction among some members of the group.' In the minds of some participants, the above paragraph on Authority came into conflict with another paragraph:

COMMITMENT: It is not seen as sufficient simply to be involved in a quantitative way . . . but also in a qualitative way in terms of cooperative, creative and dynamic participation.

The degree of commitment, and what exactly might be meant by the 'qualitative component', is a frequent cause of friction and distress in drama in education too, between the authority source and participants – the teacher and students. In the case of this youth theatre project, it led to five students leaving the group, three apparently without rancour. A fourth left 'unhappy with the direction the show was taking'. The fifth was excluded by the leaders, without, as it turned out, sufficient negotiation with the group. The leaders believed that they were fulfilling Neelands's fifth function:

A hassle it was, and a few of the group organised a meeting to discuss it, as well as other, less defined problems. We had the meeting, and things seemed to be resolved.

The mismatch of expectations was not resolved, with some participants believing that the writer was not incorporating the group's wishes sufficiently: 'an example of this is the group's desire to have a female or androgynous central character'. This was expressed 'time and time again' (this from a group member). The playwright had a different perception: 'It's billed as Michael Doneman and company, but I have led the writing. It's not group-devised.' These tensions remained throughout the production, and at least two members of the audience noted them as contributing – not necessarily negatively – to the final result:

> I had assumed wrongly that the text was devised by the kids and put in order by Michael, but what I discovered was that he had in fact written it which explained the complexity. I felt there was a gap between the text and those delivering it.

> *The Great Circle* . . . for the group a far from easy or happy experience . . . blazed with the energy of those real tensions; the compromises and trade-offs resulted in a varied, kaleido-scopic style.

This dis-ease is not uncommon in youth theatre projects, and it partly comes from the difficulty of matching sets of different expectations and priorities. This may be paralleled with drama in education. The drama teacher is faced with the need to provide 'the play for the children', while at the same time pursuing 'the play for the teacher'. If the children do not get a measure of their play, they will pull out of the contract. The youth theatre leader does not have to be so solicitous to the group, for they are volunteers, usually very enthusiastic. However, the leader faces two priorities even more difficult to match: the 'play for the participants' and the 'play for the audience'. The participants need to have a useful, challenging and satisfying learning experience, especially in developing the skills of the medium, and they want to perform. As well as this, a piece of theatre must emerge which is interesting, accessible and qualitatively accept-able to a paying audience, some of whom are unconnected with the performing group. The familiarity of the audience is crucial in defining *their* contract. Two written audience responses to *The Great Circle* make an interesting comparison.

Recently I had the pleasure of attending *The Great Circle*, at La Boîte and was delighted with the work of the whole company.

This was from a spectator familiar with the leaders and some of the young participants – the whole text of this response concentrates on the company.

I am writing to you to complain about the dreadful garbage served up supposedly as 'entertainment' in the awful play *The Great Circle* . . . This play was so terrible that I demand my money back.

This from a stranger, and it concentrates on the material, with a predictable demand.

CONTRACTS IN THEATRE IN SCHOOLS

Doneman and this group at least had the advantage of working in a theatre, whose primary function is producing drama. Teachers working in performance work in schools find these problems exacerbated by external constraints of expectation and of the limited time inevitably available in schools. Teachers, naturally, usually have a strong commitment to the educational function of youth theatre. Accordingly, some of them subordinate to this their group's responsibility to their audience. They carefully select the audiences to be unthreatening – groups of other students, parents and friends, or people in institutions unlikely to be critical, such as primary schools and old people's homes; those in other words who will not drive a hard bargain contractually. A phrase commonly used in invitations to performance work in schools is 'work in progress', which is supposed to negate for the audience any expectation of finished performance product.

However, teachers work within a system where theatre is often seen as either extra-curricular or peripheral and ornamental. A survey of drama teachers indicated that for a clear majority of respondents the greatest source of stress in their teaching lives was the imperative to 'put on the school play or musical'.[5] Most teachers saw the annual school musical as peripheral to their own work, and though some enjoyed the experience, a large number perceived that its purposes and expectations had little to do with what they regarded as important. They perceived Principals as wanting a high-finish product that would please and impress an audience, and thus show the school in a good light. For many schools, the school play or musical is seen as the cultural highlight, or even yardstick. The choice of plays and musicals also makes very clear that the school rarely wants its audiences to be challenged intellectually or morally (a purpose important to most drama teachers); rather, the teachers perceive that the Principals expect nothing more educational than demonstrating a high level of performing skills, and providing an enjoyable and unexceptionable audience experience. Of this part of the contract, teachers are usually in no doubt.

Along with this, the teachers themselves usually have a stake in their own work being seen by outsiders to be effective and impressive. Their self-esteem, their esteem among their colleagues, their promotion prospects, their desire to establish or raise the status of drama within the school, all put the teacher under considerable pressure to 'perform' and make sure the students perform. Only the very strongest and most self-confident resist this pressure and maintain a 'work-in-process' ethic or affirm the negotiability of subject matter and allow the students to create their own. This can easily backfire, and, ironically, lead to the subject being seen as self-indulgent, not sufficiently concerned with artistic standards inside and outside the school. It is a truism of competitive drama festivals that improvised work rarely wins prizes.

Even fewer teachers use the annual school production to present material intellectually challenging to the audience, and, in a further irony, risk their opprobrium by involving the audience in an educational, polemical or satirical event. Part of the audience contract clearly understood by school managers and audiences of parents specifies a good-humoured experience with all tensions resolved by the end, and no discomforting questions left hanging.

CONTRACTS IN DRAMA IN EDUCATION

Drama teachers usually reserve those dramatic purposes which relate to intellectual or conceptual matters for the classroom, for the genre of drama in education. The constraints here, and the contracts which must be negotiated, are very different from those of the school musical or of the youth theatre. Unlike the school musical, the constraints are not imposed arbitrarily for purposes in the **real context** quite unrelated to the activity of drama – that is, for the cultural image of the school. Nor, on the other hand, can the teacher rely on the advantages of the **context of the medium** which are implicit or explicit in youth theatre. A school, and the classroom inside it, provide a very specific **context of setting** which to a large extent pre-empts and dictates the nature of the **contexts of medium** and **fiction**.

As the last chapter showed, the percipients and the location need to be perceived together. For instance, in a western conventional theatre the function of an audience is clear, and primary – to sit and spectate. Any other function has to be specially negotiated. and a new contract set up. A theatre only exists as that 'special place'. Even in other cultures, such as an Aboriginal corroboree, the location is specially chosen for its theatrical qualities.[6] In medieval Europe the marketplaces and carts used daily by Mystères or Guilds as part of their working environment were physically transformed to endow them with the special quality of the occasion for the Mystery cycles. A classroom has some of the locational qualities of an auditorium, but others which belie those.

Similarly with the participant group, and the functions of audience. Certainly for a percentage of the time students are used to being treated as listeners and watchers. However, the expectations of a class of schoolchildren are not confined to comparatively passive spectating. Participatory activity is very much on the agenda. During a typical day, the class may be required to discuss, to hypothesise, to write tests, to cut up frogs, to paint, to bath a baby, to cook, to question a visiting policeman, to throw bean bags, to make measurements with rulers or thermometers, to square dance, and to speculate on baths full of water. These activities are accepted as they are perceived, explicitly as fitting into a recognisable learning purpose or process called History, or Science, or English. Implicitly they are an accepted part of that consistent, closed system of interacting belief and action called schooling. This can permit the teacher to work in role without any further difficulty than that imposed by the limitations of the space. Participation in drama may be perceived as just another natural activity, an extension of the hypothesising and proto-dramatic activities which the children have been used to engaging in since they set up cubby houses in the preschool classroom or, a little later, practised shopping transactions with simulated money.

It can also cause initial management difficulties for teachers, particularly in a schooling system where drama is often perceived as a novel or a fringe subject. These difficulties can frequently seem endemic to the art form, and daunt those teachers with limited understanding of how drama works, and the conditions necessary for it to operate. The problem is very often expressed in terms of 'these children have never done drama before'. That is most unlikely to be true, at least for normal children, who have been engaged in dramatic play and role-play since they first played peekaboo. Any school yard during recess is full of examples of solo, intimate, collaborative and epic role-play containing all the elements of dramatic form. That is part of the expectation of the playground. In schools where a strong implicit distinction is made between what happens within and beyond the classroom, this may well mediate against its acceptance in the classroom. In practical terms this is likely to be expressed by the children bringing in the rules of the play-ground: the teacher has unaccountably removed the boundaries of acceptable behaviour in the classroom, and the children use the release to explore the new situation to see if there are limits – and also to test out how worthy of their conventional respect that teacher still is. In the classroom, that constitutes misbehaving.

In other words, before the contract of the dramatic ellipsis can be invoked, the participants must negotiate a contract within the **context of setting** that will allow it to become the **context of the medium**. A renegotiation of the contractual expectations of the classroom may be necessary. The boundaries of acceptable behaviour and of appropriate action need to be clearly defined. The first steps may be taken explicitly. In most cases the word 'drama' appearing on the timetable as a distinct 'subject' is the first indication to the participants that the location is to be 'made special' and that certain events for which they may have a range of synonymous expectations will occur in that location and timeslot.

The scope of this is limited. The very fact of drama being a subject means that it is lined up with other activities, each in their own way special, but contributing to the ordinariness of schooling. It is the dilemma, not only of the drama teacher, but of all subject-based teachers in schools, that they simultaneously strive to engage their clients with the uniqueness of their discipline, and to emphasise its necessary place in the total curriculum. Since that curriculum is explicitly concerned with signification and significance, all these special events for which the classroom – or school site – provides a negotiable environment are commonplace exactly to the extent that they are significant.

This paradox partly has to do with the language used to describe the events, the signifiers that define which area of knowledge is embodied in each 'subject'. In the western Newtonian tradition of nominalisation (expressing reality in the static and 'objective' form of nouns), the dynamic process of *knowing* is redefined in the language of educational institutions as *knowledge*, then further categorised into nouns called subjects like History, Geography, Science, Art, each apparently distinct, and each purporting to deal with a separate area of experience (or being). The natural process of adding to experience and making complex textures of meaning from it, which Richard Courtney disingenuously calls 'curricking',[7] is turned into a noun-abstraction, a 'curriculum'; most usually, with the definite article – '*the* curriculum'. Usage makes for ease, as much as etymological justification; the word 'curriculum' is a word commonly and easily used by teachers, the verb 'to currick' is not.

This progressive nominalisation is embedded and explicit in the very structures of schooling. In Early Childhood Education, the notion of distinct subjects is hazy, and often officially discouraged.[8] Then through the primary years subjects are taught with dwindling degrees of integration, but still with one teacher. In secondary schools, subjects are mostly taught as separate entities by different teachers with specialist training, with the students in separate class groupings. This process is normally replicated at tertiary level, with subjects further broken down into specialised sub-disciplines – such as physics and chemistry, medieval literature and the Reformation, or voice and movement. The more the specialisation, the higher the status, from the lowly 'general' degree through to the arcana of the PhD. Specific attempts to break down this nominalised framework by providing alternative educational frameworks, such as A.S. Neill's Summerhill school in England, or the alternative primary schools dotted sporadically about Australia, have rarely achieved great status in popular terms, or much success beyond the rhetoric for most of the community. This is because a whole system of certifying and validating is attached to this nominalisation process (or more accurately, anti-process). Exams are in subjects.

The network of assumptions and practices derived from that ultimately dictates the behaviour of the participants in the classroom setting. It is not entirely fixed in concrete, and at least since Jean-Jacques Rousseau educators have been trying to alter the action of the classroom by changing the accompanying noun-based language: 'childhood has ways of seeing, thinking, and feeling, peculiar to itself'.[9] This Romantic terminology has been significant in drama in education – in for instance the language of the 1950s pioneer Peter Slade. A more recent post-Romantic attempt to re-evaluate the nature of drama in education writes of 'not human beings, but humans being'.[10] More influentially, the notion of 'curricking' is taken up within the movement, but on a broader front, in the phrase 'negotiating the curriculum' – that is, re-verbalising the noun.[11] This phrase reflects a significant amount of practice taking place in schools across the whole range of 'subjects', and in particular a fluidity of subject definition which may be observed within many primary school classrooms.

As we have seen, many primary teachers experienced in drama prefer not to schedule it as a separate 'subject' and timeslot, on the very specific grounds that they incorporate it within the framework of other curriculum areas. Categorisation of drama as a subject causes particular contracts to be drawn up relating to the operation of this separate discipline, its rules and limitations. Those contracts are invariably constrained by time available for it as a separate subject. The contracts are also bound to be congruent with the contracts for all other subjects, which removes any pretensions drama has to being 'special'.

This has already been noted, but those teachers may express another purpose, substituting cause and effect. If it is part of the very nature of the group activity called drama to 'make special' an event, then to make a piece of learning in another subject area significant one may use drama. For negotiating this kind of contract within the **context of the setting** which transforms it unobtrusively into that of the **medium**, and simultaneously sets up the **fictional context**, a number of conventions specific to drama in education have been developed. Necessarily so, for these complex processes which subsume building the theatre, contracting the percipients, writing, rehearsing and performing the play, have to be condensed within the concentration span and initial interest of thirty students, as well as the time available for this total event – which is most likely to be subdivided into a number of shorter time-spans of perhaps fifty minutes each, some days apart.

Practice in drama in education has evolved sophisticated approaches through the use of *questions*. As we have seen in chapter 4, questions immediately create tension. The teacher can structure the material into a **fictional context** by framing questions which both focus the action and provide an initial tension to sustain the expository activities which clarify the fiction – 'What, I wonder, could drive anyone to commit that murder?'

This is clearly exemplified in a widely used set of teacher's planning materials.[12] The accompanying teachers' notes, broaching the subject matter, immediately address themselves to the reader in the form of a focussing question: 'What is your personal response to the following material?' – which is a brief paragraph of documentation incorporating an inscription:

MARY ELLIS
Died August 7th 1845
Age 2 months

This is immediately followed with questions redolent with tension, still addressed to the teacher:

> It would be useful to write down some of your responses under the following headings:
> WHAT DO YOU KNOW ABOUT THE CHILD AND THE CIRCUMSTANCES SURROUNDING HER DEATH?
> WHAT MIGHT YOU INFER OR INTUIT?
> WHAT DO YOU WANT TO ASK OF THE MATERIAL?
> WHAT FEELINGS DOES IT INVOKE?

The author notes, as one of the key features of the inscription, that 'its terseness and incompleteness generate many, many questions'. He then goes on to describe as an exemplar one way in which the material has been used – in fact how he himself used it. Though this description gives little indication of the **context of the setting** and how familiar the students were with the medium of drama, it is significant here for two reasons. Firstly, it clearly shows how the teacher's initial question was transferred to the students, and in turn generated further questions which would lead into a **dramatic context**. Less obviously, it indicates a highly *negotiative*, processual approach. The teacher's way of framing the questions gave the students the opportunity individually and collectively, and the tension embodied in the questions themselves gave them the motivation, to engage in the dramatic ellipsis which is the most direct contract among the participants and without which drama cannot take place. The following account of the actual use of these materials is part of the accompanying documentation. It indicates the manifold and complex use of questions generating further questions to create through negotiation a **fictional context** contractually acceptable to children and teacher.

Here is a brief account of how the material was used with a class of thirty 11-year-olds in a city middle school. The teacher introduced the topic . . . and collected from the group all that 'they already knew' about the 'Wild West', 'Cowboys', etc. The teacher then introduced the material with a narrative . . . The sign was introduced and, working in small groups, the class were asked to address two questions:

'What information can you get from this sign; what does it tell you, what sense can you make of it?'

'Secondly, I wonder if there are any questions you would like to ask, things that are unanswered that you would like to know more about – about this sign or about the people or about the moment when this was put up.'

After a short time discussing the sign, the groups came up with the following questions:

'Who was Mary Ellis?'

'How did she die?' . . . [etc.] . . .

The teacher asked the group to order the questions in terms of their own interests, and then invited the group to form hypothetical answers for each, based on what they knew about wagon trains, that period of history, etc. The teacher made it clear that he didn't have the answers, the sign was only a fragment.

Chapter 7

Language, gesture and action

LANGUAGE IS POLYFUNCTIONAL

Since language and gesture, as the media for expression of the **fictional context**, are the most immediately recognisable of the elements of drama, a great deal of analysis has been done on both: on language mostly by literary theorists, on gesture mainly by theatre practitioners. Currently, theorists are attempting to find paradigms which can cope with the many simultaneous dimensions and functions which operate as language and gesture: among them semiotics,[1] sociolinguistics[2] and ethnography.[3] The trouble which semiotics has found, referred to in the Introduction, is that language in drama is so polyfunctional that analysis quickly becomes incomprehensibly obscure to anyone but the analyst, or turns into counting sand – endless and useless. Some progress has been made by those who have chosen to make language and gesture the centre of their concentration, but that is frankly beyond the scope of this book. In all drama, language and physical action are polyfunctional, multi-dimensional, with all their constituents dependent on each other; furthermore, in process drama those constituents are constantly being renegotiated. To boil these down to one chapter is to do them a disservice; to do otherwise is to unbalance the book entirely. Accordingly, the disservice which I will do is to isolate and concentrate on one dimension as if it had an existence independent of all the others. A dimension particularly relevant to the scope of this book is that of *purposiveness* – within the range from the functional to the aesthetic – since this dimension crosses contextual boundaries.

FROM CONTEXT TO TEXT

The purposes of the participants in drama are made manifest through the primary elements of the medium: language, movement and gesture. Together, these form the dramatic text.

The text of drama may be said to be all the action which happens within the **dramatic context**. As already noted, another difficulty which literary analysts find with drama is that only a part of that text is ever recorded, and is by that action severely transformed. The practitioner and theorist Martin Esslin notes the primacy of the non-verbal indicators over verbal text: 'If there is a contradiction between the words and the action, the action prevails.'[4] The extent of the corruption which dramatic performance text undergoes when its action is transposed into the written text of a playscript may be compared with that which it undergoes when the visceral action is recorded on video or film – the scholarship of semiotics has to some extent grown out of the recognition of this mediation, which in effect turns the drama into another art form. Esslin goes on to stress that in fact, 'drama being action, the verbal element in drama must also function primarily as action'.

This will suffice as a starting point, though it should be treated with caution. Drama as action is something of an oversimplification, and, within the field of drama in education, something of a cliché, as Gavin Bolton mischievously highlighted in his title for a conference address: 'Drama is Not Doing'. Commenting on this, he goes on to

> invite readers to accept a paradox that is the central component of good drama generally and of good improvised drama in particular. It is this: that when an action in drama achieves a moment of heightened significance it does so because the meaning created is largely released from its dependence on that action.[5]

The implications of this caveat are taken up in chapter 8, within a discussion of symbolisation in drama.

However, starting with Esslin, the movement and gesture by which dramatic narrative unfolds itself, together with the verbal and paralinguistic internal communication, comprise the action. The action in conventional performance gives rise to a surface text and subtexts that are communicated to an external audience.

In drama in education the action is readily conceptualised as the *tasks* that the characters undertake, which embody verbal and gestural activities. Since the audience function is also embodied in the participants, and the **fictional context** is much more an integral part of the **context of the medium**, how those participants receive and construe the surface and subtexts are more complex processes, subject to constant renegotiation in both contexts.

FUNCTIONS OF DRAMATIC TEXT

As indicated in the Introduction, there are three contextual functions of language. These categories need to be further defined.

1 *Expressive* Ben Jonson gives a pertinent definition of this function: 'Language most shows a man: speak that I may see thee.'[6] In terms of this book, the expressive function forms both part of the surface text and at least one level of subtext, as the following extract from a critical commentary on a play exemplifies: 'Karl's language characterises him. This expressive self-characterisation is in part intentional, but it is in part involuntary and unintentional.'[7]

2 *Purposive* This comprises the language and gestures by which the dramatic narrative unfolds, and through which the characters pursue their tasks, their internal purposes.

3 *Communicative* This implies communication with the audience, and comprises three sub-categories. The first of these is the *referential*, by which the playwright, through the actors, conveys information to the audience beyond what can be inferred by the characters themselves in their interactions. This is usually expository, as when a character, or an external narrator, uses language whose primary purpose is to give the audience background information to the situation and relationships. While a muse or prologue is handy, most playwrights embed their exposition in what is ostensibly purposive language, and even in the most skilled hands it can often prove tyrannous:

Nay, but this dotage of our general's o'erflows the measure . . .

The two characters whose conversation starts *Antony and Cleopatra* only exist to give the audience a setting and a point of view, and they open and close the scene with observations which they would not need to share with each other, since they both know the score.

On the other hand, *referential* language may be, so far as the characters are concerned, subtextual, where the audience knows what the characters don't: for example in *The Winter's Tale*, the ambiguity of Leontes's 'All's true that is mistrusted', by which Leontes intends that all he had feared about his wife's infidelity is proved, but which the audience knows to mean the opposite. Soliloquies, such as Iago's, turn subtext into surface text briefly, for a character to make the audience his confidant. Speaking across the boundary between the **contexts of the fiction** and the **medium** he apprises them of motives and intentions which must be hidden from other characters, and which he is unlikely realistically to articulate to himself.

The second sub-category of communicative language is the *poetic*, which denotes those aspects of the language action that draw attention to the structure and the artifice of the fiction. Like the *referential*, this is addressed to the audience beyond the **fictional context**.

The third sub-category, particularly relevant to drama in education, is the *reflective*. This denotes that text which focusses on other parts of the dramatic text, or on the whole event within the **fictional context**. As such, it properly belongs outside, as part of the text of the **context of the medium**. However, frequently in the genre of drama in education it happens as a function of the dramatic text itself for reasons which will become clear below.

For many actions, including virtually all talking and physical gesture, the purposive entails a communicative function. This may seem very obvious when considering drama as 'acting' for an audience. However, the 'actor' is only the secondary enactor, reinterpreting the contextual purposive action as communication. Where there is no external audience, as in experiential role-play (where the participants are, as it were, their own audience, held during the time of the action under the level of consciousness) the distinction between these needs to be clear.

There are subtle interplays: a participant role-playing a character will be seeking to act purposively – to do – as that character in that situation. However, the roleplayers are not just the characters; their roles in the **context of the medium** entail the management of their roles within the **fiction**. They need to make simultaneous communicative acts, that is, to give signals to the other participants which indicate enough of the nature of the purpose of their character's action for the other role-players to maintain the drama – and for *their* characters to maintain their tasks. The participants need to be able to move smoothly and naturally between the two contexts and to some extent to control and monitor the operation of the dual affect – that is, to 'weep as a patient and simultaneously revel as a player' *and* at the same time shape the conditions that bring this about.

That may occur within the **fictional context** where the 'player' shapes the text by his or her very participation and interventions; it may occur concurrently, between episodes, while the players as playwrights plan and shape the structure of the next piece of text. Drama in education workers have sometimes underestimated the complexity and sophistication of the skills appropriate for this particular form of the art, and ways in which effective participants, particularly good teachers, manage the communication patterns.

Drama in education is a particularly episodic genre. This is, no doubt, partly the result of the time-spans available for its operation in schools – where a sustained drama may have to operate with days between each fifty-minute segment. It is also the result of the desire of drama leaders and participants to negotiate the structure of the dramas, to interweave the functions of playwright, participant and audience. Typically, each scene within the drama is negotiated afresh, and the **context of the medium** reasserted. Participants have to speak and do out of role to create a new internal location, and regroup for a new set of interactions.

Even within one scene, the tasks may engender language and action which move rapidly from one context to another – in other words from the expressive and purposive mode to the communicative. In *The Nativity* (described in detail in chapter 3), during the art work, making presents, though the task was more-or-less in role, the children were more-or-less out of role (shop assistants don't make the presents they sell). The modality of the last sentence is not imprecise, but accurate. During the session, much of the language and action were text within the **context of the medium** concerned with the art work. Not a little was back in the **real**, concerned with classroom management, or the children's school and home lives. However, almost all the children frequently dropped back into language from within, too. One sub-group invented a song as they worked – 'We're going to Bethlehem: you can come too'. Part of their game included addressing me as Caspar, and even attempting to provide a further layering of dramatic deception – 'You're not allowed to see what I'm making: not till this afternoon.' Not wishing to confuse them, I refused to be drawn into role at this point, as 'Caspar' had promised the 'shop assistants' that he would not return until the afternoon. This in fact seemed to confuse the children more. They could slide in and out of role at will; why wasn't I now playing the game?

As is not uncommon, the teacher was underestimating the students' ability to manage levels of role and deception *at will*. The artistic quality of the text generated should not be under-estimated, either. Children may have limited knowledge of the registers of language appropriate to situations in the **real context**, but by school age they are adept at those with which they have had contact, and adept too at using their play to practise and develop an awareness of the congruous and the incongruous.[8] Already embedded is a range of behaviours including language that relate to motives and intentions across a range of situations: 'few, if any of these children had ever tried to hide from a policeman. But we can appeal to the generalisation of exper-ience: they know what it is to try to hide. Also they know what it is to be naughty and to want to evade the consequences.'[9]

The following fragment of recorded transcript may serve to indicate a little of the spontaneous aesthetic shaping which was sustaining the dramatic action in purely expressive and purposive terms (with a caveat, indicated in the Introduction: transcribed verbal text is just a partial schema for the original dramatic action; and improvised text is even less responsive to documentation, being much looser, more complex in its auth-enticity than playtext, and often involving many characters).[10] The children were playing 'themselves' (see chapter 2) and the teacher was playing a dinosaur who had slipped through a time warp and ended up, frightened and amnesiac, in the school yard. After the tension of the hunt, and the first fearful contact with the dinosaur, they were taking Dino in hand to find him a home, and explain something of life in a twentieth-century school. These helpers were located in the (real) school library, showing Dino a book on dinosaurs containing a picture of a Tyrannosaurus rex with great teeth – with which they promptly endowed Dino, and started discussing dentists.

Helper: It's where you go – to the dentist – to get your teeth fixed.

Helper: *These* are teeth.

Helper: They make sure your teeth are clean and that.

Helper: They pull them out if they are bad . . . and fillings, you get fillings. But I haven't got any.

Dino: Is it good to have fillings or bad to have fillings?

Most: Bad!

Helper: It's good! If you've got holes in your teeth, that is.

Dino: Where do they come from?

Helper: The dentist.

Dino: Holes come from the dentist?

Helper: No! They come from bacteria in your teeth. If you eat too much sweet things, and you don't clean your teeth properly you get holes in your teeth.

Helper: That's probably what happened to dinosaurs. They got holes in their teeth and died out.

Dino: When did dinosaurs die out? Before people or after people?

Helper: Before, when there's no people.

Helper: Millions of years.

Helper: And now there's just little tiny bones.

Helper: Fossils.

Helper: Hundreds and hundreds of years ago.

Dino: Would dinosaurs have had big swimming pools and schools?

Helper: No, they just had swamps.

Helper: Would *you* like to come with us to the museum next week and see some dinosaur bones?

Dino: I'm not sure.

The dramatic economy and tight focus of this passage is an outcome of the purposiveness, combined with the need to maintain a comprehensible dialogue and modified by the number of potential speakers. The part played by the teacher in shaping the text is worth noting. The video camera may have modified a fraction the children's action – though they had much earlier incorporated it into their perception of the **context of the setting** and were to all intents and purposes oblivious of it. It probably affected the teacher's action more significantly. Apart from this, there was no external audience, so the poetic quality which may be detected existed for the shared internal pleasures of the participants, as their own audience within the **context of the medium**. This kind of 'revelling' in the structure and elegance of the text is a key feature of successful drama in education, which participants frequently remark upon afterwards.

In perhaps the most famous recorded language action in the history of the genre, a fragment from an improvised drama on the biblical story of Elijah, there was, untypically, an external audience, as well as the camera.[11] It is worth quoting in full, not only because of its power to move, twenty years after its only performance, but because the children's observations on language are documented too; moreover its salient features bear analysis in terms of this dimension of purpose, and the power of the language is largely contained in the vocabulary. Viewers frequently comment on two non-verbal aspects – the combination of real passion and control, evident in the clarity of the dialogue; and the power of one character who never speaks, but holds a significant proportion of the focus: the bejewelled Queen Jezebel.

Scene: The Court of King Ahab

Servant:	My lord, I gave them an order and they will not obey it.
Ahab:	I do not believe this. Your King has given you an order.
Townsman 1:	My Lord, can you not see – what is wrong with you? Ever since She came it started – that Jezebel.
Townsman 2:	We don't want her here.
Ahab:	You don't want her here, but you've got her – and be grateful.
Townsman 1:	My Lord, you aren't going to let this happen. I've lived in this city since the beginning. I've seen every house built. It takes months, sometimes a year, to build a house. And people have lived in them from the beginning as well. Would you let your house go, My Lord?
Ahab:	What Baal needs, Baal gets.

Townsman 1:	There's plenty of room in the Palace grounds – build Baal's temple there . . .
Townsman 3:	. . . There'll only be you using it.
Townsman 2:	There are women in this city – what will they do?
Ahab:	Well, let your women talk.
Townswoman 1:	Jezebel, there's women in this city with babies – what do you think is going to happen to them?
Townswoman 2:	They'll probably die.
Townswoman 3:	What if they get a fever?
Townswoman 2:	You don't care.
Townswoman 1:	We haven't enough clothing – you should know that by now. Why do you think we need our houses? To keep them warm. (*Hubbub of agreement.*)
Ahab:	Yes I realise that – you can't let them go, but you will.
Townsman 3:	I wonder how you can call yourself a king.
Townsman 5:	A king who doesn't care.
Townsman 3:	Who doesn't care for children who might die in the streets if you pull down their houses.
Ahab:	They will not die.
Townsman 3:	That is why we need our houses, to keep the children warm. Don't you understand?
Townsman 6:	(*To Jezebel*) I wonder why you call yourself a queen?
Townsman 3:	A queen that paints her face. And a thing like this happens. (*A disturbance in the crowd and murmurs:*) Elijah! – it's Elijah. (*Elijah makes his way through the crowd, which gives way.*)
Ahab:	Who are you? What do you want?
Elijah:	And you know. I am Elijah. The Prophet. And the only Prophet at that. I have been outside this crowd, listening to your arguments . . .
Ahab:	. . . Listening like a spy – is that all you are good for? Or can't you do anything better with your time?

Elijah:	And you call yourself a king. Doing this to my people.
Ahab:	And you call yourself a prophet – living in the mountains shut up in a cave – like a wild beast.
Elijah:	I live in the mountains because I am nearer God.
Ahab:	Nearer God?
Elijah:	Your Baal . . .
Ahab:	You call them your people – well, why don't you live among them? I'll tell you why – you could not live among them because you are frightened of them – you could not rule over them.
Elijah:	(*Holds up scroll.*) Do you know what they are?
Ahab:	Yes, I know.
Elijah:	The Law.
Ahab:	My father's Law.
Elijah:	The Law. (*To people*) And your king is disobeying them. You call yourself a king, you call these your people and you'd do such a thing to them. What have you got to say to that?
Ahab:	Not half as much as you have. But before we go any further, I would like to know why you are here. And once more, what you want.
Elijah:	To solve this problem.
Ahab:	It's none of your business. You aren't a part of these people. You don't live among them. Why don't you stop pretending? You're no prophet. Why don't you get it into your head?
Elijah:	These are the Laws . . .
Ahab:	I'll tell you why. Because you want to keep on going. Never stop – until the world ends.
Elijah:	Until you change the Laws they shall be kept.
Ahab:	Is that a threat?
Elijah:	That is a threat.

Ahab: You people: listen – as well as you – if
                            Elijah interferes: I'll fill the well in. Collect
                            all your belongings – I want you out of your
                            houses by noon. (*To Elijah*) And as for you
                            – interfere any more and I'll have your
                            hands off.
                            Guards!
                            (*Ahab and Jezebel exit, through the silent
                            crowd.*)

That this dialogue is being entirely improvised is stressed by the
film narrator and by an audience member, who had seen a
segment of the same scene enacted earlier, with entirely different
dialogue.

The first level of text is entirely *purposive* – energetically
living-through in role the events of the narrative, the characters
speaking and responding entirely appropriately to their tasks.
The language is fluent, the answers and interruptions instinctive
and immediate, it is unselfconsciously authentic to the situation.

Simultaneously, on another textual level the language is
expressive within the **fictional context**. An enormous amount of
aesthetic shaping is taking place as the language emerges: the
children are selecting, modulating and managing a language
register appropriate to their understanding of the status of the
characters and the gravity of the situation. Very occasionally the
intensity of the personal engagement – and their limited
knowledge of the chosen register – causes this to slip: 'Not half as
much as you have' is scarcely kingly – the child behind the
character is clearly taken aback by Elijah's blunt question. On
the other hand, they are capable of deliberately changing register.
After the breathtaking grandiosity of 'Because you want to keep
on going. Never stop – until the world ends,' Ahab's peremptory
'And as for you – interfere any more and I'll have your hands off'
is brutally, purposefully colloquial.

There is a further important level of expressive subtext, within
the **real context** of the children and only apparent within the
fictional context to those who know the children's background.
In order to create a 'play for the children' within the rather
esoteric biblical story, the teacher had focussed this scene of
evictions to clear a site for the temple of Baal. The school where
this drama took place was on a new housing estate, and many of

the children's families had recently moved, some compulsorily after a slum clearance scheme. They knew what it was to be moved on. The section of dialogue dealing directly with that issue is very direct and down-to-earth, especially from the women (the girls); it is also the section where they are most actively involved, and in fact where some quieter members of the class are moved to speak, instead of leaving the action all to the star players.

The extent to which communicative language is used, and the presence of the external audience has modified the text, is questionable, probably considerably less than appears. The children are certainly recreating *referentially* the historicity of the situation, instinctively using whatever background knowledge they have: 'We haven't enough clothing – you should know that by now', 'living in the mountains – shut up in a cave', 'I'll fill the well in.'

The *poetic* nature of the language is perhaps its most immediately recognisable quality. However, in the strict sense of this chapter, the Formalist sense of language which exists to draw attention to itself, it is not primarily poetic, and there is little evidence in the film that the children were conscious of using that language for the audience's benefit. There is poetic repetition, in for example the rolling '. . . how you can call yourself a king?', '. . . a king who doesn't care . . .', '. . . who doesn't care for children', but this is purposive language too, the desperate arguments of characters united in their need to persuade the king, with the language expressing that unity. The refrain-like 'How can you call yourself a king/queen/prophet?' has the same function as an acrobat's platform – a secure base for the character to regroup while getting ready to launch the next spectacular tirade; again purposively rather than poetically. There is vivid imagery, and a care for the choice of words evident throughout: Ahab and Elijah show particular mastery – 'And you call yourself a prophet – living in the mountains – shut up in a cave – like a wild beast.' 'I live in the mountains because I am nearer God' – but the immediacy of the confrontation, and the totally unhesitating answer, again belong to the purposive and expressive modes. The children also show sophisticated understanding of the power of variation and skill in its use: the simplicity of 'they'll probably die' and 'The Law.' 'My father's Law.' 'The Law' is certainly an artifice, but an entirely implicit and instinctive one, which also operates purposively in the **fictional context** as the characters struggle to put their point across in a public forum across the grandest of status gaps.

The children's own reflection on the drama is significant, in that they are concerned totally with the purposive and expressive, and by implication even deprecate the notion of the drama in conventional terms – their aesthetic response is entirely absorbed in the game of drama itself, not its effect on others:

Narrator: Does Mr Stabler tell you what to say?
Child 1: No – we just think it up . . .
Child 2: . . . as we go along.
Child 3: If it was Mr Stabler's idea it wouldn't . . .
Child 1: It wouldn't be right.
Child 2: It wouldn't feel right.
Child 1: It wouldn't be our drama – like a parrot repeating words – or a play – a script. If he told us what to say it wouldn't be our drama, it would be a play.
Child 3: I'd rather do drama than a play . . . because if you do a play you have to learn the words and if you forget it might ruin the whole thing. But in drama you just think the words as you go on.
Child 1: It's more fun . . . in a play you can't say what you want to say . . . what you feel.

MULTIPLE FRAMING

A further complication in analysing the text of drama in education, and separating the communicative functions from the expressive and purposive, is that the genre employs multiple frames, and multiple dramatic conventions to activate those frames. This may entail partial or total re-enrolment of the participants. In a drama with tertiary students entitled *The Mind of the Terrorist* a group of 'freedom fighters' were engaged in planning a mission involving their probable suicide.[12] I interrupted their quite deep enrolment for a dramatic exercise in order to distance and examine the characters' motivations. I broke the participants into pairs, and asked each in turn to take the role of a hostile news reporter, interviewing the 'terrorist', while their partner, maintaining the original role, justified his or her actions as 'freedom fighter'. This artificial convention broke the flow of experiential role-play, and demanded conscious management of the text, yet the interviewees were able to use their previous empathy, and this new constraint, to continue to generate quite authentic text.

A common device to introduce a reflective dimension is to actually introduce a performance component within the **fictional context**. In the *Zola Budd* drama referred to in chapter 3, the participants had been in role in a scene framed on the edge of the action, as athletes in the changing room after the ill-fated race that was the drama's focus event. For the next scene they were completely re-enrolled as a television current affairs team, with a range of political attitudes to that event, and asked to prepare a feature on the event 'including the fracas in the changing room'. This involved processing, reflecting on and transforming their previous expressive and purposive text into communicative text within the **fictional context**. As this task took nearly an hour in real time, the participants frequently renegotiated the **context of the medium** and also often lapsed into text within the **real context** and **context of setting**, that is, talked about their own real lives, without destroying the dramatic frame. This device is often used if the experiential action has been particularly intense and emotional: *Utopia* (see chapters 2 and 3) used just such a device to permit the participants, for whom the fiction had become out of control and spilled over into the **real context**, to rediscover the dramatic text slowly and cautiously, and then recreate a new, manageable version of that text which kept it firmly anchored in the **fictional context**.

The following drama on Northern Ireland, *The Fields of Orange and the Float of Ignorance*,[13] very clearly shows the relationship between *expressive, purposive* and *communicative* texts in drama in education – in fact each section of the drama was coincidentally structured to generate those dimensions of text in that order.

Expressive text

Joint leaders Jacq Hamilton and I first lightly enrolled the participants as Australian tourists, and we asked them to put together from a collection of books, songs and maps 'your Ulster ancestry, of which you are proud'. The dramatic text had the

primary *expressive* purpose of giving them some initial engagement with the situation of people in Northern Ireland, of which
they had little direct knowledge, and of allowing them a familiar
role as Australian adults. Because this task involved considerable
time, and only light enrolment, a considerable amount of activity
belonging to the **setting** and **real contexts** occurred simultaneously, though the students stayed on task – that is, within the
fictional frame. Irish songs were playing throughout and formed
a deliberate layer of resonant text, both *expressive* and – in the
sense that the participants were also audience – *referential*.

Purposive text

For the second session the group was split up and re-enrolled, the
larger group retaining their characters of session 1 as Australian
tourists holidaying in Ulster to rediscover their roots. In role as
an apparently jovial tour operator – but in fact a UVF partisan
using these innocents as publicity for the cause – I invited them
to take part in a traditional July festival whose 'origins were lost
in history'. Their task was to design and decorate a gaily orange
'Irish-Australian Friendship Float', and learn a 'traditional jin-
gle' – in fact the marching song 'The Sash My Father Wore'. Six
women participants meanwhile were being re-enrolled elsewhere
as Catholic Irishwomen, deeply committed IRA supporters.
They too learned a song, 'The Patriot Game'.

When the two groups eventually confronted each other during
the 12 July Parade, it was through those two songs, which for a
considerable time formed almost exclusively the verbal text. The
gesture and paralinguistic dimension was consonant with this –
the Australian/Orangemen danced and waved bright favours as
they sang, the IRA women stood silently, clad in black shawls.
Eventually the quiet intensity of 'The Patriot Game' outfaced the
brasher strains of 'The Sash', the unwitting Orange Paraders
realised the deception implicit in what they were singing, and the
web of conflicts became explicit in speech and violent action.
That interchange through songs was paradoxically not poetic at
all, but *expressive* and *purposive*. The songs were – as they are in
the real Irish context – both assertively *expressive* of the motives
and ideologies of the antagonists, and used in this transaction
with the deliberate *purpose* of winning or resolving the conflict.

Communicative text

We cut the dramatic role-play short, unresolved, and immediately asked the participants to get into four groups including members of both sub-groups. Using the tune of 'Shanagolden', a song they had learned during the first session, each of the groups was given ten minutes to write one stanza of 'the ballad which would have been written about this event', in other words to create a piece of text outside the previous frame, but still within the **fictional context** of Ulster, for *communication* – the projected audience for this also only existed within that fiction – this drama had no external audience. The groups worked quite separately, one with the instruction to begin the ballad, two to continue it, and the fourth to finish it. The following was the result – the title was negotiated among the whole group retrospectively, but the text is unchanged apart from minor punctuation adjustments.

The Ballad of the Fields of Orange and the Float of Ignorance

There were some young Australians, they ventured to the
  North
They knew not what they entered, they knew not what they
  sought.
Led through fields of Orange so blindly did they go
They did not see the shamrock, they did not see the woe.

We were innocently singing about lives we did not know
Confronted by six women who saw us as their foe;
They were mourning for their menfolk, their loved ones who
  had died.
We Aussies stood there dumbly, not knowing why they cried.

The Orange float it halted, the people disembarked –
These tourists did not understand the women's troubled
  hearts,
Who sang of their dead husbands, who sang of their distress –
How could the Aussies understand on the float of ignorance?

And as the bright sun faded, their eyes were left with tears.
They left us with confusion, our minds with unknown fears.
A thousand words were spoken, yet most was left unsaid,
And our ignorance left with us, of the living and the dead.

This text is both explicitly poetic and functionally *poetic* and *referential*. It also forms a dramatic symbol *within* the context of the whole dramatic event, and as such it embodies for its participants a measure of the transformed dramatic meaning. The juxtaposition of the first- and third-person plural pronouns is particularly worth noting. They are interchanged throughout: stanzas 1 and 3 place the narrative entirely in the third person; stanza 2 in the specific point of view of 'We Aussies'; stanza 4 uses them equivocally – at the moment that we cut the dramatic action, neither group had in fact 'left' the scene. Two factors are significant about this interchangeability of pronoun and narrative viewpoint: (1) each composition group consisted of participants from *both* role sub-groups; (2) this composition task followed immediately after the action, with no formal de-roling. The participants were aware of the shift out of the central fictional frame (they had, among other things, to shift to another room). There was clearly some residual effect from that enrolment which manifested itself in the poetic text.

Synthetised text

The final activity of the drama consisted of the whole group learning and singing the song, in unison. We had intended this to be a *reflective* activity within the **context of the medium** but, like the final re-enactment in the *Utopia* drama, it took on for the participants an added expressive dimension, difficult to analyse, but for which one of the participants retrospectively quoted the phrase 'emotion recollected in tranquillity' – which as the participant was well aware was Wordsworth's definition of the origin of poetry, and sums up well the aesthetic synthesis embodied in that final dramatic text.[14]

Chapter 8

Negotiating meaning

The word 'meaning' has already been used often during this book, invoking a number of apparently different dimensions. What the word 'meaning' in the arts actually means has been variously defined, including among the more portentous: 'satisfying the need for identity and community',[1] and 'defamiliarisation to recover the sensation of life'.[2] Exponents of drama in education spend a considerable time wrestling with the word, as part of their artistic and professional responsibility for 'learning'; our definitions range from the early 'development through drama'[3] and 'learning through drama'[4] – where meaning is specifically and totally attached to the pedagogical aims – through 'change of insight (or understanding)'[5] where it is attached to the individual's personal meaning systems – via 'deconstructing or reconstructing official reality'[6] to 'subverting the theatricality of schooling'[7] – which ascribe a social construction and even a pro-active component to the dramatic meaning.

At this point, another grammatical caveat is necessary. 'To mean' is a transitive verb – you can't just mean, you have to mean something. Along with nominalisation, intransitivity is a curse of western scholarship, particularly beloved in the upper levels of the education industry. Teachers aim to teach something, and children learn that – or something else. The meanings they share are specific and contextual – or they don't share anything. On the other hand, the teacher-education place where I work has a subject called 'teaching and learning', and believes those lead towards 'understanding'. Teaching what? Learning what? Understanding what? It is all to do with seeking to generalise towards some received or universal truth. When you generalise about knowing, you remove any direct object – knowing geography, the internal combustion engine and Shakespeare are all knowledge. Or are they? Any literate school student knows that when you have a subject and a transitive verb without a direct object, you don't have any meaning. The crucial importance of contextual knowledge in considering dramatic meaning – and the light which it actually sheds on learning theory – will emerge through this chapter.

Artistically speaking, dramatic meaning is inevitably a product of the elements of drama, the outcome of the purposes of the percipients within the totality of the simultaneous contexts in which they are operating. In this chapter I shall try to show that the negotiability of meaning in drama in education is 'limited'. This is in apparent contradiction of Barthes's attractive notion, referred to in the Introduction, that each individual has limitless capacity for renegotiating any artist's meanings. The processuality of meaning in drama is not without bounds. This is because the art form is *collective*, depending to a great extent on specific contractual obligations for its very existence, and upon a very close sharing of participants' purposes made manifest in the management of the **fictional context**. A proportion of the meaning which emerges is therefore shared – as social meaning, at once a part of and apart from the personal constructions of meaning which each individual negotiates within the experience. 'Rites [including drama] cannot exist in an aesthetic or formalist vacuum; they require the context of community.'[8] The signification emerging from the **fictional context** is mediated and transformed through the **contexts of the medium** and **setting**, then further transformed within the participants' **real context**.

AESTHETIC MEANING

Dramatic meaning, like any other, is not a passive construct, nor is it static to be defined. A scholar of more conventional genres of performance drama notes: 'Drama has an operative function . . . rather than mirroring life passively, drama is a means of thinking about life, a way of organising and categorising it . . . not a mirror held up to nature, but a gauge.'[9] The very titles of the two main genres explored in this book, '*in education*' assert that their practitioners believe this to be true. This would seem to be true across the arts, with particular reference to their function in education. An influential report, *The Arts in Schools*, claims that the arts 'make vital contributions to children's education in six main areas':

1 In developing the full variety of human intelligence
2 In developing the ability for creative thought and action
3 In the education of feeling and sensibility
4 In the exploration of values
5 In understanding cultural changes and differences
6 In developing physical and perceptual skills[10]

The arts in education philosophers Peter Abbs and Malcolm Ross make similar claims into similar manifestos.[11] Some of the claims have been touched upon explicitly, all of them by implication, in this book – though to define and justify or dispute them is beyond its scope. However, there is a consonance through all the definitions within this paragraph which suggests that drama shares with the other arts some qualities of meaning which may be labelled *aesthetic*.

MOOD AND AESTHETIC MEANING

Just what happens in a work of art, the experiences which lie between purpose and meaning, and the functions of those involved, have been a major preoccupation of this book, embodied in constant distinctions between percipients, participants, playwright, audience, actors, etc. They are also a preoccupation of many aesthetic education philosophers, and usually resolve themselves into about three or four basic functional modes, within what American visual arts educator Elliott Eisner calls the fourth governing principle of creativity: *aesthetic organisation*.[12] British music specialist Keith Swanwick still uses the terms specific to his art form *composer*, *performer* and *listener* but stresses that these really are interdependent functions – all humans can take on any function – and that negotiation of meaning can happen in any direction among them.[13] He also emphasises the social nature of the creation of meaning in music.[14] In Australia, dance education scholar Warren Lett started the terminological ball rolling a decade ago with *making*, *remaking* and *receiving*.[15] Presumably independently in Britain, literature specialist Abbs came up with *forming*, *presenting*, *responding* and *evaluating*.[16] In other words, similar categorisations have occurred across the arts and across the globe.

Down the ladder a rung, the policy-makers also use shared terminologies frequently derived from the philosophers. A comparison of terms used in official Australian arts education documents clearly shows this:

- Victoria classifies the dimensions *perceiving, transforming, expressing* and *appreciating* (in this rather puzzling order).
- Western Australia has *creating, performing, appreciating* and *managing*.
- New South Wales distinguishes *improvising, organising, performing* and *observing*.
- The Queensland arts manifesto modifies Abbs's categories into *forming, presenting, responding* and *valuing*; the same state's senior drama syllabus further modifies this into *forming, presenting, responding* and *transforming*.[17]

Part of this constant refinement concentrates on the definition of 'responding' or 'appreciating'. For Abbs the word specifically refers to the initial, intuitive, spontaneous and affective response on perceiving and experiencing a work of art without which, for him, there is no aesthetic dimension. This response precedes the conceptualising, symbolising functions which together with it make up the totality of meaning (or meaning potential) inherent in the art work. Where the responding is exclusively that of a spectator to a moment, this may be simply seen – such as the response to a painting, to a haiku, to a song. Where the art work exists more substantially in time for an audience, it becomes more complex: although the totality is not visible until the end, the spectator at a three-hour play or the reader of a novel has time to process his or her first responding, and incorporate this into the continuing responding. In drama in education the responder is simultaneously one of the makers, and even sometimes a presenter. That response, its processing and re-incorporation into the art work, which then produces more responding, provides a self-generative emotional current which contributes not only to the totality of apprehension, but to the tension of the dramatic action itself. This current is in fact the *mood*. It is necessary to find another term at this point, for the word 'response' can easily be interpreted as applying to an *individual*. Drama being a group art, this feeling quality of response is generated not just in individuals, but within the group, a group mood, the atmosphere of the play.

The words 'response' and 'appreciation' sound passive or reactive. Where the participant group are *characters* as well as *audience*, mood's self-generative function makes it a pro-active force. This may sound abstract, but it is actually one of the key indicators to participants and leaders of whether the drama is engaging the group, and providing an appropriate level of tension. Managing mood is therefore a key element of the negotiation of drama, though inevitably it operates at the intuitive and affective level of apprehension. Intervention within the drama whether by the leader or other participants must be made with due concern for the mood. A drama cannot in fact start until the participants are in an appropriate mood. The dominance of the **context of the setting** in schools has led to the whole apparatus of 'warm-up games' and 'starter exercises' developed for the express purpose of creating a congruent responsiveness. The class which has just come into the drama session excited and agitated over an argument with another teacher in the playground is in no mood to continue with a gentle drama on the need to be kind to animals. The students' mood might well be channelled into a play about injustice and authority, or might force that into the 'animals' drama as a theme; the wise teacher usually avoids this apparent opportunity, however, for the students in such a case are at their *least negotiable* and the metaxis which feeds into the drama is unlikely to lead to any negotiability of understanding – that is, their sense of injustice will be transferred straight on to the protagonist of injustice in the drama and lead to closed, inflexible understandings.

DRAMATIC SYMBOLS AND AESTHETIC MEANING

Louis Arnaud Reid, influential in the field of aesthetic education for forty years, wrote two studies separated by over a decade called *Meaning in the Arts*. In the second, after canvassing a number of semantic and referential interpretations, he concludes that aesthetic meaning is multiple and interwoven: a work of art is itself an 'embodiment of meaning'.[18] While it is partially referential, the meaning cannot be entirely extrapolated to the field of reference – which may seem to leave the adherents of instrumental role-play in drama teaching without a rationale. He further asserts that 'the division between a) feeling and the rest of the functioning mind as b) thinking, knowing . . . and as c) being actively interested . . . has been disastrous for the understanding both of feeling and of knowing'. This then leads him to distinguish between comprehension and *apprehension*, which seems to him to be a more accurate word to denote the privileging of the sensuous and affective components of meaning pertaining to an art work, over the rational and cognitive.

Reid's influence may be seen in the thinking of key educators in the arts,[19] including drama. Gavin Bolton takes up Reid in his understanding of the notion of the 'meaning-embodied symbol'.[20] The dialectic which is created between the aesthetic symbol and its referent is another aspect of the *responding* dimension. Bolton's paradox referred to in the previous chapter is relevant here: 'when an action in drama achieves a moment of heightened significance it does so because the meaning created is largely released from its dependence on that action.' Bolton uses the example of a group in a drama about a 'primitive tribe' using marked sweatbands to denote the particular responsibilities within the tribe – in other words *purposively*. 'Gradually people became identified by the sweatbands . . . the sweatbands marked our territory.' In other words they took on an *expressive* function. In both cases they were still closely referential, mimetic signs. The *context of the setting* provided the fortuitous opportunity to turn the sweatbands into dramatic symbols. Two children were absent for one session; their sweatbands were 'found . . . ceremoniously carried back to the cave . . . we sat round them and . . . deciding our fellow tribesmen had met their death, we buried the bands. A succession of meanings had accumulated round the bands, so they became, in the artistic sense, symbolic objects.' Bolton notes the negotiability of the symbols: 'The operative word is "became", because as teacher I am not in a position to predecide, "let's use some sweatbands so that later they can represent the dead bodies of their owners".'

TRANSFORMING MEANING FOR USE

This is a clear exemplar of the processuality of the emergence of dramatic symbols in drama in education, of the social and collective nature of the emergence of meaning in drama, and incidentally of some very deft management of dramatic signs. However, in terms of usable meanings it is problematic. While those symbolic meanings which the sweatbands had accrued had become less narrowly referential to the dramatic action which had produced them, they were still closely tied to and within the **fictional context**. They did not directly set up any dialogue or resonances with the **real context** nor the **context of the medium**. In fact, assumptions embedded in the fiction served to exclude an important element from the **real context**. This is dealt with in more detail below under 'unofficial meanings'. It may also be contrasted with another dramatic symbol which emerged in a drama of Bolton's, a handshake – to be described later in this chapter – far more powerful, and of more far-reaching significance because of its metaxis with all the external contexts.

As Bolton's sympathetic yet critical commentator David Davis observes: at this point in his writing (1978) he 'appears to equate symbolisation with art'.[21] In recent years, like most workers in the genre, Bolton has become significantly more structuralist in his concern to reveal the elements of the form, more daringly post-structuralist in the Brechtian juxtaposition of **fictional context** and **context of the medium**. In 1978, however, rather than taking the further Brechtian step of 'making the world controllable', Bolton took a phenomenological stance, 'regarding the outside world, via the art form, as the means whereby "our deepest levels may be touched" '. This may be contrasted significantly with TIE playwright Geoff Gillham's analysis of a dramatic symbol, described in the Introduction. The play starts with a woodcutter's axe as a tool in the hands of a strong workman and finishes with it transfigured into a weapon of the woodcutter-turned-soldier. Writing from a Trotskyist ideology, Gillham explicitly relates this to the **real context**, and claims that the symbolic gesture only has significant power if it is related by the audience to their own lives. Whether in terms of the impact of any piece of theatre upon the lives of any audience, particularly one strongly influenced by a dominant **context of setting**, this proposal is somewhat specious, will be examined later in this chapter. However, it serves to illustrate the contrasting perceptions of two workers who in their practice and in their use of symbols in that practice are not dissimilar and who admire each other's work.

This may to some extent be resolved in the notion from the world of education of 'transformational' learning, which accords

Negotiating meaning   223

comfortably with the recent use of this word in arts and drama
education circles – both Victoria and Queensland use 'transformation' in their arts documents as one of the dimensions of aesthetic
experience. In educational philosophy the phrase 'transformational learning' is used as a concept oppositional to 'reproductive
learning', and this has influenced current thinking in drama in
education, or at least current terminology.[22] Transformational
learning may be simply defined as that which is capable of being
used in other contexts. For any learning to be useful to the learner
(in Piaget's language, fully assimilated or internalised) meanings
created in the arts and drama must be capable of transformation
into other forms *and other contexts*. In other words, it must be
socialised. This proposition would be a truism to Marxists like
David Davis and Geoff Gillham, and entirely consonant with
Bolton's own practice, which is far less individualistic than his
earlier writing implies.

MEANING AND IDEOLOGY

It is not, however, necessary to take an inflexible ideological
position before one can approach drama in education with some
expectation of creating meanings which may fulfil the 'education' part of the title of our genre. It is of course quite possible for
any teacher to take varying ideological standpoints according to
the purposes of the moment, the particular **context of setting** and
educational objective – as regional drama resource consultant
one colleague was simultaneously working in a school developing narrowly pedagogical drama resources for manual arts
teachers and devising a radical and possibly subversive approach
towards educating young people forced by the employment
situation to stay at school.[23]

From the standpoint of a local authority Drama Adviser, Jon
Neelands shows a pragmatic tolerance for the range of ideological standpoints likely to pertain to teachers, and demonstrates
neatly that drama is an appropriate medium for exploring issues
across that range.[24]

The phenomenologist standpoint*

in terms of a *neutral* stance we can . . . establish with the class

* My terminology, not his.

> . . . a range of informed points of view which are representative of the whole spectrum of opinions, and which challenge the group's existing perceptions.

An example of this is the range of attitudes to military conscription shown in Dorothy Heathcote's *Crossroads* drama.[25] The adolescent students were encouraged to explore and demonstrate a wide range of attitudes towards the notion of military call-up. The drama itself crystallised these in action, with the students, in role as Ancient Greek villagers, accepting or rejecting a traditional potsherd, symbolic of accepting one's duty to the country. In the reflective discussion following the drama, the teacher is entirely accepting of the choices made by the students in the drama, and of their justifications for those choices made afterwards. She allows the students to negotiate and reinforce their own ideologies through the drama. At no time (at least, so far as is revealed in the film and accompanying commentary) was the question of the Vietnam War mentioned, although at the time – 1970 – the American and Australian drafts, as well as Britain's non-involvement, were very pertinent issues. Heathcote was concerned with issues in 'universal' terms, not particularities.

The liberal reformist standpoint

> in terms of a *balanced* stance we can represent the context so as to emphasise the complexity and duality of the disputed issue and so avoid the tendency to polarise as in 'us and them'.

An example of this would be *Forest Park*, a drama with upper primary children from a city suburb about the issue of forest conservation versus the timber industry.[26] The children had been camping and studying the topic of conservation, and had become very committed to this side of the debate. The teachers accordingly put them in the roles of top woodcraft workers and artists. The scene was set round the opening of a new theme park and tourist attraction in a rainforest area, where the tourists would be able to watch the crafts workers at work, and buy their products. At the 'opening ceremony', the 'Environment Minister' unexpectedly attacked the notion for its despoliation of the environment and refused to open the Forest Park. The children

were thus put in the dilemma between their genuine commitment to conservation, and their equally genuine commitment to
their roles as crafts workers dependent on quality timber for their
livelihoods. Half an hour's problem-solving later, in the drama
they were allowed a resolution of the problem, through intelli-
gent compromises and solutions, although after the drama, the
real-life implications of their choices were explored more con-
frontingly in discussion. In fact, this subject matter and the
dramatic ambush were entirely controlled by the teachers, so no
explicit negotiation occurred with the children. However, what
dictated the starting points and structuring of the drama was the
initial attitudes of the children. Had this drama taken place in a
timber town, it would have been structured entirely differently,
and with a quite different **fictional context**.

The radical standpoint

in terms of a *committed* stance we can demonstrate the
contexts that have generated our own perspectives on the
issue, so that our commitment is seen in context. We can
demonstrate the social consequences of, and alternatives to,
attitudes . . . '

A good example of the use of drama in this way is Kathy Joyce's
descriptions of her overt policy as a Drama Adviser, to 'tackle the
problem of gender role stereotyping in school, family and
society' with the intention of 'using and creating the opportunities to counter [it] whenever possible, but in such a way that the
children themselves become aware, yet do not reject the ideas'.[27]
She stresses that, although she has seen *direct* engagement with
the issue – 'I recollect watching a group of fourth year boys
sensitively changing and powdering "babies" in a fictitious
society where men ran the creche and women went out to work' –
most of her work during the project involved 'such issues [being]
implicit within the dramatic content and the degree to which
they are explored depends on the level of awareness of the teacher
and his/her relationship with the class'. This account is particularly interesting as it is directly challenging of established
social mores. Had she been, like Gillham, explicitly revolution-
ary, she would have been unlikely to have been appointed to, or
have held long, her position, and would have been unable to

engender such projects formally within a male-dominated system.

Each of these three major standpoints involves a slightly different renegotiation of the **fictional context** with the students, and in that difference of negotiation lies the *learning* that is likely to be achieved, the particular 'change of understanding' . . . from what to what. Each of the **contexts** will generate a different meaning, or set of meanings, which is in line with the ideological framework of the teacher and/or the institution. *That*, however, is also mediated by the ideological frameworks of the students, and their attitudinal starting points.

UNPREDICTED MEANINGS

There's the rub. We've already seen that drama is an oblique medium – not a mirror, but a gauge. This quality, added to the uncontrollability of where the students are coming from, makes for unpredictable meaning outcomes. It could be said that the very word 'education' to some extent limits negotiability. Throughout this book I have emphasised the leader, the teacher and the playwright. The teacher may cede some of the playwright's function to the group, but in practice this is usually far outweighed by his or her own greater command of the elements of dramatic form, by the convention of schooling that the teacher is the focus of action in the classroom, and most of all by the dominance of the **context of the setting**. Where negotiation of subject matter or form exists, it is invariably mediated by the teacher's objectives, aspirations and level of acceptance of students' contributions. It is part of the nature of formal education to negotiate children towards outcomes acceptable to the teacher. That this can cause contractual problems even outside a school setting has been examined in regard to *The Great Circle* where the participants expected a greater acceptance of their contributions than they received from the very dominating leader (who was a teacher).

Dramatic meaning, however, has a maverick quality. Most formal education works on explicit assumptions, expressed in the 'objectives' for lessons and units of work. The word 'objectives' implies a whole grammar of assumption in education (educational grammar lesson number 3!). Schooling follows our society in attempting to subdue or deny the dynamic (verbal) and deeply subjective nature of knowledge by reifying (another word for nominalising – turning doing into things) and objectivising knowledge. The very word 'subject' as it is used in schools has been objectivised into a nominal construct denoting a compartmentalised area of knowledge, with 'objectives', no less. It is usually assumed, implicitly and unquestioningly, that if the lesson or unit has been successfully completed, *those* objectives have been fulfilled – the apparatus of evaluation and assessment in education exists primarily for the purpose of checking and ratifying this. What is very rarely assessed is what other, divergent meanings may have arisen, not part of the original objectives at all. These learnings occasionally receive the red pen treatment 'this was not asked for', but far more often pass unnoticed. The likelihood of such uncontrolled meaning-making in drama in education is accentuated both by the oblique nature of drama and by its direct appeal to the students' attitudes as starting points. The arts philosopher Robert Witkin elegantly reveals this in a study of *Dragons*, a theatre in education programme for infants.[28] The team's explicit central objective was to 'counter stereotyping' by showing that things are often not what they seem. To achieve this they took a dragon as their central character, and set out to deconstruct the stereotypic frightening image of a dragon. Witkin deconstructs the dramatic action to demonstrate the paradox that in the very process of achieving their objective they were strongly reinforcing other stereotypes, such as that of a mother as a figure of safety, security and wisdom. Witkin takes pains to stress that this in itself is useful knowledge, which would have been a perfectly acceptable objective had the team been aware that they were focussed on it.

OFFICIAL AND UNOFFICIAL MEANINGS

Such maverick meanings may not always be so congruent with what is educationally acceptable. The problematic nature of drama within education is accentuated when it is used for specifically polemical purposes. This may be seen clearly in a piece of performance theatre in education: *Mia v. Trike*.[29] The playwright, Pat Cranney, regards himself as a processual playwright, explicitly concerned with assisting audiences to use drama as an expression of their social identity. He also regards himself as an educator, with social values he wishes to share with his audiences. In particular, his general social position, which he wanted this play to illustrate, is that 'the social barriers which our capitalist society puts up are also human barriers. The social structures dictate the human values.' It is open to question whether the tension between those two general purposes was resolved in the play.

Four sets of specific purposes, or objectives, were canvassed in devising this play, as is not uncommon in TIE.

1 *Education systems* TIE companies are often given very specific objectives to work to by groups of teachers, company education advisory committees or curriculum advisers. In this case the only directive from this quarter, to 'get the children to use their imaginations', was felt by the playwright to be unhelpfully generalised.

2 *The company*: Sidetrack Theatre provided a number of parameters for acceptable objectives. It is a company with a strong commitment to being an agent of radical social change. It is particularly concerned with (a) repression, (b) multi-cultural issues in Australia, (c) the communities within and around Sydney.

3 *The audience*: Cranney took the highly negotiative step of selecting two socially contrasting high schools, to research the concerns and interests of children from the age group (years 7 and 8). He workshopped ideas and discussed with the children what they might like the play to be about. Their decisions were that they wanted the play to be futuristic, big, an adventure, and about the world of video.

4 *The writer himself*: One perception of some of the children helped to refine one of Cranney's own purposes, about the exploitative nature of society. The children, especially at the predominantly white Anglo-Saxon girls' high school, voiced the opinion that 'on the dole you're bludging'. The time of this research was during the period of the 1987 stock market crash, and the International Year of the Homeless. Cranney, a writer who believes in the impact of drama upon the **real context**, decided to incorporate an exploration of the nature of homelessness and unemployment into his own purposes. He wanted the play to explore the destructive force of tourism, the drift which tourism creates from manufacturing to service industry, and the unnecessary exploitation of natural resources. His generalised

objective of 'reaching into an aspect of the children's culture and causing reflection on that culture' became refined into exploring the theme of video culture offered to him by the schoolchildren, *'to set up genres of video culture, and the clichés of the culture, and then subvert them'*. This last quotation reveals the underlying polemical intent.

This implies a lot of objectives. Attempting to weld them together in terms of the children's interests, Cranney created a play which was an adventure, big, about video culture and futuristic, as they had requested. However, in terms of his and the company's ideological objectives, it was very problematic.

The play finished with a resolution of tension, which embodied the polemic – the play gave answers to the questions it had raised, which were explicitly concerned with power and control. The affirmative statements or answers implicit in that resolution of tension were evident in the action of the play, and confirmed by the playwright himself: (a) that individual resourcefulness and initiative can change society; (b) that individuals together are stronger than inhuman systems; (c) that human values can triumph over official oppression; (d) that youth is not powerless to oppose social evil, perhaps even change it.

These statements are in line with the rhetoric of both liberal and radical education. I believe it is questionable to what extent any of them are confirmed by the real-life experience of most of the young audiences, though the questions which preceded these answers are obviously of concern to the youngsters. *If* it is questionable, then it might be suggested that a more genuinely educational approach would be neither to assert it explicitly (which Cranney does not do) nor to assert it implicitly through the resolution of dramatic action (which he does), but to offer it to them to examine as a proposition; in other words, to leave a question, not an answer. To provide an explicit answer invites rejection, to provide an implicit answer invites the maverick response, exemplified in a brief analysis of this programme's action.

The action does implicitly raise questions for the audience about the nature and usefulness of defiance:

• What is the nature of property, and what gives any one section of the people private rights to that property?

- Has an agent of unjust laws the right to power?
- Are vandalism and the protest of spraycan graffiti automatically wrong?

All three questions are raised in the narrative, which could be said to illustrate the anarchic aspect of art – validating rebellious thoughts among the audience, like Punch defying morality, Indiana Jones defying probability or Robin Hood defying oligarchy. Another viewer could see it as a safe outlet, for a one-hour excursion into a **fictional context** is highly unlikely to affect the real behaviour of the audience and turn them into assaulters of police, expert spraycan protesters, or computer hackers – three actions depicted approvingly in the drama. A further question arises, then, as to whether in the guise of a social medicine this play is actually providing a cathartic placebo. A closer analysis of the audiences would be necessary to see whether the meaning they derived was in fact that which the playwright proposes.

Another alternative meaning, or at least a corruption of the author's intent, could be derived from the glamorising of the use of graffiti as a protest. It is not necessary here to make a value judgment about the appropriateness of spraycan graffiti on railways, a common practice of young people in Sydney. However, the play does. It validates this as a way, the only way, for the oppressed protagonists to fight back against their oppressors. In the final scene, the two heroes return, in danger, to finish their graffiti; the message derived might well be that to do so is both successful *and sufficient*.

Both the female heroes use martial arts against the male agents of repression; this is portrayed as admirable and successful, and it is designed to make a feminist statement. It could equally be construed as glamorising and validating the use of personal violence as a means of opposition, upon one's brother as well as on the police.

The writer's attempt to 'subvert the video culture' is equally suspect in terms of the action. On one level, this does occur: the hero, Mia, rejects video culture and saves her fellow from the strong, gratuitously violent influence which it exerts, leaving her unlovely brother as its sole supporter. However, to show Mia triumphing over her oppression with the means at her disposal, namely her own knowledge of video technology, carries two messages:

1 the 'official' metaphor: that the resourcefulness of the human spirit will use whatever means are at its disposal to get out of its prison.
2 an 'unofficial' meaning: Mia has already been shown to have rejected formal education. Her success in hacking into the monorail computer, which saves the heroes, validates the time she has herself spent in video parlours getting to know the technology.

The company itself was divided about the meanings emerging from the ending. Originally, Cranney had intended the secondary, more privileged hero, Sue, to return and use the power of her privilege to save Mia. The team thought this ending was sentimental, and that it carried an ideologically unacceptable subtext of legitimising the power structure and leaving Mia in an 'Uncle Tom' position. The ending was changed for the girls to use their own martial arts skills to get even, and then to make their own graffiti protest on Parliament House, with the consequences left up in the air. Even with that question left unanswered, this more open ending carries the message of legitimising what might be said to be a simplistic rhetorical gesture, without in any way exploring why this action is genuinely liberating and not just futile and self-destructive.

This critique does not assert that all these alternative meanings were taken up by the students, just that they were available to them. Their responses to the meanings inherent in the dramatic action would have been conditioned by two key factors:

1 The **real context** of their own values and attitudes, part individual, part shared within the community of those watching (the age, social perceptions, class orientations and group interests and preoccupations).
2 This in turn would be mediated by the very strong **context of the setting** within which the students were responding, the values and mores of the specific school where the performance took place.

Drama in education is susceptible in just the same way to maverick meanings and unacknowledged assumptions. Gavin Bolton's 'tribal sweatbands' drama appears very much of its period, when 'primitive tribe' dramas were a commonplace device to provide a simplified **dramatic context** for the class to examine a particular aspect of group behaviour, such as survival skills or leadership. Some unacknowledged assumptions inherent in the phrase 'primitive tribe' would make that drama less acceptable these days, particularly in Australia. Aboriginal observers of drama in education have pointed out strongly that, in the whole field of social education, the word 'primitive' carries derogatory associations and is not even accurate – so-called primitive societies across the world are being shown to be primitive only in their prior grasp of western technology and weaponry.[30] Moreover, the concept of tribality, where it is not derogatory, implies a particularity of social behaviour that an Anglo-Saxon teacher and children would be unlikely to have access to. In their terms, by even using the words 'primitive tribe', Bolton was unconsciously reinforcing racist attitudes.

Bolton is the most assiduous of workers in the genre of drama in education in constantly re-evaluating his work. In his book *Drama as Education*,[31] in a chapter actually entitled 'In Context', he showed a cautious shift away from inward-looking phenomenology, where the learner is the 'passive observer of the given world', to one where 'learning is a process of finding a frame through which to make connections'. In this he acknowledged his debt to David Davis, in the work of whose students he found an example of drama in education which 'epitomises what this book has been about'. The work was a lesson plan for a drama on 'rape'. Ironically, the considerable debate which this very example aroused caused him deep uneasiness. The lesson was challenging but protective; it left the questions it asked unanswered to be taken up in discussion, but it also contained an unspoken, at the time unnoticed, assumption: that by dressing attractively, girls are inviting rape. Later he published a recantation of his former approval, along with a warning about the dangers of unforeseen assumptions.[32]

SYMBOL, CONTEXT AND MEANING

This chapter concentrates to some extent on the work of one drama educator, Bolton, because both his practice and his writing have a clarity that is extremely useful and can also be beguiling, and reveal maverick meanings of its own, which can lead to further discoveries about this evanescent and slippery quality called dramatic process. To conclude this study, there's a

famous dramatic moment which occurred in another drama
which Gavin Bolton, who is white, was leading in South Africa
in 1980 with a class of black children and a lot of mainly white
adult onlookers. It is significant that this moment was created by
the participant, not the leader. Here's his description:

> I was recently working with a class of fourteen year old
> coloured and black children in South Africa. Towards the end
> of the drama lesson, for which these politically aware pupils
> had chosen a topic painfully close to their everyday exper-
> ience, I role-played a journalist interviewing, seventy years
> after the 'terrible incident', an old man of 84 who had been but
> a 14-year-old boy at the time, inviting him to recall what had
> occurred seventy years previously – in fact a few minutes
> earlier in the lesson. The black boy adopted an old man's
> rambling mode of dredging up from his memory, but then I
> switched the angle of the topic. The dialogue went something
> like this:
>
> JOURNALIST: This is now the year 2050. You must have seen a
> lot of changes in South Africa in the past seventy
> years.
> OLD MAN: I have.
> JOURNALIST: Would you mind telling me, Sir, what for you has
> been the greatest change?
> OLD MAN: We are equal now. (The old man looked the
> interviewer in the eye, not with resentment nor
> hostility, not even triumph but with self-assur-
> ance, dignity and pride. Spontaneously the
> journalist and the old man shook hands.)[33]

Bolton goes on to note that 'the attendance of the rest of the class
and all the black teachers watching was riveted by that simple
action. It was what Dorothy Heathcote calls "a moment of awe",
for it had so many implications for all who were present.' It
should not be too difficult to see this piece of process drama as an
example of dramatic art form, a climactic moment negotiated
spontaneously, but minutely focussed and subject to tight
control of the elements of situation and role, of narrative and
tension, and of dramatic mood and symbol. As he points out: 'It
was indeed Drama: a simple action embodying significance – the
basic medium of drama is embodied in that handshake.'

This moment is a graphic demonstration that the metaxis

between the **real** and the **fictional contexts** always exists where there is powerful drama. There's nothing more universal than the **real context** – you can't get beyond that.

Let's suppose this dramatic moment had happened, as it might well have, not in Johannesburg in 1981, between a white adult and a black child with a group of black participants and a group of white onlookers, but between two children in an Australian school, in a drama class of well-off white Anglo-Australians. It would still have been a moment of dramatic significance, a genuine dramatic symbol – but it would not have been 'a moment of awe'.

If we strip the mystical rhetoric away from the phenomenological belief in 'universal essences fundamental to man's humanity',[34] those two Australian children could certainly have recognised that this moment had currency in other human contexts beyond their experience, and thus it would give them a sense of affinity with others. This generalised apprehending is significant, but perhaps no more so than the similar recognition of shared significance which a joke brings – and that's not to denigrate drama or jokes.

The individual meanings, too, which emerged would be entirely different, according to what the Australian children brought into the lesson – for Bolton himself and all the South African participants the personal meanings were bound up with the **real context**.

And that points to the deepest artistic meanings being not the most universal, but the most *specific*, being inextricably woven into and part of *that* **real context**. The **fictional context** allowed reality to be suspended, but it stayed very, very present, and the power of the drama was the resonances between the two contexts, the metaxis. In their real life of 1980, South African black and white rarely touched, whites scarcely ever deferred to blacks, children and teachers did not shake hands, they were patently not equal. The boy was making, and participants and onlookers were actively accepting, an ethical statement of significance in their real world, highlighting *what should be* by presenting *what could not be*, within the permission granted by the fiction. It was only a moment of awesome significance because all those participants together made and acknowledged the shared meaning, and in that moment at least endorsed the ethical message. Unarguably this was a *social* making of meaning, arising from the climax of this social event that was the drama. It was simultaneously highly theatrical; from the similar moment that happened to me two years later (referred to in chapter 4) I would vouch that the boy was not just role-playing in the dramatic context but was deliberately making the statement within the real context, as playwright and actor, both to his classmates, who identified with and endorsed the gesture, and especially to the onlookers *and the teacher*, who were at that moment a real audience.

More specifically in fact, the moment was a climactic resolution of tension in the **fictional context** – that is, it answered the questions within that context – which simultaneously drew attention to the unanswered questions in the **real context**:

- Will what happens in South Africa in the next seventy years bear any similarity to the events of our drama?
- Will there ever be a moment when black and white are able to say 'with self-assurance, "we are equal now" '?
- What will our own involvement be in striving to bring this about?

It therefore carried a double tension, the tension embodied in those very questions of power and control, and the tension *between* that tension and the resolved drama itself. The awesomeness in that moment lay entirely within the processual artistry – of leader and participants – that created the whole dramatic event.

Notes

INTRODUCTION

1 See M. Esslin (1987) *The Field of Drama*, Methuen, London, p. 38.
2 For a glimpse into the sense of dynamism and kinship which permeates aboriginal knowledge, see J. Miller (1985) *Koori: A Will to Win*, Angus & Robertson, Sydney, p. 1.
3 J. Belo (1970) *Balinese Culture*, Columbia University Press, New York.
4 M.A.K.Halliday is a leading and influential figure in sociolinguistics who has been involved in the detailed definition of genre in language.
5 For further information about this debate, and how the word genre is used particularly by linguists, see, e.g. G. Kress (1985) *Linguistic Processes in Sociocultural Practice*, Deakin University Press, Geelong.
6 Dr John Carroll, Charles Sturt University, New South Wales (1991).
7 See T. Jackson (1980) *Learning Through Theatre*, Manchester University Press, Manchester, and J. O'Toole (1977) *Theatre in Education*, Hodder & Stoughton, London.
8 Aristotle (*c.* 330 BC) *The Art of Poetry / The Poetics*, variously translated and published, section 6.
9 This model was originally devised by myself and a colleague for a schools' textbook, J. O'Toole and B. Haseman (1988) *Dramawise*, Heinemann, London, though it has been embroidered for this book.
10 For operative fantasy, see A. Davidson and J. Fay (1972) *Fantasy in Childhood*, Greenwood, Westport, Conn. For conscious adoption of role see, e.g. M. Banton (1965) *Roles*, Tavistock, London, and E. Goffman (1971) *The Presentation of Self in Everyday Life*, Penguin, London. For the dramatic components of ritual, many writers since Jung have analysed these, including R. Hornby (1986) *Drama, Metadrama and Perception*, Associated University Press, Cranbury, NJ.
11 See M. A. K. Halliday (1985) *Spoken and Written Language*, Deakin University Press, Geelong.
12 See R. Barthes (1977) *The Death of the Author*, Fontana, London.

13 This phrase was coined by M. Pfister (1988) *The Theory and Analysis of Drama*, Cambridge University Press, Cambridge, p. 19.

14 Esslin, op. cit., p. 11.

15 The relevant bits of Aristotle and Horace, and their descendants from early Renaissance times (e.g. Scaliger and Minturno), through to playwright-scholars Lope de Vega and Calderón, are anthologised in B. Clark (1955) *European Theories of the Drama*, Crown, NY, pp. 38–69.

16 Sir Philip Sidney (1595) *In Defence of Poesie*, also known as *An Apologie for Poetrie*, reprinted 1951, Cambridge University Press, Cambridge; John Dryden (c. 1670) *A Defence of Dramatic Poesy*, Dent, London.

17 Ben Jonson (c. 1620) *Discoveries*, reprinted 1889, Cassell, London, p. 141.

18 Useful popular introductions which chart this discovery include T. Eagleton (1983) *Literary Theory: An Introduction*, Blackwell, Oxford, and R. Selden (1984) *A Reader's Guide to Contemporary Literary Theory*, Harvester, Brighton.

19 A. Marshall (1992) 'Comparative studies in performance training in traditional Aboriginal ceremony and contemporary Australian theatre', *Journal of the Queensland Association for Drama in Education* 16(2), Brisbane.

20 W. Benjamin (1973) *Understanding Brecht*, New Left Books, London.

21 Augusto Boal (1979) *Theatre of the Oppressed*, Pluto Press, London.

22 For example, *New Theatre Quarterly* (no. 14) consisted of features on: the ideological constraints on theatre in Thatcher's Britain; a Shakespearean rediscovery through production; a poem by a street theatre entertainer; a study of a nineteenth-century genre in its historical context; an article on games and their theatrical application; a comparison of spaces for two Shakespearean productions; a comparison of two productions of a play by Ibsen; an account of theatre and social issues in Malawi; a comparative analysis of actor training in Italy.

23 C. Marowitz (1990) *The Marowitz Shakespeare*, Boyars, New York, variously performed by students.

24 J. Derrida (1978) *Writing and Difference*, Chicago University Press, Chicago.

25 Seminar session chaired by me: 'The nature of playwriting', Interplay '85 1st International Festival of Young Playwrights, Sydney, 1985.

26 I have assessed for the Australian National Playwrights' Centre since 1984, and my perception is confirmed by the two directors during this period, Terry Clarke and Kingston Anderson.

27 S.T. Coleridge (1817) *Biographia Literaria*, chapter 13.

28 This word, now current usage in writing in drama in education, is first used in this way by Boal, op. cit.

29 R. Chorley and P. Huggett (1967) *Models in Geography*, Methuen, London.

30 R. Walford (1970) *Games in Geography*, Longmans, Harlow.

31 C. O'Neill (1987) 'Mapping meaning', keynote address to the 12th
    NADIE Conference, Brisbane, and J. McLeod (1987) 'Drama as
    metaphor', conference workshop, NADIE, Brisbane.

32 M. Banton (1965) *Roles*, Tavistock Press, London, p. 2.

33 Sir J. Frazer (1922) *The Golden Bough*, Macmillan, London.

34 E. Goffman (1971) *The Presentation of Self in Everyday Life*,
    Penguin, London; R.D. Laing (1966) *The Divided Self*, Penguin,
    London; E. Berne (1975) *Games People Play*, Penguin, London.

35 Plato (c. 360 BC) *The Republic*, variously translated, including B.
    Jowett (1947) Penguin, London, p. 82.

36 Aristotle, op. cit. (Introduction), p. 36.

37 Horace, in B. Clark (1918) *European Theories of the Drama*, Crown,
    New York, p. 29.

38 Gavin Bolton himself draws attention to this paradox, in his essay
    (1983) 'Drama in education: learning medium or arts process', in D.
    Davis and C. Lawrence (eds) (1986) *Gavin Bolton: Selected Writings
    on Drama in Education*, Longmans, London.

39 *Disbelief* by La Boîte Youth Theatre, 1988, reviewed in *Lowdown*
    10(4), Carclew, Adelaide.

40 E. Goffman (1974) *Frame Analysis*, Harper & Row, New York.

41 Sir Philip Sidney (1595) *In Defence of Poesie*, also known as *An
    Apologie for Poetry*, variously published. In the Cambridge
    University Press (1951) edition this quotation appears on p. 53. I
    have added the emphasis.

42 G. Bateson (1955) 'A theory of play and fantasy', in J. Bruner *et al.*
    (eds) (1976) *Play: A Reader*, Penguin, London, p. 123.

43 Ibid., p. 127.

44 D. Heathcote (1975) 'Drama and learning', in L. Johnson and C.
    O'Neill (eds) (1984) *Dorothy Heathcote: Collected Writings on
    Education and Drama*, Hutchinson, London.

45 This analogy is how we tried to elucidate the word for secondary
    students, in O'Toole and Haseman, op. cit.

46 Or variations, as the classicist scholars like de la Paille and Boileau
    disputed the details.

47 G. Bolton (1990) 'Constraint in drama', *SCYPT Journal* 19, Standing
    Conference of Young People's Theatre, London.

48 Particularly by Dorothy Heathcote, op. cit., p. 94, by Chris Lawrence
    (1982) 'Teacher and role', *2D: Journal of Dance and Drama* 1(2): 21,
    Leicester, and by a group of in-service teachers including Chris
    Lawrence (1982) 'Dramatic Tension', *London Drama* 6(6): 15–17.

49 *Be Aware* (1985) participation TIE for intellectually disabled second-
    ary students devised by Jacq Hamilton and myself. Queensland
    Special Education Workshop 1985 (documenting video).

50 L. Vygotsky (1933) 'Play and its role in the mental development of
    the child' in Bruner *et al.* (eds) op. cit.

51 For example the structuralist M. Pfister (1988) *The Theory and
    Analysis of Drama*, Cambridge University Press, and the post-

Freudian psychologists H. and S. Kreitler (1973) *The Psychology of the Arts*, Duke University Press, Durham, NC.
52 O'Neill, op. cit.
53 B. Bettelheim (1976) *The Uses of Enchantment*, Alfred Knopf, New York, p. 5.
54 E. Bentley (1965) *The Life of the Drama*, Methuen, London, p. 12.
55 These phrases were coined by the educational linguist James Moffett (1968) *Teaching the Universe of Discourse*, Houghton Mifflin, Boston, p. 62, and taken up for drama in education by Ken Byron (1986) *Drama in the English Classroom*, Methuen, London, p. 74.
56 This drama, taught by Gavin Bolton in 1977, is described in detail in chapter 4.
57 Dorothy Heathcote developed the convention and coined the phrase; though it was in common currency for some years previously, the first reference in print that I can find is in Heathcote (1984) 'Drama as context for talking and writing', in Johnson and O'Neill (eds), op. cit., p. 144.
58 E. Hirsch 'Validity in interpretation', in Eagleton, op. cit. The British critic of this ilk, F.R. Leavis, was very influential on a generation of English literature teachers.
59 See O'Toole, op. cit., chapter 6: 'The perils and pleasures of participation'.
60 Bolton Octagon TIE programme (1974) *Holland New Town*, described in detail in my book *Theatre in Education* (see n. 7 above).
61 P. Davies (1988) *Storming St Kilda by Tram*, performed by Theatreworks Melbourne. See chapter 5.
62 *Yarranlea Years* (1989) Brisbane CAE. See chapter 4.
63 R. Tulloch (1982) *Year Nine Are Animals*, Heinemann, Melbourne (and reprinted in the UK as *The Fourth Year Are Animals*).
64 *Bruvvers*, Bruvvers Community Theatre Company, Byker, Newcastle upon Tyne.
65 Aristotle, op. cit., pp. 14–18.
66 This framework is derived and modified from the work of Pfister, op. cit.
67 In a drama on *Prisoners of War*, featured in the film *Three Looms Waiting* (1971), BBC Films, London.
68 The precise definition in this book of that very loose portmanteau word 'emotion' appears in chapter 4.
69 R. Barthes (1984) *The Rustle of Language*, Blackwell, Oxford, p. 77.
70 See S. Langer (1953) *Feeling and Form*, Routledge & Kegan Paul, London, and Esslin, op. cit.
71 Quoted by N. Morgan (1991) 'The place of learners in the teaching process', *NADIE Journal* 15(2), Sydney.
72 G. Gillham (1980) 'Symbols in drama', *SCYPT Journal* 10, Standing Conference of Young People's Theatre, London.
73 See D. Morton (1984) *Drama for Capability*, National Association for Drama Advisers, Banbury, and D. Davis (1990) 'In defence of drama in education', *NADIE Journal* 15(1).
74 Bolton originally expressed this slightly differently as 'drama for

change of insight' in (1979) *Towards a Theory of Drama in Education*, Longmans, London, p. 41.

75 See chapter 1, n. 6 below for a detailed list of the prominent works in this movement.

76 Aristotle, op. cit., p. 20.

77 *Bill Rogers Mining Company* (1980) taught by Brad Haseman, video, Brisbane South Region Drama Resource Project.

1 THE DRAMATIC CONTEXTS

1 M. Esslin (1987) *The Field of Drama*, Methuen, London, p. 38.

2 P. Slade (1954) *Child Drama*, Cassell, London, pp. 40–51. Slade was a Drama Adviser in Birmingham, England, and had a great influence on the next generation of drama teachers, including later pioneers like Dorothy Heathcote.

3 Ibid., p. 48.

4 C. Jung (1958) *Psychology and Religion*, quoted in R. Courtney (1968) *Play, Drama and Thought*, Cassell, London, p. 136.

5 B. Butler (1983) 'Drama in education versus the theatricality of schooling', *SAADYT Journal* 5(2), South African Association for Drama in Education, and A. Hunt (1976) *Hopes for Great Happenings*, Eyre Methuen, London.

6 J. Holt (1968) *How Children Fail*, Penguin, London; I. Illich (1976) *Deschooling Society*, Penguin, London; N. Postman and C. Weingartner. (1981) *Teaching as a Subversive Activity*, Penguin, London; E. Reimer (1971) *School Is Dead*, Penguin, London; P. Freire (1970) *Pedagogy of the Oppressed*, Seabury Press, New York.

7 G. Lang (1979) 'Far more fundamental than the fundamentals', *NADIE Journal* 4(2): 56.

8 The place of Slade *et al.* in the history of drama in education, along with educational and ideological perspectives on that history, may be found in G. Bolton (1984) *Drama as Education*, Longmans, London, or J. Deverall (1975) 'Drama, subject and service', *Young Drama* 3(1) and 3(2), Thimble Press, London.

9 P. Stevenson and J. O'Toole (eds) (1988) *Pretending to Learn*, Brisbane CAE.

10 For instance, by the arts education philosophers Malcolm Ross (1984) *The Aesthetic Impulse*, Pergamon Press, Oxford; and Peter Abbs and his drama specialist contributor Chris Havell (1987) *Living Powers*, Falmer Press, London.

11 This drama, described on pp. 183 ff of Stevenson and O'Toole (eds), op. cit., was devised by a student, Margaret Guy, with almost no practical experience of drama teaching.

12 Originally devised by Kathy Madden for her class of year 7 (12-year-olds), this drama was subsequently used almost identically with a group of year 12 (16-year-old) students, to the professed satisfaction of both teachers and sets of students.

13 In Australia at the time of writing (1991), this is happening both

informally, through the influence of scientific humanists like Dr David Suzuki receiving popular media time, and formally, with the presentation of the Government's Speedie Report.

14 This has been particularly vigorous in the UK, partially in response to the social changes and changes in education imposed by the Thatcher Government (for explicit confirmation of this, see the Joint Conference Report *Positive Images* (1985), National Association for Drama Teachers, St Albans England). It has been less of a mainstream preoccupation in Australia and Canada.

15 Butler, op. cit.

16 Documented in the classic film *Three Looms Waiting – an account of Dorothy Heathcote at Work* (1971), BBC Films, London.

17 This has been strong in Australia, see R. Perry (1984) *Makebelieve Play and the Preschool Child*, Queensland Preschool Curriculum Project, Brisbane.

18 Slade, op. cit., p. 45.

19 G. Boomer (1984) 'The politics of drama teaching', *NADIE Journal* 8(2), Melbourne.

20 Observations reinforced by descriptions in the *NADIE Journal* 7(2): 25–8.

21 J. O'Toole and B. Haseman (1988) *Dramawise*, Heinemann, London, including the prototype for the model forming the basis of this book, is an attempt to address this critique.

22 See G. Bolton (1977) 'Creative drama as an art form', reprinted in D. Davis and C. Lawrence (eds) (1986) *Gavin Bolton: Selected Writings on Drama in Education*, Longmans, London.

23 Both these quotations are from E. Bentley (ed.) (1981) *The Brecht Commentaries*, Eyre Methuen, London, the first on *The Good Woman of Setzuan*, p. 88; the second on *Mother Courage* p. 120.

24 This quotation, together with a cogent gloss on it, appears in J. Neelands (1985) 'Issues or contexts?' in *Positive Images* (see n. 14 above).

25 H. Rosen (1980) 'The dramatic mode', *NADIE Journal* 5(2), Brisbane.

26 This drama I have on report from the teacher, Debbie le Bhers (1989), at Brisbane State High School.

27 Tynewear TIE Co. (1980) *Labour for the Lord*, writer Phil Woods.

2 ROLE

1 For example, Erving Goffman and Michael Banton: see nn. 3 and 2 below.

2 M. Banton (1965) *Roles*, Tavistock Press, London, p. 2.

3 E. Goffman (1974) *Frame Analysis*, Harper & Row, New York.

4 B. Wilshire (1982) *Role and Identity*, Indiana University Press, Bloomington, pp. ix and 245.

5 M. van Ments (1983) *The Effective Use of Roleplay*, Kogan Page, London.

6 G. Bolton (1990) 'Constraint in drama', *SCYPT Journal* 19, Standing Conference of Young People's Theatre, London.

7 Among writers who evince these fears are: P. Abbs (1987) *Living Powers*, Falmer Press, London; M. Ross (1983) *The Development of Aesthetic Experience*, Pergamon Press, Oxford; D. Hornbrook (1990) *Education and Dramatic Art*, Blackwell, Oxford.

8 W. Wohlking and P. Gill (1980) *Instructional Design Library: Roleplaying*, Educational Technology Publications, Englewood Clifts, NJ, USA.

9 K. Jones (1980) *Simulation: A Handbook for Teachers*, Kogan Page, London.

10 See, for example, E.J. Burton (1955) *Drama in Schools*, Herbert Jenkins, London.

11 A good introduction to this field is the anthology *Play: A Reader* collected by J. Bruner *et al.* (1976), Penguin, London.

12 I. and P. Opie (1984) *Children's Games of Street and Playground*, OUP, Oxford; I. Turner and L. Spatchcock (1978) *Cinderella Dressed in Yella*, Heinemann, Melbourne.

13 See B. Watkins (1981) *Drama and Education*, Batsford, London, and G. Bolton (1984) *Drama as Education*, Longmans, London, from which the quotation is taken (p. 92).

14 C. O'Neill (1987) 'Mapping meaning', keynote address to the 12th NADIE Conference, Brisbane.

15 I first heard this phrase from Paul Stevenson: see n. 17 below.

16 I also refer briefly to this drama in J. O'Toole (1977) *Theatre in Education*, Hodder & Stoughton, London.

17 Paul Stevenson (drama in education) uses the term 'simulation' when training Further Education teachers and police cadets.

18 G. Shirts (1969) *Starpower: A Simulation*, Western Behavioral Sciences Institute, La Jolla, California.

19 C. Freestone (1978) *Using Roleplaying as an Educational Strategy*, Macquarie University Press, Sydney.

20 D. Heathcote (1968) 'Role-taking', in L. Johnson and C. O'Neill (eds) (1984) *Dorothy Heathcote: Collected Writings on Education and Drama*, Hutchinson, London. The emphasis is added.

21 Dealt with at greater length in O'Toole, op. cit., chapter 6: 'The perils and pleasures of participation', and in J. O'Toole, 'Will TIE die?' (1981), *2D* 1(1). An example of a TIE programme which included the students participating in a board game was *Country Hicks and City Slicks* (1981) performed by the Queensland Theatre Company Roadworks team.

22 Coventry Belgrade Theatre in Education *Rare Earth* (1973), later published by Methuen, London.

23 David Pammenter, in his preface to *Ifan's Valley* (1975), published in P. Schweitzer (ed.) (1980) *Theatre in Education: Five Infant Programmes*, Methuen, London, p. 102.

24 For instance Gavin Bolton expresses strong doubts in 'Drama and emotion: some uses and abuses' (1977), reprinted in D. Davis and C. Lawrence (eds) (1986) *Gavin Bolton: Selected Writings on Drama in*

Education, Longmans, London; also Pammenter himself (in informal conversations 1989). A detailed description of an artistically very elegant 'Adventure Programme', *Holland New Town* (1973), may be found in O'Toole, op. cit., pp. 134-7. A more detailed critical analysis of *Ifan's Valley* is found in T. Jackson (ed.) (1980) *Learning Through Theatre*, Manchester University Press, Manchester.

25 It would not be fair to identify this teacher and Principal, particularly as they are both excellent teachers, but untrained in the use of drama in the classroom.

26 *Forest Park* (1990) a drama in three visits, with sixty year 6 children of St Edward's Primary School, Daisy Hill, Queensland, and their teachers Kathy Hogan and Marie Garrigan; this drama is documented on video at Griffith University, Brisbane.

27 This phrase was coined by Dorothy Heathcote, and is used in her essay 'The authentic teacher and the future' (1984), in Johnson and O'Neill (eds), op. cit., though the phrase had already been in currency for some years.

28 *Farms* (1987), Lesley Thompson, Brisbane, observed by Paul Stevenson (see n. 29 below and p. 85).

29 *Goldilocks Revisited* a drama for year 2 children, by Kathy Kiernan, documented in P. Stevenson and J. O'Toole (eds) (1988) *Pretending to Learn*, Brisbane CAE, from which this introduction is taken.

30 Most notably by Dorothy Heathcote, in a film with the title *Building Belief* (1974), Northwestern University, Evanston, Ill.

31 Cf. B. Haseman and J. O'Toole (1990) *Communicate Live!* Heinemann, Melbourne, a book not for infants, but for Senior Secondary students.

32 The central characters of Sophocles' play *Philoctetes*, variously translated and published.

33 Cf. G. Dean (1988) 'Human relations policing skills: training for reality', *Queensland Police Journal* 42(3), Brisbane, and J. O'Toole (1989) 'Police academy', *NADIE Journal*. 14(1), Melbourne. Similar exercises have existed elsewhere: see J. Hale (1978) 'Police cadets', *NADIE Journal* 4(2).

34 This has been further documented in J. O'Toole (1979) 'Hard journeys to Utopia', *NADIE Journal* 4(2), Melbourne.

3 PURPOSE AND FOCUS

1 As J. Bruner and V. Sherwood (1975) 'Peekaboo and the learning of rule structure', in J. Bruner *et al.* (1976) *Play: A Reader*, Penguin, London, pp. 277ff, have shown.

2 Quoted in C. Cazden (1973) 'Language and Metalinguistic Awareness', in Bruner et al. op. cit., p. 606.

3 A. Koestler (1969) *The Act of Creation*, Pan, London, p. 39.

4 J. Bentham (1840) *Theory of Legislation*.

5 C. Geertz (1972) 'Deep play: the Balinese cockfight', in Bruner *et al.*, op. cit., p. 668.

6 K. Groos (1896) in 'The play of animals: play and instinct', reprinted in ibid., p. 67.
7 L. Vygotsky (1933) 'Play and its role in the development of the child', in ibid., p. 553.
8 J. Bruner (1972) 'The nature and uses of immaturity', in ibid., p. 38.
9 Vygotsky, op. cit., p. 549.
10 Among the many such commentators are Peter Slade (1954) *Child Drama*, Cassell, London; Gavin Bolton (1977) 'Creative drama as an art form', in D. Davis and C. Lawrence (eds) (1986) *Gavin Bolton: Selected Writings on Drama in Education*, Longmans, London; David Davis (1983) quoted by C. Havell (1987) 'The case for drama', in P. Abbs (1987) *Living Powers*, Falmer Press, London, p. 172.
11 H. Rosen (1980) 'The dramatic mode', paper delivered at the NADIE Conference, Brisbane (tape transcript).
12 Vygotsky, op. cit., p. 548. The phrase was originally coined by Nohl.
13 From a survey of over 100 drama teachers which he carried out, Brad Haseman (1989) 'Working out', *NADIE Journal* 14(2), extrapolates this point.
14 Havell in Abbs, op. cit., p. 180.
15 D. Heathcote (1980) 'Material for significance', in L. Johnson and C. O'Neill (eds) (1984) *Dorothy Heathcote: Collected Writings on Education and Drama*, Hutchinson, London.
16 E. Dodgson 'Working in a South London school', in M. Wootton (ed.) (1982) *New Directions in Drama Teaching*, Heinemann, London.
17 L. Arnaud Reid in M. Ross (1981) *Assessment and Aesthetic Education*, Pergamon, London, p. 9.
18 Abbs, op. cit., p. 55.
19 This phrase was coined by G. Gillham (1974) in his 'Report on the Condercum Project', unpublished; it has been used extensively, particularly by Gavin Bolton.
20 D. Heathcote in *Three Looms Waiting* (1971), BBC Films, London.
21 *The Industrial Revolution* (1980) documented in P. Stevenson and J. O'Toole (eds) (1988) *Pretending to Learn*, Brisbane CAE.
22 T. Stabler in *Three Looms Waiting*. The exceptional ability to be able to formulate this kind of question on the spot is one of the qualities for which Heathcote is respected as perhaps the pre-eminent teacher of drama in education, as B.-J. Wagner points out (1976) *Dorothy Heathcote: Drama as a Learning Medium*, National Education Association, Washington, DC, chapter 6. It is also recognised, by Wagner and others, to be a crucial skill of the teacher/playwright.
23 B. Brecht from 'Theatre for pleasure or theatre for instruction', from *Brecht on Theatre* (1977), trans. F. Willett, Eyre Methuen, London, p. 69.
24 N. Morgan and J. Saxton (1987) *Teaching Drama*, Heinemann, London, pp. 158–9.
25 Ken Byron (1986) *Drama in the English Classroom*, Methuen, London, pp. 44–6.

26 The teacher was Gavin Bolton, and the drama sequence is recorded on video (1978) *Hijack*, Kelvin Grove CAE, Brisbane.
27 This comment (1985) was reported to me, as a visiting lecturer, by the supervising teacher, Isobel Deeble.
28 Byron, op. cit., p. 44.
29 Morgan and Saxton, op. cit., in their 'Contextual Structure for Drama Planning', pp. 158–9.
30 *The King and the Fountain* taught jointly with Brad Haseman, Buranda State School, 1982.
31 G. Bolton, documented in K. Robinson (1980) *Exploring Theatre and Education*, Heinemann, London, pp. 82ff.
32 Morgan and Saxton, op. cit., p. 158.
33 Wagner, op. cit., chapter 6, and Morgan and Saxton, op. cit., pp. 67ff, have observed and further codified these questions.
34 J. Carroll (1986) 'Framing drama: some strategies', *NADIE Journal* 10(2): 5.
35 Byron, op. cit., p. 83.
36 Carroll, op. cit., p. 5.
37 J. O'Toole and B. Haseman (1988) *Dramawise*, Heinemann, London, p. 39.
38 Ibid., pp. 35ff.
39 Aristotle (c. 330 BC) *The Poetics*, variously translated.
40 Horace (20 BC) *On the Art of Poetry*, variously translated.
41 Byron, op. cit., p. 149.
42 P. Stevenson (1988) *INCA: An Integrated Arts Program*, Brisbane CAE.
43 R. Barthes (1975) trans. R. Miller, *The Pleasure of the Text*, Cape, London. Its applicability to this particular dramatic context was pointed out by T. Collitt (1989) in an unpublished paper, 'King Lear and cruelty', presented to the Australasian Drama Studies Association Conference 1989.
44 This macabre piece of business reportedly occurred in a fringe theatre production during the 1970s, for which I have been unable to find any references.
45 *The Nativity* (1982) Year 2, Burnie, Tasmania, 1982, documented in Stevenson and O'Toole (eds), op. cit.
46 This phrase was coined by J. Moffett (1968) *Teaching the Universe of Discourse*, Houghton Mifflin, Boston. The application of this principle to role-play is lucidly dealt with in Byron, op. cit.
47 This convention was much used according to the recipes of E.J. Burton (1955) *Drama in Schools*, Herbert Jenkins, London.
48 G. Bolton (1977) *The Bolton Workshops*, vol. 1, printed by Kelvin Grove CAE, Brisbane.
49 G. Bolton (1988) 'Drama as art', *Drama Broadsheet* 5(3), National Association of Teachers of Drama, London. The phrase 'fixed statement' in this context is also attributable to Bolton, *The Bolton Workshops*, op. cit.
50 This drama is documented on video: (1980) *Videokit No. 1: Stone Age*, Queensland Association for Drama in Education, Brisbane.

51 Perceptively demonstrated by G. Little (1982), in an unpublished paper delivered to the Conference of the National Association for Drama in Education, Hobart.
52 Byron, op. cit., p. 129.
53 These teachers' evaluations, which for obvious reasons are unpublished, are from Tynewear Theatre in Education, Newcastle upon Tyne (1980), and Queensland Arts Council, Brisbane (1989).
54 Coventry Belgrade Theatre in Education (1967) *The Belgrade's Bones: 1st Annual Report*, p. 7.
55 G. Tyler (1969) 'Open letter to the Arts Council', *Outlook* 1, British Children's Theatre Association, London.
56 B. Manning, to a conference of drama teachers in Sydney, *c.* 1982.
57 Tynewear TIE was attached to the local Civic Theatre. *Labour for the Lord* was written by Phil Woods with the team.
58 Leeds Playhouse TIE (1973) *Spacemen Have Landed in Leeds*, directed by Roger Chapman. The actor was John Surman.
59 Unnamed programme (1972) referred to in J. O'Toole (1977) *Theatre in Education*, Hodder & Stoughton, London.
60 Durham TIE (1974) *Out of the Casebook* with David Griffiths, see ibid.
61 For example, London Education Authority during the 1980s.
62 For example, Queensland Education Department during the 1980s.
63 For example, Newcastle Stagecoach and Durham TIE, UK, during the 1970s.
64 For example, KITE TIE, Brisbane, during the early 1980s.
65 Tynewear TIE (1980) *Time Please*, written by Phil Woods with the company, directed by Chris Bostock.
66 Tynewear TIE (1980) *Play Shadows*, written by John O'Toole with the company, directed by Roger Chapman.

4 TENSION, TIME AND AUDIENCE

1 For example, in H. Kreitler and S. Kreitler (1973) *The Psychology of the Arts*, Duke University Press, Durham, NC.
2 C. Lawrence (1982) 'Teacher in role', *2D* 1(2), and in an unsigned article written by a group of Durham University post-graduate students(1982) 'Tension in drama', *London Drama* 6(6).
3 This term was coined by B. Bloom *et al.* (1964) *A Taxonomy of Educational Objectives*, McGraw-Hill, New York.
4 For example, current Queensland Senior Music Syllabus, written with four categories of objectives: Content, Process, Skill and Affective.
5 J. McKenna (1981) 'Teacher intervention and the relationship of work and play', *NADIE Journal* 6(1): 33 – the quoted passage is by Dorothy Heathcote.
6 G. Ryle (1949) *The Concept of Mind*, Longmans, London, as pointed out by G. Bolton (1984, written in 1981) 'Emotion in drama', in D. Davis and C. Lawrence (eds) (1986) *Gavin Bolton: Selected*

Writings on Drama in Education, Longmans, London, p. 112. The word 'inclinations' is Ryle's, the word 'dispositions' is Bolton's.

7 Kreitler and Kreitler, op. cit.

8 These words are from E. Bentley (1965) *The Life of the Drama*, Methuen, London, p. 15. The same point is made by Bruno Bettelheim (1976) *The Uses of Enchantment*, Alfred Knopf, New York, p. 45.

9 I am indebted to my brother Professor Michael O'Toole for these terms and translations; see also L.M. O'Toole, and A. Shukman (eds) (1977) 'A contextual glossary of Formalist terminology', *Russian Poetics in Translation* 3, Holdan Books, Oxford, and Essex University.

10 I am indebted to Brad Haseman, the teacher concerned, for this anecdote about his typically elegant hands-on research into the nature of drama in education.

11 See, for example, Bentley, op. cit., and M. Pfister (1988) *The Theory and Analysis of Drama*, Cambridge University Press, Cambridge.

12 This phrase was coined by J. Moffett, (1968) *Teaching the Universe of Discourse* Houghton Mifflin, Boston.

13 K. Byron (1986) *Drama in the English Classroom*, Methuen, London, p. 74.

14 See, for example, D. Booth (1982) 'Storytelling', *Emergency Librarian* 10(2), Ontario; N. Morgan and J. Saxton (1987) *Teaching Drama*, Hutchinson, London; P. Verriour (1986) 'Creating worlds of dramatic discourse', *Language Arts* 63(3) UMI, Boston.

15 W. Gaskill 'Working with actors', in K. Robinson (ed.) (1980) *Exploring Theatre and Education*, Heinemann, London.

16 A. Marshall (1992) 'Comparative studies in performance training in traditional Aboriginal ceremony and contemporary Australian theatre', *Journal of the Queensland Association for Drama in Education* 16(2), Brisbane.

17 See, for example, R. Barthes (1977) *The Death of the Author*, Fontana, London.

18 *Yarranlea Years* (1988), Brisbane CAE, written by me, and performed in the Old Yarranlea School with an audience of ex-pupils of that school.

19 This is a subject which I have written on in more detail, in J. O'Toole (1977) *Theatre in Education*, Hodder & Stoughton, London, and (1981) 'Will TIE die?' *2D* 1(1).

20 C. O'Neill (1987) 'Mapping meaning', keynote address to the 12th NADIE Conference, Brisbane.

21 J. McLeod (1987) 'Drama as metaphor', conference workshop, NADIE Conference, Brisbane.

22 P. Abbs (1982) *English Within the Arts*, Hodder & Stoughton, London p. 33.

23 S. Langer (1953) *Feeling and Form*, Routledge & Kegan Paul, London, p. 308.

24 Bentley, op. cit.

25 E. Goody (1978) *Questions and Politeness*, Cambridge University Press, Cambridge.
26 A. Boal (1979) *Theatre of the Oppressed*, Pluto Press, London, p. 155.
27 Structuralist critics analyse it in exactly the same way: this quotation is by Pfister, op. cit., p. 95.
28 From B. Brecht (1930) *The Exception and the Rule* quoted in A. Hunt (1976) *Hopes for Great Happenings*, Eyre Methuen, London, p. 154.
29 Boal, op. cit., p. 155.
30 The first quotation is from B.-J. Wagner (1976) *Dorothy Heathcote: Drama as a Learning Medium*, NEA, Washington, DC. p. 60. The second is from J. Neelands (1984) *Making Sense of Drama*, Heinemann, London, p. 36.
31 *Spacemen Have Landed in Leeds* (1974), Leeds Playhouse Theatre in Education, filmed and distributed by Leeds Polytechnic Film Unit, England.
32 These words form voice-over comments by a team member, John Surman.
33 Boal, op. cit., p. 122.
34 See with specific relevance, G. Little (1984) in *Drama, Language and Learning*, NADIE, Hobart, and J. Carroll (1988) 'Drama and language', unpublished PhD thesis, University of Newcastle upon Tyne.
35 *Labour for the Lord* (1980), Tynewear TIE, Newcastle upon Tyne, written by Phil Woods with the company (also referred to in chapter 3).
36 *Dealing With Drugs* (1982), SAADYT Conference, Witwatersrand University, with St Barnabas's Secondary School students.
37 *Outlaws* (1977) Gavin Bolton, documented on *ILEA Drama Work-In Video Unit No. 1*, Inner London Education Authority.
38 *Be Aware* (1985), Queensland Special Education Cooperative Workshop TIE, written by Jacq Hamilton and John O'Toole.
39 Quoted in R. Courtney (1968) *Play, Drama and Thought*, Cassell, London, p. 20.
40 Langer, op. cit., p. 324.
41 Tom Stabler, Headmaster of Kingsley County Primary School, Hartlepool, England, in *Three Looms Waiting* (1971), BBC Films, London.
42 R. Linnell (1985) 'Theatre in education: a personal view', *London Drama* 7(1): 9.
43 Ibid., p. 10.
44 O'Neill, op. cit.
45 Pfister, op. cit., p. 98.
46 D. Heathcote (1975) 'Drama and learning', reprinted in L. Johnson C. O'Neill (eds) (1984) *Dorothy Heathcote: Collected Writings on Education and Drama*, Hutchinson, London, p. 92.
47 *Nuclear War* (1986) by students of Brisbane State High School, Queensland – quoted in J. O'Toole and B. Haseman (1988) *Dramawise*, Heinemann, London, p. 140.

48 The TIE 'adventure programme is referred to on p. 81 above, and more extensively in *Theatre in Education*, pp. 133–7. It has also been dealt with by Gavin Bolton (1977) 'Drama and emotion: some uses and abuses' reprinted in Davis and Lawrence (eds), op. cit., 95–8.

49 I am indebted to Brad Haseman (1989).

50 *Dealing With Drugs* (see n. 36 above).

51 As Brendan Butler (1983) 'Drama in education versus the theatricality of schooling', *SAADYT Journal* 5(2), South African Association for Drama in Education, and Esther van Ryswyck (1983) 'TIE for political growth' *2D* 2(2): 15, point out.

52 Esther van Ryswyck, the SAADYT President, in taped conversation one week following the drama.

53 Heather Jacklin, a white teacher from Namibia, ibid.

54 Athol Fugard, ibid.

55 Goody, op. cit., p. 22.

5 LOCATION – RENEGOTIATING EXPECTATIONS

1 M. Esslin (1987) *The Field of Drama*, Methuen, London, p. 19.

2 Ibid., p. 38.

3 M. Pfister (1988) *The Theory and Analysis of Drama*, Cambridge University Press, Cambridge, p. 19.

4 J. Kott (1984) *The Theatre of Essence*, Northwestern University Press, Evanston, Ill., p. 133.

5 Ibid., p. 132.

6 L.M. O'Toole and A. Shukman (eds) (1977) 'A contextual glossary of Formalist terminology', *Russian Poetics in Translation* 3, Holdan Books, Oxford, and Essex University.

7 G. Gillham (1980) 'The dramatic symbol', *SCYPT Journal* 10, Standing Conference of Young People's Theatre, London.

8 This and the following quotations by Paul Davies either come from 'Location theatre' in R. Fotheringham (1987) *Community Theatre in Australia*, Methuen, Sydney, or from informal conversations during the following year.

9 J. O'Toole J (1977) *Theatre in Education*, Hodder & Stoughton, London, chapter 5: 'The perils and pleasures of participation'.

10 J. O'Toole (1981) 'Will TIE die?', *2D* 1(1): 65, Leicester.

11 We have outlined in detail a set of activities deconstructing the particular messages of a secondary school assembly, in B. Haseman and J. O'Toole (1990) *Communicate Live!*, Heinemann, Melbourne.

6 THE PARTICIPANT GROUP

1 I am indebted to Robby Nason, *World EXPO On Stage*, for this information.

2 J. Neelands (1984) *Making Sense of Drama*, Heinemann, London, p. 27. The italics are his.

3 Ibid.

4 La Boîte Youth Theatre (1987) *The Great Circle*, devised with the group by Michael Doneman. The quotations throughout are from either A. Jones (1987) *Almost the Full Circle: Report on the Great Circle Project*, La Boîte Theatre, Brisbane, or from informal conversations with Michael Doneman and the theatre director, Jim Vilé.

5 B. Haseman (1989) 'Working out: a survey of Queensland drama teachers', produced for the Queensland Association of Drama in Education', *NADIE Journal* (1990) 14(2).

6 A. Marshall (1992) 'Comparative studies in performance training in traditional Aboriginal ceremony and contemporary Australian Theatre', *Journal of the Queensland Association for Drama in Education* 16(2), Brisbane.

7 Richard Courtney, in a lecture delivered at Melbourne State College, Australia *c.* 1978 – information supplied by Paul Stevenson.

8 In Queensland, for instance, the Early Childhood Division was founded in the early 1970s with an aggressively integrative policy – separate subjects were not permitted to be taught.

9 Most capital cities have one, such as Brisbane Independent School, usually founded in the late 1960s or early 1970s, now mostly struggling financially.

10 J.-J. Rousseau (1760) *Émile*, variously translated and published.

11 G. Lang (1979) 'Far more fundamental than the fundamentals', *NADIE Journal* 4(2): 56, Melbourne.

12 G. Boomer (1982) *Negotiating the Curriculum*, Ashton Scholastic, Sydney. Garth Boomer is a prominent educational administrator, with a background of English and drama teaching.

13 K. Byron (1985) *Indians and Pioneers*, 2D Publications, Leicester.

7 LANGUAGE, GESTURE AND ACTION

1 See, for example, K. Elam (1980) *The Semiotics of Theatre and Drama*, Routledge, London.

2 J. Carroll (1987) 'Language in drama in education', unpublished PhD thesis, University of Newcastle upon Tyne, takes a sociolinguistic paradigm to provide the most coherent study so far of the area: Carroll is primarily a practitioner.

3 Significant ethnographical work on the language of drama in education is documented in H. Felton and G. Little (1984) *Drama and Language: NADIE Working Paper No. 1*, NADIE, Hobart.

4 M. Esslin (1987) *The Field of Drama*, Methuen, London, p. 83.

5 G. Bolton (1978) 'Drama is not doing' reprinted in D. Davis and C. Lawrence (eds) (1986) *Gavin Bolton: Selected Writings on Drama in Education*, Longmans, London, p. 145.

6 B. Jonson (*c.* 1620), reprinted 1889, *Discoveries*, Cassell, London, p. 119.

7 M. Pfister (1988) *The Theory and Analysis of Drama*, Cambridge University Press, Cambridge, p. 105.

8 As many writers on language and learning have noted – e.g. K.

Chukovsky (1963) 'The sense of nonsense verse', in J. Bruner *et al.* (eds) (1976) *Play: A Reader*, Penguin, London, p. 596, documents the awareness of incongruity.

9 J. Donaldson (1978) *Children's Minds* Fontana, London, p. 24 (quoted to make this same point by M. Fleming 'Language development and drama', in M. Wootton (ed.) (1982) *New Directions in Drama Teaching*, Heinemann, London).

10 *Dino the Dinosaur* (1981): the teacher was Brad Haseman. The words are recorded in *NADIE Journal* 6(2): 49, and a videotape exists of the event, published by Brisbane South Region Drama Resource Project.

11 *Elijah* (1970) by the fourth-year children of Kingsley County Primary School, Hartlepool, England, teacher Tom Stabler. Recorded in *Three Looms Waiting* (1971), BBC Films, London.

12 *The Mind of the Terrorist* (1983). Documented on video, Brisbane CAE Audio-Visual Department.

13 *The Fields of Orange and the Float of Ignorance* (1988) fully documented in H. Smigiel (ed.) (1991) *Drama Down Under*, NADIE Publications, Melbourne.

14 W. Wordsworth (1805) Preface to *The Lyrical Ballads*, variously published.

8 NEGOTIATING MEANING

1 P. Abbs (1982) *English Within the Arts*, Hodder & Stoughton, London, chapter 5.

2 V. Shklovsky (1965) *Art as Technique*, quoted in R. Hornby. (1986) *Drama, Metadrama and Perception*, Associated University Press, Cranbury, NJ.

3 The title of Brian Way's very influential teacher's textbook, (1968) *Development Through Drama*, Longmans, London.

4 The title of the book to emerge from the UK Schools Council Drama 10–16 Project, another influential text for teachers: L. MacGregor, M. Tate and K. Robinson (1977) *Learning Through Drama*, Heinemann, London.

5 G. Bolton (1979) *Towards a Theory of Drama in Education*, Longmans, London.

6 David Pammenter, a British pioneer of theatre in education, in an unpublished lecture (1989) 'Community drama and social deconstruction', Brisbane CAE

7 Brendan Butler, a young South African drama teacher (1983) – see chapter 1. above.

8 R. Hardin – clearly derived from Jung – (1983) *The Ritual in Recent Criticism*, quoted in Hornby, op. cit., p. 62.

9 Hornby, op. cit., p. 26.

10 K. Robinson (ed.) (1982) *The Arts in Schools: Principles, Practice and Provision*, Gulbenkian Foundation, London.

11 P. Abbs (1987) *Living Powers*, Falmer Press, London, p. 208, and M. Ross (1980) *The Arts and Personal Growth*, Pergamon Press, Oxford, p. 18.

12 E. Eisner (1969) 'A typology of creative behaviour in the visual arts', in E. Eisner and D. Ecker *Readings in Art Education*, Xerox Coll., Lexington, Mass.
13 K. Swanwick (1979) *A Basis for Music Education*, NFER–Nelson, Windsor.
14 K. Swanwick (1988) *Music, Mind and Education*, Routledge, London.
15 W. Lett (1982) 'From actual to virtual: children's thinking and making in the arts', *NADIE Journal* 7(2).
16 Abbs, *Living Powers*.
17 Victoria: J. Benson (ed.) (1988) *Arts Curriculum Framework P-10: For Total Growth*, Victorian Ministry of Education; Western Australia: (1990) as provided by NADIE WA Liaison Officer, Robin Pascoe; New South Wales: (1988) *Draft Drama Syllabus K-6*, NSW Department of Education; Queensland: (1) L. Blundell (ed.) (1990) *P-10 Arts Framework*, Queensland Department of Education; (2) (1991) *Senior Syllabus in Drama*, Queensland Board of Senior Secondary School Studies.
18 L. Arnaud Reid (1980) 'Meaning in the arts', in M. Ross (ed.) *The Arts and Personal Growth*, Pergamon, Oxford.
19 Both Malcolm Ross and Robert Witkin use Reid's term 'the intelligence of feeling', the latter as the title of a book which had some influence in drama in education during the late 1970s and early 1980s: R. Witkin (1974) *The Intelligence of Feeling*, Heinemann, London.
20 G. Bolton (1978) 'Symbolisation in improvised drama', reprinted in D. Davis and C. Lawrence (eds) (1986) *Gavin Bolton: Selected Writings on Drama in Education*, Longmans, London, pp. 147–8.
21 D. Davis (1986) Introduction to ibid., p. 134.
22 F. Marton *et al.* (1985) *The Experience of Learning*, Scottish Educational Press, Edinburgh.
23 Brad Haseman, consultant to Brisbane South Region Drama Resources Project.
24 J. Neelands (1985) 'Issues or contexts?', in *Positive Images*, NATD, St Albans, p. 16.
25 D. Heathcote in *Three Looms Waiting* (1971), BBC Films, London.
26 *Forest Park* (1989), leaders Cathy Hogan, Marie Garrigan and myself, with sixty year 6 children of St Edward's Primary School, Daisy Hill, Queensland.
27 K. Joyce (1987) 'Confronting sexism through drama', *2D* 6(2): 33–50.
28 R. Witkin (1981) *Analysing Drama: Five Workshops*, Brisbane South Region Drama Resource Project, p. 25.
29 *Mia v. Trike* (1989) by P.P. Cranney, devised with and performed by Sidetrack Theatre, Sydney. The quotations and descriptions of the playwright's process which follow are from a transcribed conversation which I had with him following a performance of the play.
30 At the 1987 NADIE Conference, a continuing workshop led by Aboriginal educators Hope Neill and Mike Williams discussed at

length these issues, and this led to the formation of an on-going NADIE Aboriginal Education Project.

31 G. Bolton (1984) *Drama as Education*, Longmans, London.
32 G. Bolton (1987) 'Off target', *London Drama* 7(4).
33 G. Bolton (1981) 'Drama in the curriculum', *2D* 1(1), Leicester.
34 Ibid. (written in 1981 and now acknowledged as inadequate).

Index

272042

DUE / DA   R